The Future of Illusion

The Future of Illusion:
Political Theology and Early Modern Texts

Victoria Kahn

The University of Chicago Press :: Chicago and London

Victoria Kahn is the Katharine Bixby Hotchkis Professor of English
and professor of comparative literature at the University of California,
Berkeley. She is the author of *Rhetoric, Prudence, and Skepticism in the
Renaissance; Machiavellian Rhetoric: From the Counter-Reformation
to Milton;* and *Wayward Contracts: The Crisis of Political Obligation in
England, 1640–1674.*

The University of Chicago Press, Chicago 60637
The University of Chicago Press, Ltd., London
© 2014 by The University of Chicago
All rights reserved. Published 2014.
Printed in the United States of America

23 22 21 20 19 18 17 16 15 14   1 2 3 4 5

ISBN-13: 978-0-226-08387-2 (cloth)
ISBN-13: 978-0-226-08390-2 (e-book)
DOI: 10.7208/chicago/9780226083902.001.0001

Library of Congress Cataloging-in-Publication Data

Kahn, Victoria Ann, author.
  The future of illusion : political theology and early modern texts /
Victoria Kahn.
      pages cm
  Includes bibliographical references and index.
  ISBN 978-0-226-08387-2 (cloth : alkaline paper) —
  ISBN 978-0-226-08390-2 (e-book)   1. Political theology.   2. Politics
in literature.   3. Theology in literature.   4. European literature—
History and criticism.   1. Title.
  BT83.59.K34 2013
  201'.72—dc23

                                            2013017961

Den Himmel überlassen wir
Den Engeln und den Spatzen.

HEINRICH HEINE

To live in a political realm with neither authority nor the concomitant awareness that the source of authority transcends power and those who are in power,
means to be confronted anew, without the religious trust in a sacred beginning
and without the protection of traditional and therefore self-evident standards of
behavior, by the elementary problems of human living-together.

HANNAH ARENDT

Contents

Abbreviations

AS   Sigmund Freud, *An Autobiographical Study*, trans. James Strachey (New York: Norton, 1989)

BPP   Sigmund Freud, *Beyond the Pleasure Principle*, trans. James Strachey (New York: Bantam Books, 1967)

CD   Sigmund Freud, *Civilization and Its Discontents*, trans. James Strachey (New York: Norton, 1989)

CP   Carl Schmitt, *The Concept of the Political*, trans. George Schwab (Chicago: University of Chicago Press, 1996)

D   Machiavelli, *Discourses on the First Decade of Titus Livius*, in *Machiavelli: The Chief Works and Others*, trans. Allan Gilbert, 3 vols. (Durham: Duke University Press, 1989), cited by book, chapter, and page number

FI   Sigmund Freud, *The Future of an Illusion*, trans. James Strachey (New York: Norton, 1989)

HH   Carl Schmitt, *Hamlet or Hecuba*, trans. David Pan and Jennifer Rust (New York: Telos Press, 2009)

MM   Sigmund Freud, *Moses and Monotheism, The Standard Edition of the Complete Psychological Works of Sigmund Freud*, ed. and trans. James Strachey, vol. 23 (London: Vintage, 2001)

NCP   Leo Strauss, "Notes on Carl Schmitt, *The Concept of the Political*," in *CP*

P   Machiavelli, *The Prince*, trans. Robert M. Adams (New York: Norton, 1977), cited by chapter and page number

PT   Carl Schmitt, *Political Theology*, trans. George Schwab (Cambridge: MIT Press, 1988)

RC   Carl Schmitt, *Roman Catholicism and Political Form* (1923),
        trans. G. L. Ulmen (Westport, CT: Greenwood Press, 1996).
        This translation is based on the second, revised 1925 edition.
SCR   Leo Strauss, *Spinoza's Critique of Religion*, trans. E. M. Sin-
        clair (Chicago: University of Chicago Press, 1965)
T   Walter Benjamin, *The Origin of German Tragic Drama*, trans.
        John Osborne (London: NLB, 1977)
TKTB   Ernst H. Kantorowicz, *The King's Two Bodies: A Study in
        Medieval Political Theology* (Princeton: Princeton University
        Press, 1957)
TM   Leo Strauss, *Thoughts on Machiavelli* (Chicago: University of
        Chicago Press, 1958)
TT   Sigmund Freud, *Totem and Taboo*, trans. A. A. Brill (New
        York: Vintage Books, 1946)
TTP   Benedict de Spinoza, *Theological-Political Treatise*, ed. Jona-
        than Israel, trans. Michael Silverthorne and Jonathan Israel
        (Cambridge: Cambridge University Press, 2007), cited by
        chapter and page number

Preface

This is a book about the relationship between political theology, art, and rational critique, both in the early modern period and in our own. It is also a book about the process of reading several times over. In my work on early modern texts, I have repeatedly encountered critical books that did not exactly seem to be part of the secondary literature—whether because the argument was unorthodox or because the function of commentary was so clearly subordinated to a different kind of argument, an argument about modernity. But precisely for this reason, these works have seemed more alive, more current, more relevant today than many of the classic works of scholarship on the Renaissance and early modern period. Some of these works are now enthroned in the canon of "theory"—Walter Benjamin's *Trauerspiel* book, Carl Schmitt's *Political Theology*—but the specificity of their engagement with early modern texts has mostly been ignored. Some take the form of commentary on difficult early modern texts—this is the case with Leo Strauss's books on Machiavelli and Spinoza—but they have been neglected by early modernists precisely because they have seemed too tendentious about the conditions of modernity. And yet, in reading the early moderns to make sense of modernity, they serve to remind us why we read at all. It's the wager of this book that the contemporary conversation about political theology has much to gain by returning to these seminal twentieth-century works and taking seriously their engagement with early modern texts.

In this book, I read the modern readings of the early modern period in order to discover the historical roots of the assumption that, as Hobbes and Vico argued, we can know only what we make ourselves. Borrowing from some of the modern figures in this book, I use the term "poiesis" to capture this concern with making as a new form of knowing. It's an argument of this book that the early modern concern with poiesis, with art broadly conceived, had an important role to play in negotiating the relationship between politics and theology, and that art is precisely what has been missing from the current debate. In focusing on art in the broad sense in which the early modern period understood it, the book challenges the view that enlightenment is predicated on purging reason of its illusions. The more radical enlightenment of the early modern period is instead the enlightenment that comes with accepting the impossibility of any such bedrock or foundation. Illusion, as Freud noted, is not simply a matter of error; it is constitutive of who we are. But Freud also insisted that some illusions are better than others. So, I will argue, do the early moderns in ways that are still exemplary for us today.

I would like to highlight at the outset the methodological decision to write this book in terms of a series of conversations: not only between the modern figures and the early moderns who fascinated them, but among the moderns themselves. If, from one perspective, the book describes the activities of two camps—one sympathetic to and the other critical of the early modern turn toward poiesis—from another perspective, the book shows all of the moderns struggling to make sense of the implications of this radical turn toward poiesis and away from transcendental justifications of human agency. In this struggle, Schmitt is deeply engaged with Strauss, Strauss with Ernst Cassirer, Ernst Kantorowicz with Cassirer and Schmitt, Benjamin with Schmitt, and Hannah Arendt with Benjamin.[1] Freud is the exception in the sense that his primary interlocutor is not one of his contemporaries but rather Spinoza. These conversations are the focus of the chapters that follow, chapters that are designed to provide a fuller context for our conversations about political theology today.

This book has benefited from the comments of a number of early modern scholars whose work I very much admire: David W. Bates, Julia Reinhard Lupton, Jane O. Newman, Graham Hammill, Don Herzog, Lorna Hutson, and John McCormick. In the course of writing, I have been particularly grateful for the lunchtime conversation and advice of David Bates. For reading drafts of chapters, sometimes more than once, I thank Rachel Eisendrath, Kinch Hoekstra, Andreas Kalyvas, Jeffrey Knapp, James Martel, Francine Masiello, William Rasch, Ethan Shagan, Richard Strier, Alan Tansman, Paula Varsano, Brett Wheeler, and Linda Zerilli. The Early Modern Sodality at Berkeley read two chapters and improved them greatly with their comments, as did the participants at the School of Criticism and Theory at Cornell, superbly directed by Amanda Anderson, in the summer of 2011. Louise George Clubb asked a probing question at just the right moment and fundamentally changed my understanding of this project. Eric Santner generously shared his then unpublished work with me. Alan Thomas was a patient and supportive editor. Jennifer Zahrt was my computer and editorial wizard in Berkeley, and Paco Brito was a wonderful research assistant. At Chicago, it was a great pleasure to work with Susan Tarcov, Isaac Tobin, Michael Koplow, and Laura Avey, who helped prepare the book for publication. Above all, Helene Silverberg helped me see who my other interlocutors were in this book and made me talk to them. For that and so much more, I am eternally grateful. This book is dedicated to the memory of my father, J. P. Kahn, MD, with whom I would have liked to discuss these ideas.

:   :   :

An earlier version of chapter 1 appeared as "Hamlet or Hecuba: Carl Schmitt's Decision," in *Representations* 83 (Summer 2003): 67–96; an earlier version of chapter 2 appeared as "Political Theology and Fiction in *The King's Two Bodies*," in *Representations* 106 (2009): 77–101; and part of chapter 4 appeared in my essay in *Political Theology and Early Modernity*, ed. Graham Hammill and Julia Reinhard Lupton (Chicago: University of Chicago Press, 2012), © 2012 by The University of Chicago. All rights reserved. I am grateful to the publishers for permission to draw on this material.

Introduction

In recent years we have seen a powerful resurgence of interest in the problem of political theology, understood as the theological legitimation or religious dimension of political authority. Political events, from 9/11 to the Arab Spring, have prompted Western scholars to revisit the relationship between religion and the state, in the process frequently castigating liberalism for cordoning off religion within the sphere of private experience. Prompted in part by the rise of religious fundamentalism in the Muslim world and in part by a sense that liberal values in the West are under threat and are incapable of defending themselves without recourse to religion, figures such as Charles Taylor, Giorgio Agamben, Slavoj Žižek, and Terry Eagleton have all recently published books addressing the upsurge of religion or the religious dimension of secular modernity.[1] While some are apologists for Christianity, and others are skeptics or agnostics, all seem to agree that we are living in a "postsecular world," a world in which the Whiggish narrative of increasing secularization in the West has come up against the fact that religion has not withered away. To the contrary, it is ever more present in political life and civil society both in the West and in non-Western countries. In response to these developments in the United States, we hear repeatedly that liberalism has failed to address the profound religiosity of

American citizens and—in a different way—has been equally incapable of addressing Jihad.

Both in the United States and in Europe, the turn to political theology is a way of talking about the crisis of liberal democracy—a crisis of values that derives from liberalism's inability to offer a substantive defense of its own principles, including formal equality, religious neutrality, and religious tolerance. In the aftermath of the terrorist attacks in New York and Washington, D.C., of 2001, some of these arguments seem to have been prompted by the guilty sense on the part of many intellectuals that liberalism has been insufficiently attentive to the powerful bonds of religion, for good and for ill. And once we are attentive to these bonds, it's argued, we see that modern Western rationalism founders on its own incapacity to defend its superiority to irrational belief.[2] Instead of validating the claims of Enlightenment reason, we're told, our "postsecular" moment demands that we once again take seriously the conjunction of religion and politics, including the religious sources of authority, affiliation, and community.

In the history of the West, the problem of political theology received its distinctively modern form in the early modern period, which saw the emergence of the nation-state and the beginnings of liberal political theory, with its secular account of human agency and its subordination of the church to the state. In this context, political theology refers not to the theological legitimation or theological essence of political authority, but rather to the *problem* of the relationship between politics and religion once this theological legitimation is no longer convincing. To this problem, liberalism and parliamentary democracy provided distinctive answers, though their efficacy is still being debated. The most important and influential twentieth-century analysts of political theology— Carl Schmitt, Leo Strauss, Ernst Kantorowicz, Walter Benjamin, Ernst Cassirer—were all acutely aware of the momentous significance of this earlier historical moment, and all returned to the early modern period to provide a genealogy of the modern problem of political theology. While not as directly engaged in political analysis, Sigmund Freud was drawn into the conversation about political theology both by the events of World War II and by his own personal experience as a secular Jew. And yet, while all of these modern figures are frequently cited by contemporary analysts of the postsecular, little attention is paid to their readings of early modern texts.[3]

This is a book about the neglected dialogue between these modern theorists and early modern texts, and its implications for our contemporary conversation about political theology.[4] I argue that what the modern critics find in the early modern period is a break with an older form of political theology construed as the theological legitimation of the state, a new emphasis on a secular notion of human agency, and, most important, a new preoccupation with the ways art and fiction reoccupy the terrain of religion.[5] In so doing, they remind us that poiesis is the missing third term in both early modern and contemporary debates about politics and religion. By poiesis I mean the principle, first advocated by Hobbes and Vico, that we can know only what we make ourselves. This kind of making encompasses both the art of poetry and the secular sphere of human interaction, the human world of politics and history. In its rejection of transcendental legitimation, this notion of poiesis also differs from the more familiar Renaissance notion that human creativity is modeled on the divine creativity of God and authorized by the principle that man is made "in the image and likeness of God." For some of the early twentieth-century figures in this book, the early modern emphasis on poiesis amounted to a harmful turn in the history of Western philosophy and political thought, while for others it described a positive form of agency that is equally relevant to the production of art and to political activity. Attention to poiesis reconfigures the usual terms of the debate and helps us see that the contemporary debate about political theology is a debate about what Hans Blumenberg called "the legitimacy of the modern age."

Poiesis vs. the Permanence of Political Theology

The centrality of poiesis both to the moderns and to early modern texts has been lost to recent critics, who have instead affirmed the "permanence" of political theology, defined as the necessity of some kind of theological imaginary to the realm of politics. They have argued that there is a mystical foundation to authority (Jacques Derrida); that belief in reason is no more rational than belief in religion (Stanley Fish); that dialectical thinking is ultimately a secularization of messianic thinking and messianic time (Giorgio Agamben); that the Kantian attempt to establish religion within the bounds of reason alone is paradoxically predicated on religion (Hent de Vries).[6] Much of this work seems to be motivated by the assumption that religion is the "real" and that it informs our being in the world whether we like it or not. Thus Michael Allen Gillespie has asserted "the enduring importance of theology for modernity" and argued that post-Enlightenment thought is utterly "parasitic on the Christian worldview."[7] Rather than seeing religion as man's first indirect self-consciousness of himself, as Ludwig Feuerbach argued in the nineteenth century, many of these critics see modern self-consciousness as predicated on the repression of the divine.

For some critics, influenced by Schmitt and Kantorowicz, but also Freud and Jacques Lacan, political theology names something more than a structural relationship between, though less than a substantial identity of, politics and theology: the persistent haunting of liberal modernity by something in excess of the law, an exception that is then analogized not only to the miracle, grace, or some other figure of transcendence but also, in the register of immanence, to mere life, creaturely life, biopower or bios. In his essay "The Permanence of the Theological-Political?," Claude Lefort writes, "Every religion *states* in its own way that human society can only open on to itself by being held in an opening it did not create. Philosophy says the same thing, but religion said it first, albeit in terms which philosophy cannot accept. . . . What philosophy discovers in religion is a mode of portraying or dramatizing the relations that human beings establish with something that goes beyond empirical time and the space within which they establish relations with each other."[8] In a gloss on this passage, Eric L. Santner identifies this "something that goes beyond empirical time" both with "an ultimate lack of foundation for the historical forms of life that distinguish human community" and with a dimension of human experience "that seems to push thinking in the direction of theology."[9] In a similar vein, Roberto Esposito refers to the residue of transcendence that immanence cannot reabsorb.[10] For Esposito, Santner, and others of this bent, political theology in modernity is under erasure, which produces a situation we could describe as having your religion and eating it too. In the new idiom, what used to be called the materialism of the signifier, the insistence of the letter in the unconscious, or the unconscious tout court is now seen as the relic or remains of the political-theological conception of sovereignty.

While contemporary critics have neglected the early modern sources of political theology, scholars of the early modern period have used the current fascination with the religious dimension of political authority to launch a "return to religion" in early modern studies. In some cases, this has taken the form of equating early modern political theology with the divine right of kings. In other cases, it has taken the form of arguing, for example, that English Renaissance poetry is informed by a "sacramental poetics" that aimed to compensate Protestant readers for the loss of Catholic ritual. In some of the most compelling work in this area, Julia Reinhard Lupton has sought to "develop an approach to political theology for early modern studies that remains faithful to the potentialities and achievements of liberalism," by tracing the emergence of a protoliberal idea of citizenship from within Pauline universalism. Finally, in an approach that is closest to the one I aim to develop here, Graham Hammill construes political theology as the relationship between politics and theology, where politics is conceived as constituent power—the power to constitute the state—and theology names the ongoing problem of legitimating or shoring up the power of the state by securing the allegiance of subjects. But for Hammill, as for Lupton, political theology is more than civil religion: it can also be a vehicle of democratic transformation. Where I take issue with Hammill is in the interpretation he offers of the theological dimension of politics. Even as he argues that early modern theological fictions help produce and sustain allegiance to the state, he wants to hold onto, or argue that Machiavelli and Spinoza held onto, the theological dimension of this democratic "imaginary" as irreducible to the human imagination. It is not enough for humans to be capable of self-transcendence through communal political action—it is not enough, in other words, for humans to be capable of poiesis; this capacity for transcendence must also be divine.[11]

What is striking about much of this recent work on political theology is the extent to which it still subscribes to the secularization narrative in the sense elaborated by a scholar such as Schmitt or criticized by Karl Löwith. According to this narrative, modern ideas of state sovereignty, historical evolution, scientific progress, and even the autonomy of the aesthetic artifact are all secularized versions of Christian concepts.[12] Sovereignty is modeled on the omnipotent God, evolution and progress on eschatology, and aesthetic autonomy on the divine creator. The implication here is that Christianity actually has an explanatory power when it comes to these modern developments, which, it's argued, would have been inconceivable without the conceptual framework first established in theological terms. Such arguments are very often functionalist: if something takes the place of religion, it must be performing the same function. But, as Hannah Arendt noted long ago, this is equivalent to saying that because I sometimes use my shoe to drive nails into the wall, a shoe is a hammer.[13]

In contrast to these arguments, the modern and early modern figures in this book are preoccupied with the critique of a theological worldview and the imagination of an entirely immanent account of human nature. Their texts validate the paradigm of Hans Blumenberg, who argues for a decisive break between modernity and theological modes of explanation. Blumenberg's analysis helps us see that the recent interest in political theology in the academy and beyond is not only a response to the rise of global Jihad, or to the problems of liberal democracies, but also—more broadly—a way of questioning what Blumenberg called the legitimacy of the modern project of self-assertion, or the assertion of rationality, without reference to transcendental norms. Blumenberg locates the origins of the modern project in the early modern period, with its new scientific, philosophical, and aesthetic modes of reasoning.[14] According to his argument, Christianity cannot explain or account for the legitimacy of scientific and philosophical curiosity in the early modern period, and this in turn means the traditional secularization narrative must be rejected. In place of secularization, he proposes the model of "reoccupation": modernity takes up medieval problems but reoccupies them in a novel way. Modernity is not so much a transformation and secularization of Christian concepts as it is a novel response to the crisis of the medieval worldview. Specifically, late medieval nominalism broke the link between God and nature, thus creating a "Gnostic" crisis about the source of order in the universe but also leaving a space for human self-assertion. In Blumenberg's analysis, too, the modern project is fundamentally poetic in the sense elaborated by Hobbes and Vico that we can know only what we have made or constructed ourselves: *verum et factum convertuntur* (truth and fact—in the sense of that which is done or made—are interchangeable).[15] This notion of poiesis, I argue, is central to the work of not only Hobbes and Vico, but also Machiavelli, Shakespeare, and Spinoza, all of whom provide powerful meditations on what it means artfully to construct the world of human interaction and political order. One of the goals of this book is to show the moderns and early moderns speaking directly to this issue. Another is to recuperate this understanding of poiesis for modern debates about political theology and secular agency.

It's important to stress that the "verum factum" principle does not deny that human beings do not create the world they come into; it does not deny the influence of contingency and necessity on our lives (or what, in a modern idiom, we would call the discovery of the unconscious, the libido, and drives). Nor does it deny that some principle of authority is necessary for a functioning state or for what we might call the political life of symbols. But even if we construe each of these very different elements as a limit on the capacity for human self-fashioning and self-determination, it still makes a difference to our understanding of human agency and "self-assertion" whether we describe these limits in theological or secular terms. As Hannah Arendt argued long ago, "The long alliance between religion and authority does not necessarily prove that the concept of authority is itself of a religious nature."[16] What is at stake for critics of the religious foundation of authority, as

Samuel Moyn has noted in commenting on this passage, is the possibility of a purely secular politics. Equally at stake, I would argue, is a purely secular conception of poiesis.

The possibility of purely secular politics goes hand in hand with a recovery of a purely human realm of the symbolic. In making this point, I take issue with the tendency, in recent debates about secularism, religion, and politics, to hand over the symbolic realm to religion. Sometimes this takes the form of suggesting that any gesture of transcendence is implicitly religious. At other times, it takes the more restricted form of arguing that "the political" is by definition religious, i.e., that religion provides the ur-repertoire of symbols that legitimates political power.[17] A spinoff of this second argument is that religious metaphors are themselves a sign that we cannot escape religion even when we want to. An example of this is Samuel Moyn's observation that Hannah Arendt "occasionally uses theological language to describe precisely the secular politics she advocates," and that "she refers to the possibility of new beginnings involved in political action as miraculous." On the basis of these metaphors, Moyn then charges Arendt with a kind of cryptotheology.[18] But why should we assume that religious metaphor is a subset of political theology, understood as the notion that there is some transcendental ground of political authority? Why not assume the exact contrary, that political theology is a subset of metaphor, that is, of purely human ways of understanding the world and negotiating its political conflicts?[19] This, I'll suggest, is the view of Benjamin, Kantorowicz, and Cassirer, as well as the view of Machiavelli, Shakespeare, and Spinoza.

Blumenberg's argument about poiesis finds a powerful echo in the work of Erich Auerbach and, in a different way, Hannah Arendt—two figures whose work has influenced the argument of this book. In *Mimesis* Auerbach charted the development of a mode of realism that broke with—or to use Blumenberg's vocabulary—reoccupied the theological assumptions of medieval Christianity and in the process produced a secular conception of literature as the product of a purely human activity of poiesis. Auerbach located a powerful example of this development in Dante, and its exemplary Renaissance achievements in the work of Montaigne, Rabelais, and Shakespeare.[20] In *Literary Language and Its Public*, he then traced his philological approach to German historicism and to Vico's theory of historical knowledge.[21] According to Vico, "the physical world—*il mondo della natura*—has been created by God; therefore only God can understand it; but this historical or political world, the world of mankind—*il mondo delle nazioni*—can be understood by men, because men have made it."[22] Auerbach, who had translated an abridged version of Vico's *New Science* into German, rebutted the charge that Vico's emphasis on poiesis produced a kind of epistemological relativism: "It is a grave mistake to suppose that historical relativism [by which Auerbach meant historicism, i.e., the historical contextualization of cultural artifacts] results in an eclectic incapacity for judgment, and that judgment must be based on extrahistorical standards." Precisely because there are no extrahistorical standards for cultural interpretation, in confronting works of culture "we do not lose the faculty of judgment; on the contrary, we acquire it."[23] In the late twentieth century, Auerbach's admirer Edward Said offered a similar appreciation of Vico's relevance for literary criticism and criticism more generally. He also famously insisted on its secular presuppositions: "Knowing is making, Vico said, and what human beings can know is only what they have made, that is, the historical, social, and secular." The critic who attends to cultural circumstances and historical context exists "in secular history, in the 'always-already' begun realm of continuously human effort," and takes as his object of investigation not only the human artifacts we know as texts but also "the worldly and secular world in which texts take place."[24] Deploring the turn to religion on the part of his contemporaries in the 1970s, Said celebrated Auerbach as a new Vico, one who fully appreciated the alliance between poiesis, literary criticism, and secular thought.[25]

As a Jew who emigrated from Nazi Germany and who produced a distinguished body of work on early modern literature, Auerbach would seem to be an obvious figure to include in this book. And yet I have not done so for two reasons. The first is that, while a compelling case could be made that his readings of Dante, Shakespeare, and others engage the question of political theology in relation to literature, they do so in a way that is fairly oblique. Auerbach nowhere refers to political theology or the crisis of liberalism, and his references to the Nazi state are few and far between.[26] The second is that Auerbach is too readily associated with arguments that assume the self-evident virtues of literature. It's arguable that literary scholars are now turning to Schmitt, Strauss, Benjamin, and others precisely because traditional humanistic defenses of literature seem so stale. By contrast, these figures invite us to think about the work of literature and of literary criticism in ways that are directly relevant to the cultural and geopolitical issues confronting us today. More than Auerbach, they help us see the stakes of a defense of poiesis, not least of all when they explicitly attack it. This is because they see poiesis not simply as a literary question but also as an explicitly political question.[27]

Hannah Arendt was similarly preoccupied with poiesis, but in contrast to Auerbach and Blumenberg, she equated poiesis with a harmful emphasis on fabrication, as opposed to the constructive activity of "worldmaking." In *The Human Condition*, Arendt was critical of the way the paradigm of poiesis or *homo faber* (both her terms) had come to dominate the sphere of politics in the early modern period. Arendt identified "modern man's world alienation with the subjectivism of modern philosophy," beginning with Descartes and Hobbes. Descartes's doubt and Hobbes's assertion that we can know only what we make ourselves both undermined the notion of an objective truth and a world of shared perception. Experimental science, with its emphasis on "making" and "fabricating," contributed as well to the demise of truth.[28] Alluding to Vico's verum factum principle, Arendt argued that "[t]he use of the experiment for the purpose of knowledge was already the consequence of the conviction that one can know only what he has made himself, for this conviction meant that one might learn about those things man did not make by figuring out and imitating the processes through which they had come into being."[29] In Arendt's account, the new science was enormously powerful, but at the cost of replacing nature with history: "the object of science therefore is no longer nature or the universe, but the history, the story of the coming into being, of nature or life or the universe."[30] In a lament that signaled an indebtedness to Heidegger's critique of the modern world picture, Arendt observed, "In the place of the concept of Being we now find the concept of Process."[31] Work was then displaced by labor, *homo faber* by *homo laborans*, whose chief function was to preserve and reproduce mere life instead of the shared life of citizens.[32]

In her later work, by contrast, Arendt recuperated a positive idea of poiesis. In an essay called "The Crisis in Culture," which I explore further in chapter 4, she argued that works of art properly understood need to be distinguished from forms of entertainment; the latter are consumed and perish, while the former endure in the world and are judged from a disinterested point of view. Such judgment is for Arendt a political faculty because it requires an "enlarged mentality," that is, the capacity "to think in the place of everyone else."[33] Aesthetic judgment, accordingly, provides the model for political judgment. Rather than "coercion by truth," such judgment involves persuasion. "Culture and politics, then, belong together because it is not knowledge or truth which is at stake, but rather judgment and decision."[34] In this way, Arendt ends up endorsing Auerbach's view that in confronting works of culture, "we do not lose the faculty of judgment; on the contrary, we acquire it." (If

Arendt had been a better reader of early modern texts, she might also have understood, with Auerbach, the way some early modern texts illustrate this positive conception of culture.) Such judgment in turn helps to construct a shared world of political action.

Early Modern/Late Modern

The central modern figures in this book shared Arendt's, Auerbach's, and Blumenberg's preoccupation with poiesis as a signature of modernity, a sign of the new anthropology that went hand in hand with liberal assumptions about politics and culture. But even more than these three, they saw their interpretations of the early modern period as a response to their own theological-political situation. In the 1920s and 1930s, this situation encompassed the crisis of the Weimar state and the rise of Nazi Germany. In his analysis of the vulnerability of Weimar to Nazi manipulation, Carl Schmitt faulted the liberal emphasis on formal equality. His chief example was the weakness of the German president Paul von Hindenburg in the face of Hitler's electoral success. Schmitt argued at the time that it was naive to give an "even chance" at the polls to a party that did not respect the rule of law, just as it was naive of Hindenburg not to establish temporary dictatorial powers in the face of the Nazi threat.[35] Under duress, Schmitt would eventually articulate an even stronger defense of the absolute dictatorial power of Hitler in "The Führer Protects the Law" of 1934.[36] Leo Strauss developed a complementary argument about the weakness of the Weimar state. Moral and cultural relativism, aided and abetted by methodological positivism of the sort defended by Max Weber, explained the inability of liberal democracies to offer a substantive defense of their own values. It also helped explain the failure of liberal democracies in the West to recognize the threat posed by Nazi Germany. As Strauss noted bitterly in his postwar critique of liberalism, *Natural Right and History*, in following Weber's thought to its logical conclusion "we shall inevitably reach a point beyond which the scene is darkened by the shadow of Hitler."[37] "The prohibition against value judgments in social science would lead to the consequence that we are permitted to give a strictly factual description of the overt acts that can be observed in concentration camps . . . : we would not be permitted to speak of cruelty. . . . The factual description would, in truth, be a bitter satire." In short, "the rejection of value judgments endangers historical objectivity. . . . it prevents one from calling a spade a spade."[38]

Kantorowicz and Cassirer, too, wanted to understand the theological-political situation of modernity, including the devastating power of the twentieth century's most horrifying political myths. They were reacting at first to the horrible carnage of World War I, which had been justified by some participants as a nationalist "holy war."[39] They were also responding to the rise of fascism and totalitarianism in the interwar period. Here, they were less worried about liberalism or relativism than about the powers of reenchantment. In the 1930s and after, these powers were regularly associated with political theology. Raymond Aron and Eric Voegelin coined the terms "secular religion" and "political religion" to refer to totalitarianism. In a similar vein, Franz Neumann referred to the Nazi ideology as a "political theology."[40] In *Meaning in History*, Karl Löwith traced the influence of messianic notions of history on modern debates, citing in particular Kantorowicz's early biography of the medieval Hohenstaufen emperor Frederick II, "with its theme of a messianic mission bequeathed to a 'secret Germany' by the struggles of the fourteenth century—until the utter profanation of this mission by Adolf Hitler."[41] By the 1950s, Kantorowicz himself seems to have shared this view of the misuse of his earlier work and pursued a fuller, more historically specific genealogy of political theology.

Benjamin, too, was preoccupied with the contemporary theological-political situation, which was bound up for him with the question of Zionism. Yet, in contrast to many of his Jewish friends, Benjamin did not believe that "the only salvation is in the Jewish state." Instead, he argued that Western European Jews could "only become part of a 'Jewish movement,' insofar as they are 'tied to a literary movement.' The Jews are 'committed to Internationalism.'"[42] Benjamin's rejection of the Jewish state may inform his critique of political theology in the "Theologico-Political Fragment" of 1920–21:

> Only the Messiah himself consummates all history, in the sense that he alone redeems, completes, creates its relation to the Messianic. For this reason nothing historical can relate itself on its own account to anything Messianic. Therefore the Kingdom of God is not the *telos* of the historical dynamic; it cannot be set as its goal. From the standpoint of history it is not the goal, but the end. Therefore the order of the profane cannot be built up on the idea of a Divine Kingdom, and therefore theocracy has no political, but only a religious meaning. To have repudiated with utmost vehemence the political significance of theocracy is the cardinal merit of Bloch's *Spirit of Utopia*.[43]

There is no spirit moving through history, history itself cannot be the vehicle of redemption, and this in turn means that there can be no religious sanctification of political power. These views would eventually inform Benjamin's increasingly pessimistic view of the political situation in Weimar Germany.

The experience of the collapse of the Weimar state and the rise of Nazi Germany eventually provoked the modern writers to take a longer view. Why do modern liberal regimes seem so incapable of mounting a robust defense of liberal values? Can this incapacity be attributed to the way liberalism dealt historically with the theological-political problem? Can it be attributed to liberal assumptions about culture, that is, about self-fashioning and autonomous agency? If modern reason is infected by relativism, Strauss wondered, is a return to a premodern idea of reason possible? What, in modern political life, Schmitt asked, can revive a genuinely existential understanding of the political, one that would surmount the vitiated conception of politics at the heart of liberalism? What resources, if any, Benjamin, Cassirer, and Kantorowicz asked, can we find in art and literature to counteract the failures of liberalism or to rethink the relationship between religion and politics? In asking these questions, the moderns were seeking to address not only early twentieth-century anxieties about the relationship between politics and religion, culture and historicism, reason and faith; they were seeking to explain the political crisis of their own time, a crisis that resulted in the Second World War. As remarkable as it seems to us now, they did so by looking to the canonical texts of the sixteenth and seventeenth centuries, during which the modern secular state, secular political theory, and secular criticism first appeared. Their innovation did not take the form of locating the origins of liberalism in the early modern period—that was part of the usual story. What was new was their evaluation of this founding moment, as well as the central role they gave to the relationship between political theology and poiesis—whether as a symptom of or resistance to the new secular political order.

According to the usual story, we can trace the origins of modernity to the sixteenth and early seventeenth centuries in Europe, and its resolution of a theological-political crisis. The religious wars of this period prompted Hobbes, Spinoza, and Locke to develop a religiously neutral discourse of rights that helped to found the modern liberal state on a distinctively secular foundation. If political theology refers to the theological legitimation of the state or a state founded on revelation, then political theology is the problem that the new secular language of rights was intended to solve. It did so by bracketing the question of religion in the state of nature and subordinating religion to the secular power of the sovereign once the commonwealth has been founded. Instead of being guided by religious principles, individuals according to the new, secular idiom of political theory are motivated by the desire for self-preservation. The contract that founds the state is simply a contract of protection for obedience. In suspending the question of a substantive common good or end of human action, the new state also removes the occasion for disagreement. Everyone is entitled to practice his religion in private, as long as his actions do not impinge on the liberties of others. Or, as modern parlance has it, we agree to disagree. This, we might say, is the self-congratulatory narrative of modern liberalism.[44]

But here, for some of the modern figures in this book, the problems begin. For Leo Strauss, the new political theory in the seventeenth century did not so much solve the theological-political problem as repress it. According to Strauss, Hobbes ultimately failed to solve the "domestic" theological-political problem because his subordination of the church to the state and his corresponding relegation of conscience to the private sphere ultimately left conscience free to oppose the claims of the state. Hobbes thus made his own absolutist political edifice unstable and unwittingly prepared the way for liberalism. In Strauss's diagnosis, because liberal political philosophy emphasized formal equality over substantive values, and because liberalism had a vitiated concept of the faculty of reason, liberalism proved unable to provide normative grounds for its own convictions, including its convictions about the relationship of religion and the state. Instead, the formal equality of liberalism was the legal equivalent—one might even say symptom—of historicism and relativism. In his early work, Strauss blamed Hobbes for the beginnings of liberalism; he would later move back in time to Machiavelli. In either case, the modern figure who best illustrated the problem for Strauss was Max Weber, with his insistence on the separation of fact and value. According to Strauss, this separation means that there can be no solution to the conflict of values, no way rationally to choose among competing ethical claims.[45] It was this liberal emphasis on formal equality and legality that in the long run left the Weimar state vulnerable to the unprincipled manipulation of the law by Hitler and his followers.

For Carl Schmitt, political theology in the early modern period referred to the theological legitimation of political authority, which the later constitutional state dismantled. But political theology also pointed beyond the early modern period to the ever-present problem of sovereignty, according to which the sovereign must be both inside and outside the law, capable of suspending the law for the sake of preserving the state. For Schmitt, then, political theology had methodological and normative connotations for thinking about politics: a genuine conception of the political always involves political theology, construed as both a sociological structure and an existential commitment. As Schmitt explained in 1922:

> All significant concepts of the modern theory of the state are secularized theological concepts not only because of their historical development—in which they were transferred from theology to the theory of the state, whereby, for example, the omnipotent God became the omnipotent lawgiver—but also because of their systematic structure, the recognition of which is necessary for a sociological consideration of these concepts. The exception in jurisprudence is analogous to the miracle in theology. Only by being aware of this analogy can we appreciate the manner in which the philosophical ideas of the state developed in the last centuries.[46]

Here and in his later work, Schmitt made it clear that by political theology he did not mean that politics is always legitimated by reference to theology or to God. To the contrary, as Schmitt's discussion of Hobbes shortly after this reveals, the early modern absolutist state was modeled on but not legitimized by reference to the omnipotent God, who had effectively been subordinated if not actually marginalized by the new political order. Rather, for Schmitt, political theology names the homology between the theological or metaphysical principles and the dominant political and juristic forms in any given era, and implies that some concrete principle must take the place of God in providing the existential basis of political order.[47] Later, in *The Concept of the Political*, Schmitt further defined the existential intensity of the political in terms of the conflict between friend and enemy, construed as two different peoples or nations. Significantly, in this work of the early 1930s, political theology also had a domestic application: it referred not only to the problem of political authority and political order but also to the necessity of combating any internal enemy who threatens the security of the state. For Schmitt in Nazi Germany, the Jews would become the internal enemy. In this way, Schmitt's concept of political theology in the 1930s dovetailed with that of others who used the term to suggest the metaphysical claims of the Nazi state.

In their diagnoses of the pathologies of modern liberalism, including its supposed inability to provide a criterion for value judgments, Schmitt and Strauss both gave a central, if negative, place to poiesis, which they associated with Hobbes. Once the theological legitimation of political authority fell by the wayside in the seventeenth century, they argued, it was gradually replaced with Hobbes's protoliberal notion of man-made authority and then with the liberal or Enlightenment idea that culture involved both the education of human nature and the mastery of external nature. For Strauss and Schmitt, this emphasis on the fundamental human capacity of poiesis was the defining feature of the early modern period. In assuming that humans are infinitely malleable, early modern writers reveal their assumption that "man is not by nature ordered towards fixed ends"; and this in turn means that "civilization or the activity which makes men good is man's revolt against nature," that is, man's violation of fixed norms and assertion of freedom as an ultimate value.[48] This violation of fixed norms inevitably results in historicism and relativism, which continues to infect modern notions of culture. For Schmitt, the modern, essentially liberal idea of culture relegates politics to one sphere of human activity among others, thereby obscuring the profound existential conflict that distinguishes politics from other human activities. For Strauss, culture or the notion that we can know only what we make ourselves deprives reason of its foundation and interest in the objective truth.

Culture so conceived amounts to a subjective fiction, in the sense of both a made thing and a mere product of the imagination. Strauss associated this view of culture not only with the early modern period but also with Ernst Cassirer, with whom he had studied. In his magnum opus, *The Philosophy of Symbolic Forms* (1953), Cassirer had announced his intention to replace the Kantian "critique of reason" with "the critique of culture."[49] We see this approach already in Cassirer's reading of early modern texts in *The Individual and Cosmos in Renaissance Philosophy* (1927), where he argued that the Renaissance was defined by a new interest in scientific, philosophical, and aesthetic form.[50] In his review of Cassirer's much later *The Myth of the State* (1946), Strauss observed that Cassirer "seems to trace the romantic revolt against the enlightenment to aestheticism. But is not aestheticism the soul of his own doctrine?"[51] "That art is a daughter of freedom," Schmitt wrote in *The Concept of the Political*, "that aesthetic value judgment is absolutely autonomous, that artistic genius is sovereign—all this is axiomatic of liberalism."[52]

Walter Benjamin also turned to the early modern period to offer a genealogy of political theology, but in contrast to Schmitt and Strauss, he offered a positive assessment of the turn toward poiesis. In *The Origin of German Tragic Drama* (1928), Benjamin argued that the emphasis on construction in the early modern "Trauerspiel" provided a model of cultural criticism, of "aesthetics as critique," that was relevant to the modern period as well. Drawing on Schmitt's *Political Theology*, Benjamin argued that baroque drama dramatized a theological-political crisis both in its themes and in its allegorical form, and he explicitly contrasted the critical potential of allegory to the romantic aesthetics of the symbol—the incarnational aesthetic—that informed not only traditional German historiography and Renaissance *Kulturgeschichte* but also the vitalist politics that Benjamin would come to associate with fascism.[53] In doing so, Benjamin elaborated a critical methodology that depended on the foregrounding of poiesis, one that resisted the totalizing narrative of traditional historiography, as well as the danger of political theology, construed as the conflation of theology and politics.[54]

Kantorowicz and Cassirer also gave a central role to poiesis in their analyses of political theology in the early modern period. For them, the Nazi manipulation of political myths constituted a whole new kind of political theology that needed to be analyzed both politically and culturally in order to be dismantled. Although in much contemporary theory this kind of manipulation of myth is often traced to a perversion of Enlightenment rationality, Kantorowicz famously turned to medieval political theology and Shakespeare in his postwar work *The King's Two Bodies*, while Cassirer, revising his earlier account of the Renaissance in *The Individual and the Cosmos*, turned to Machiavelli and Hobbes.[55] While Cassirer seems to have thought that early modern political theory contributed, in part, to the modern abuse of myth and political theology, Kantorowicz found in Shakespeare's art a critique of political theology that looked forward to the tradition of Anglo-American constitutionalism. Like Benjamin, Kantorowicz wanted to salvage a critical notion of art against the cultural relativism and historicism of his contemporaries. For both, art had an important role to play in dismantling the fetish of political theology, understood as the theological legitimation of political power; and for both the early modern period proved to be exemplary of this critique.

In the late 1930s, Freud, too, was drawn to the early modern period to think about political theology. An admirer of Jacob Burckhardt, Freud wrote two early essays on Italian Renaissance figures, one on Leonardo da Vinci (1910) and the other on Michelangelo (1914), both of which exemplify Burckhardt's thesis about the period's invention of the secular individual. But, unlike Schmitt and Strauss, Freud's engagement with the earlier period was not prompted by a desire to uncover the origins of the modern crisis of liberalism, nor was it, in the first instance, motivated by political concerns of the sort articulated by Benjamin, Kantorowicz, or Cassirer. Nevertheless, in his encounter with Leonardo and Michelangelo, Freud too emphasized poiesis, which he understood in explicitly secular terms. In particular, Freud viewed Leonardo the artist and scientist as a kind of Spinoza avant la lettre, and he interpreted Michelangelo's statue of Moses as an allegory of the civilizing process, which he identified with "Kultur," and which he would later oppose to the barbarism of Hitler's Germany. Freud, I argue, was drawn into the orbit of questions of political theology by the Nazi state, and he addressed them explicitly in his last work, a reading of Moses inflected by Spinoza's understanding of political theology. Just as Spinoza had argued that the Bible was a purely human artifact and Judaism a political theology with a historical shelf life, so Freud saw Judaism as the theological-political creation of "the man Moses," a *homo faber*, who "made" the Jews.

A Different Paradigm: Political Theology, Culture,
and the Jewish Question

The historical trajectory I have just traced from the 1920s and '30s suggests a different paradigm for thinking about political theology, one that was familiar to all of the modern figures in this book. It was not just Freud and Benjamin who were preoccupied with their own versions of the Jewish Question. In the 1920s and '30s, and arguably well after this, Schmitt and Strauss were equally concerned with this question, as was Cassirer in 1946, and Kantorowicz in 1957. In the context of this question, as we'll see below, "culture" (*Bildung* or *Kultur*) names the vexed intersection of positive and negative versions of poiesis. Precisely because the Jewish Question was a central question for many of the figures in this book, but also because their understanding of this question differed, it's worth saying a word about it in conclusion.

   In nineteenth-century and early twentieth-century Europe, the Jewish Question was the most visible debate about political theology, construed as the relationship of politics, religion, and culture. Strictly speaking, the Jewish Question concerned the granting of the legal rights of citizenship to Jews and their assimilation to mainstream European culture. As such, the resolution of the Jewish Question was the fulfillment of the Enlightenment ideal of *Bildung*.[56] But as all who debated the question recognized, the Jewish Question was not just about the cultural assimilation and citizenship of the Jews. The broader issue involved the relationship of the liberal state, culture, and religion tout court. Bruno Bauer, a left-wing Hegelian, argued that "[a]s long as the state remains Christian, and as long as the Jew remains a Jew, they are equally incapable, the one of conferring emancipation, the other of receiving it. With respect to the Jews the Christian state can only adopt the attitude of a Christian state."[57] For Bauer, political emancipation for Jews and Christians alike presupposed emancipation from all religion.

In his famous response to Bauer, "On the Jewish Question" of 1843, Karl Marx argued that Bauer's critique of religion did not go far enough. Bauer "subjects *only* the 'Christian state,' and not the 'state as such' to criticism, [that is,] he does not examine *the relation between political emancipation and human emancipation.*"[58] In advocating political emancipation from religion, Bauer failed to recognize that such emancipation left all the problems of the liberal state intact, including the division between public and private that was the basis of social, political, and economic inequality. In a move that is particularly relevant to the argument of this book, Marx added that the cultural interests of the bourgeois individual had failed to ameliorate these problems. In Marx's analysis, the bourgeois realm of culture—understood as a private, apolitical realm of individual improvement—was a corollary of the new division of public and private spheres. Civil society was now made up of "on the one hand *individuals*, and on the other hand the *material and cultural elements* which formed the life experience and the civil situation of these individuals."[59] And yet the condition that prevailed in this state was not individual fulfillment or self-realization through culture (*Bildung*) but alienation.[60] In Marx's view, then, we could say that culture plays the role of bad poiesis.

Marx's solution to this dilemma was the abolition of capitalism, which he notoriously described in this essay as Jewish "huckstering."[61] The anti-Semitism of this turn was partially alleviated by Marx's claim that, in contemporary society, "the practical Jewish spirit has become the practical spirit of Christian nations. The Jews have emancipated themselves in so far as Christians have become Jews."[62] Only when society has emancipated itself from Judaism, understood as capitalist huckstering and the liberal separation of politics and the civil sphere, Marx argued, will we be truly emancipated. When this happens, the Jew's "religious consciousness" will "evaporate, like some insipid vapour in the real, life-giving air of society." Religion, in short, will stand revealed as a mere epiphenomenon.[63]

For the early twentieth-century critics in this book, Marx's take on the central theological-political question of the nineteenth century was just one of the possible approaches and not the most convincing. Although figures on both the left and the right were sympathetic to Marx's critique of liberalism, in particular to his argument that liberalism had failed to solve the Jewish Question, they rejected the slide from the Jewish Question to the question of capitalism. Especially after the experience of Nazi Germany, it was impossible to argue that religious or other ideas could be reduced to mere epiphenomena of the market. For these writers, the situation of the Jews in Nazi Germany was not ultimately about economics but about the power of ideology to trump economic interests.[64] For the moderns, then, the Jewish Question was not a poorly framed question, as it was for Marx. Instead, it raised the issue of political theology more generally, that is, the genuine question of the relationship between religion and the state. It was this issue that prompted the moderns to return to the early modern period—the period that saw the beginnings of liberalism—in order to better understand the strengths and weaknesses of the modern liberal state. This was equally true of writers who thought of religion as the prime instance of ideology and of those who saw in religion the fulfillment of spiritual needs that liberalism, with its emphasis on formal equality, could not satisfy.

Equally important for the early twentieth-century figures, but neglected by more recent critics, the Jewish Question demanded a reconsideration of the relationship between politics, religion, and culture. In nineteenth-century Germany, these questions were at the heart of the debate about historicism, a methodological approach in the social sciences that many felt was producing cultural relativism and undermining the absolute claims of religion.[65] As we've seen, twentieth-century figures such as Schmitt, Strauss, and Benjamin were also preoccupied with the problem of historicism and its relation to culture. Schmitt and Strauss accepted Marx's argument that the isolation of a private realm of culture was symptomatic of the structural deficiencies of liberalism, though they rejected his economic determinism. Benjamin accepted Marx's diagnosis of the ills of modern culture but tried to extricate an idea of art—as distinct from bourgeois culture or from the progressivist assumptions of *Bildung*, with its notion of a coherent self that develops through time—that had the power to resist historicism and relativism and offer a principled critique of politics.[66] Kantorowicz, Cassirer, and Arendt were similarly preoccupied with rescuing a positive idea of culture from the charge of complicity with the status quo.[67]

In the following pages, I use the "Jewish Question" to refer to this constellation of issues, which prompted Strauss, Benjamin, Kantorowicz,

Cassirer, and others to turn to the early modern period to rethink the relationship between religion, culture, and the state. Reading the moderns' interest in the question of political theology through the Jewish Question is not only historically accurate; it also has the methodological advantage of not assuming the traditional narrative of secularization, where this is understood as the appropriation of Christian ideas for putatively nonreligious purposes. Finally, the Jewish Question has a striking contemporary relevance if we do not construe it too narrowly: it is worth pointing out that what the nineteenth- and twentieth-century intellectuals and politicians called the Jewish Question, we could now call—for reasons I discussed at the beginning of this introduction—"the Muslim Question."[68] In other words, the problem of the relationship of religion and the state is not simply a Jewish question, as Bauer and Marx recognized in their different ways. Moreover, it has not withered away but has reappeared in ever new forms to test the liberal commitment to religious tolerance.

: : :

The following chapters provide a typology of the modes of poiesis that emerge in the encounter of the modern and early modern figures. I use the term to refer both to the new anthropology elaborated by Hobbes and Vico, with its emphasis on making, and to the attendant emphasis on works of art as exemplary of this human capacity. Schmitt and Strauss call this idea of poiesis aesthetics, though, as we've seen, they are clear about its early modern origins in Hobbes and Vico. Chapter 1 focuses on Schmitt's analysis of aesthetics as exemplified by Hobbes and countered by Shakespeare. Schmitt's early modernity is thus internally divided, at once the paradigm of the genuinely political and the locus of its demise. Chapter 2 turns to Kantorowicz's very different analysis of Shakespearean poiesis in the context of legal and literary fiction. Chapter 3 analyzes Strauss's critique of Machiavelli's art of politics, while chapter 4 reads Strauss on Spinoza's critique of revelation and defense of liberal assumptions about culture in the *Theological-Political Treatise*. In chapter 5, I argue that Freud draws on Spinoza to develop his own critique of political theology and his own defense of the human capacity for poiesis in his late work. In this way, these chapters enact the debate about poiesis on the terrain of aesthetics, legal and literary fiction, politics, and culture, but always with reference to early modern texts.

For all of the modern figures I focus on in this book, as we'll see, the history of political theology is inseparable from reflection on the human capacity for creating artistic fictions, including the fiction of a theologically grounded political order. In *The Future of an Illusion*, Freud famously described religion as an illusion, which he defined not as error but as the fulfillment of "the oldest, strongest, and most urgent wishes of mankind." But as he proceeded in the essay, he gradually distinguished religious from artistic illusion. Art is an illusion that is acceptable to Freud because, rather than prompting belief, it invites the suspension of disbelief—a knowingness about illusion as the wish for a consolation that only humans, in their cultural activity, can provide one another. Not all of the moderns were as interested as Freud in art as a form of consolation, but all found in the human capacity for poiesis a powerful and defining characteristic of the early modern, protoliberal view of human nature, for better or worse. For some of the twentieth-century writers, the early modern turn to poiesis was a sign of a loss of transcendence; for others, this turn held out the promise of an immanent critique of the existing order or status quo. Yet for all of the modern critics, debates about political theology were debates about the future of illusion, understood in Freud's terms as the realm of fantasy, imagination, and desire: what kind of illusion we should foster, what kind of work illusion can do, and how we can distinguish one kind of illusion from another.

The Future of Illusion draws inspiration from Freud's unsparing, rationalist critique of religion in his late work, as well as from his reflection on the relationship between religious and artistic illusion. It does not, however, offer a psychoanalytic reading of early modern texts; nor do I subscribe to Freud's own rather limited conception of art. Instead, in using the word "illusion," I want to conjure up the realm of the imagination that religion and literature share, and also raise the question of how to distinguish between them. In their readings of early modern texts, the modern figures in this book uncovered a genealogy of this preoccupation. For the early moderns, too, the question of the relation of politics and theology prompted reflection on the uses of illusion and the role of art in sustaining what, with hindsight, we can call the new liberal—or even liberal humanist—order. This insight into the at once constructive and critical role of art in the realm of politics is not a twentieth-century invention. As we will see, the human capacity to forge new, ideologically powerful myths is in many ways at the heart of Machiavelli's and Shakespeare's visions of politics and theology, just as the rational capacity for ideology critique is central to Spinoza's great revision of Machiavelli. It's a premise of this book that, in revisiting these late modern engagements with early modern texts, we can recover, for the present conversation about political theology, the terrain of art and the entirely human capacity to make at least part of the world we live in.

1   Hamlet or Hecuba: Carl Schmitt's Decision

Carl Schmitt's interest in the early modern period is well documented from his earliest works. Hobbes and Bodin play an important role in *Political Theology*, and Machiavelli figures significantly if briefly in *The Concept of the Political*. Then, in the 1950s, in a burst of attention to the early modern origins of the liberal state, Schmitt devoted a monograph to Hobbes's *Leviathan*; he made early modern legal theory and state formation central to his account of the new world order in *Nomos of the Earth*; and he wrote a short book on *Hamlet*. Until recently, Schmitt's analysis of the early modern period has received relatively little attention.[1] But it becomes central to his work once we realize that, for Schmitt, the early modern period marks the emergence of liberal political theory, with its attendant concept of a separate sphere of aesthetics and its evisceration of any genuine understanding of "the political." Shakespeare's most famous play has an important role in this analysis since, for Schmitt, *Hamlet* dramatizes a world before liberalism and aesthetics, a world—though Schmitt does not use this term—before the turn to poiesis that emerged in tandem with Hobbes and the early modern state.

Schmitt's analysis of liberalism was entangled with his own anti-Semitic version of the Jewish Question. As I noted in the introduction, Schmitt's antiliberal definition of the political targeted the Jew as the internal enemy of the Nazi state. Pace Schmitt's defenders, this anti-Semitism was not merely occasional: it found vitriolic expression throughout his work and persisted until his death.[2] Consistent with his early modern genealogy of the crisis of the Weimar state, Schmitt traced the origins of liberalism to Spinoza, who makes a disturbing cameo appearance in the 1938 work on Hobbes as "the Jew" who fully realized the liberal implications of *Leviathan*. I will discuss Schmitt's view of Spinoza and its relevance to the Jewish Question more fully in chapter 4. For now, I wish only to stress that the rise of aesthetics and the vitiation of "the political" discussed below were for Schmitt inseparable from what he clearly saw as the Jewish dimension of liberalism. It's in this light, I argue, that Schmitt's argument about *Hamlet* can be read as defending Schmitt's own response to the Jewish Question during the Nazi period.

Aesthetics and Politics

Schmitt saw the emergence of aesthetics as part of the increasing rationalization of politics and the increasing dominance of technology in all spheres of life. In an important essay entitled "The Age of Neutralizations and Depoliticizations" (1929), Schmitt charted the historical process of Western secularization, depoliticization, and "aestheticization" from the sixteenth century to the present. By depoliticization, Schmitt meant the creation of a neutral sphere—initially modeled on the natural sciences instead of theology—in which parties could reach agreement through discussion and consensus. This process of depoliticization involved four steps: "from the theological to the metaphysical sphere, from there to the humanitarian-moral and finally to the economic sphere."[3] Along this trajectory, Schmitt located "an apparently hybrid and impossible combination of aesthetic-romantic and economic technical tendencies" in the nineteenth century. That is, the aesthetic was "an intermediary stage" between eighteenth-century moralism and nineteenth-century economism, "a transition which precipitated the aestheticization of all intellectual spheres." Moreover, "romantic aestheticism promoted economic thinking and is a typical attendant phenomenon."[4]

For Schmitt, the irrationalism of the aesthetic—its resistance to conceptual formulation—was the underside of the ostensibly rational mechanisms of economic production. As Schmitt wrote in *Roman Catholicism and Political Form* (1923, revised 1925): "Modern technology easily becomes the servant of this or that want and need. In modern economy, a completely irrational consumption conforms to a totally rationalized production. A marvelously rational mechanism serves one or another demand, always with the same earnestness and precision, be it for a silk blouse or poison gas or anything whatsoever" (*RC*, 14–15). In Schmitt's account of the historical development of capitalism, the indifference of technological production to its material—whether "a silk blouse or poison gas"—found an analogue in the indifference of aesthetics to ethics and politics, or at least in the aesthete's inability to come to a decision about any concrete course of political action.[5] The political equivalent of such indecision was liberalism, with its doctrine of formal equality before the law, and its preference for parliamentary debate or discussion over any concrete course of action. In Schmitt's diagnosis, the modern age of technology, liberalism, and aesthetics was antithetical to any genuine conception of "the political," which he defined as a state of crisis and existential confrontation that is beyond—or before—positive law. The genuinely political involves a decision about an exceptional state of affairs, and sovereignty must accordingly be defined as the power to decide the exception.

As numerous critics have remarked, in his critique of liberalism Schmitt himself fell victim to the aestheticism he criticized. In *Political Romanticism* Schmitt condemned the "occasionalism" and "subjectivism" of romantics such as Friedrich Schlegel, for whom there were no longer any objective religious or ethical norms. With the secularization of modern society, according to Schmitt, the church becomes a theater; the artist takes over the function of the priest, and "instead of God, the romantic subject occupies the central position." Rather than coming to a decision, the romantic turns the world into an aesthetic occasion for self-expression.[6] As Karl Löwith noted in an early essay, in opposing the decision "to the bourgeois and to romantic existence," Schmitt was drawing on Marx and Kierkegaard. Although Schmitt referred positively to Kierkegaard in *Political Theology*, Löwith charged that Schmitt was in fact far closer to Schlegel. Like the romantics, Schmitt in his decisionism negated "every commitment to norm." Instead, his was merely "a decision in favor of decisiveness."[7] Peter Bürger argued in a similar vein that Schmitt's "exception" is the political equivalent of the Kantian aesthetic, which resists the categories of the understanding, and that the sovereign who freely decides is the political equivalent of the Kantian genius who gives rules to himself. Bürger also called attention to Schmitt's aesthetic preference for the decision as more "interesting," more novel, and stranger than the norm.[8] More recently, Richard Wolin has extended these insights by noting that "in *Political Theology*, Schmitt attempts to justify his exaltation of the exception in terms explicitly culled from the vitalist aesthetics of suddenness or rupture." Wolin then points to the connection between Schmitt's "vitalist aesthetics of violence" and the "fascist aesthetic of violence" analyzed by Walter Benjamin in the 1930s.[9]

In the following pages, I want to take a different tack toward the aesthetic dimension of Schmitt's work. Instead of deconstructing Schmitt's own unwitting aesthetic ideology, I want to explore Schmitt's reading of two foundational texts of the early modern period—Hobbes's *Leviathan* and Shakespeare's *Hamlet*—that were crucial to his account of political theology, as well as to his genealogy of liberalism and the aesthetic. As we saw in the introduction, for Schmitt the aesthetic is part and parcel of a liberal notion of culture, according to which individuals form themselves just as they artificially create the state.[10] It is in this sense that we can understand Schmitt's notion of aesthetics as a version of early modern poiesis. And, in fact, Schmitt increasingly located the turn to aesthetics in the early modern period. Although he had positive things to say about Hobbes in *Political Theology* and *The Concept of the Political*, under the influence of Leo Strauss Schmitt came to understand Hobbes as prefiguring the development of aesthetics and a corresponding vitiated sense of politics. By way of contrast, Schmitt located a real drama of "the political" in *Hamlet*. There is, however, another way of interpreting the aesthetic and poiesis that makes them a locus of the genuinely political. I'm thinking here of Walter Benjamin, for whom the formal qualities of German *Trauerspiel* or tragic drama allow for a political critique of the status quo. Attention to questions of poetic form, I argue, forces us to revise Schmitt's account of the early modern period and his critique of aesthetics. At the same time, it prompts us to ask about the contribution of the romantic aesthetic—as analyzed by Benjamin and Kierkegaard—both to Schmitt's political theology and to his "apologia" for his decisions during the Nazi period.

Hobbesian Decisionism vs. Parliamentary Representation

In *Political Theology*, Schmitt singled out Hobbes as an exemplary theorist of early modern sovereignty: "The classical representative of the decisionist type . . . is Thomas Hobbes," for whom "*auctoritas, non veritas, facit legem*."[11] Hobbes was preliberal in the sense that in the Hobbesian commonwealth, the law is a function of authority. This authority is modeled on the absolute power of God rather than on any disinterested concept of the truth. But, according to Schmitt, Hobbes was also protoliberal. In asserting the division between public and private, sovereignty and the individual conscience, he articulated the bases of the modern liberal state. Hobbes thus stands on the cusp of the modern era, defined both in terms of its break with older theological conceptions of sovereignty and in terms of its anticipation of the mechanisms of representative or liberal democracy.[12]

Despite his anticipation of liberalism, in *Political Theology* Hobbes still represents the correct understanding of sovereignty. According to Schmitt, "All law is 'situational law'": it depends on the sovereign's bringing about a situation in which norms can apply.[13] There is no a priori legal norm, no natural or moral law to which the sovereign refers; rather the sovereign creates the conditions of security in which law can come into being. Because there can be no law regarding exceptions, exceptions have to be decided by the authority that is above the law (or who constitutes the law), and that authority resides in the sovereign. This sovereign must be absolute—there can be no liberal or constitutional division of powers. Such a division of powers merely obscures or "represses" the question of sovereignty, the question of who decides. Hobbesian decisionism is thus also a personalism—that is, it locates the power of decision in the person of the sovereign.[14]

Against this exemplary decisionist Hobbes, Schmitt counterposed Lockean constitutionalism and eighteenth-century rationalism, which are—according to Schmitt—incapable of conceptualizing or dealing with the exception. In Schmitt's reading of Locke, the law creates authority (rather than vice versa as Hobbes argued); but Lockean constitutionalism cannot designate the person to whom it gives authority. The law dictates how decisions should be made, but not by whom. Schmitt thus assimilates Lockean rationalism to technological, formal, or instrumental reason, or what he calls "a goal-oriented interest that is essentially material and impersonal."[15] He also assimilated Lockean rationalism to a kind of "aesthetic" rationality, which is concerned with the production of artifacts, above all with the state as an artifact. In this analysis, technological reason and aesthetics are two sides of the same debased coin. In his critique of the Weimar jurist Hans Kelsen, Schmitt then recasts this argument in specifically political terms. Now liberal democracy and technology, or representative democracy and the epistemological model of the natural sciences, go hand in hand. Just as the sciences are governed by instrumental reasoning, so liberal democracy involves a conception of politics as merely the instrument for harmonizing conflicting interests. Liberal democracy amounts to "political relativism."[16]

In the conclusion to *Political Theology* Schmitt returned to the link between technology and aesthetics. Here he condemned modern society as a whole for having turned politics into technology on the one hand and aesthetics on the other: "Whereas, on the one hand, the political vanishes into the economic or technical-organizational, on the other hand the political dissolves into the everlasting discussion of cultural and philosophical-historical commonplaces, which, by aesthetic characterization, identify and accept an epoch as classical, romantic, or baroque. The core of the political idea, the exacting moral decision, is evaded in both."[17] Technology and aesthetics alike frame the world for contemplation but conceal the sphere of genuine politics. Concentrating on means rather than ends, peace rather than war, and production or contemplation rather than political action, they encourage a formalism and historicism that deprive politics of its urgency and sublimity.

The urgency and sublimity of the political (as opposed to the weakness of parliamentary and aesthetic notions of representation) receive fuller exploration in Schmitt's *The Crisis of Parliamentary Democracy* (1923,1926), *Roman Catholicism and Political Form* (1923), and *The Concept of the Political* (1927, 1932, 1933).[18] In *Parliamentary Democracy*, Schmitt described how, in the Marxist theory of the dictatorship of the proletariat, "a rationalism conscious of its own historical development clamors for the use of force."[19] In advocating this direct use of force, Russian Marxism drew inspiration from new forms of irrationalism, associated with intuition, instinct, and Bergsonian vitalism. Schmitt then links Bakunin's vitalist preference for art over reason and science to Georges Sorel, whose "theory of unmediated real life" and "theory of direct, active decision" in *Réflexions sur la violence* provided the manifesto of the new politics.[20] According to Sorel, the bourgeoisie, "ruined" by skepticism, relativism, and parliamentarism, had rejected the power of myth. Only the proletariat had a myth in which it believed—the myth of the general strike—and so only the proletariat was capable of effective political action.

It was in this context that Schmitt singled out Mussolini for special praise. Mussolini's Italian fascism appealed to Schmitt precisely because, like Sorel, Mussolini realized the power of myth to mobilize the masses. Schmitt was fond of quoting the speech Mussolini gave in Naples in 1922, before his march on Rome: "We have created a myth, this myth is a belief, a noble enthusiasm; it does not need to be a reality, it is a striving and a hope, belief and courage. Our myth is the nation, the great nation which we want to make into a concrete reality for ourselves." The power of Mussolini's fascist myth was a "symptom of the decline of the relative rationalism of parliamentary thought," but it was

also potentially "the foundation of another authority . . . an authority
based on the new feeling for order, discipline, and hierarchy." Like Machiavelli, to whom Schmitt alludes in this discussion, Mussolini's myth
gave "expression to the principle of political realism." Mussolini's myth
was not true—he even declared openly that it was not true—but it had
what Machiavelli called "verità effettuale": it would become true by
virtue of mobilizing the masses. In its emphasis on action, Mussolini's
myth differed from the liberal lie of representative democracy, the lie of
representation.[21]

We can further gloss this lie by turning to Schmitt's remarks on representation in *Roman Catholicism and Political Form*. In this account
of what Catholicism had to offer politics, Schmitt focused on what he
called representation "from above"—the idea that the pope or priest
represented or mediated a higher truth to the faithful.[22] This idea of
representation differs from liberal and quantitative notions of representation at work in electoral politics, where the representative stands
for the number of people who have voted for him or her "below." The
Catholic representative also mediates a "public," substantive idea, in
contrast to the electoral representative who stands for the aggregate of
private interests, of private individuals who have voted in the private
space of the voting booth.[23] Above all, the Catholic representative is
eminently personal:

> The [Catholic] idea of representation is so completely governed
> by conceptions of personal authority that the representative
> as well as the person represented must maintain a personal
> dignity—it is not a materialist concept. To represent in an emi-
> nent sense can only be done by a person, that is, not simply a
> 'deputy' but an authoritative person or an idea which, if repre-
> sented, also becomes personified. God or 'the people' in demo-
> cratic ideology or abstract ideas like freedom and equality can
> all conceivably constitute a representation. But this is not true
> of production and consumption.[24]

Catholic representation joins office and personality, objective and subjective, the juridical and the normative: the office of the vicar of Christ is
neither charismatic nor merely the quantitative aggregate of individual
interests; instead it represents the *civitas humana*, the dignity of human nature. This notion of the dignity of human nature is linked to the
idea of tradition, that is, the public, historical manifestation of an idea
of humanity that transcends mere individual existence. Neither purely

transcendent, nor purely immanent (or what Schmitt calls materialist), the paradigm of representation is the incarnation.[25] I will return to
these remarks about the vicar of Christ and the incarnation when I discuss Hobbes's *Leviathan*. The important point, for now, is that Schmitt
wanted to distinguish this Catholic notion of representation from the
form of representation characteristic of liberal democracy—whose "ab-
stractions" and "mere fictions" he associated with the autonomy of the
aesthetic.[26]

In *The Concept of the Political* Schmitt also equates liberalism with
an aesthetic approach to politics. He begins by defining the political, in
contrast to the liberal ideals of formal neutrality and depoliticization,
as an "intensification" of differences and allegiances to the point where
"public collective enemies" are willing to fight each other on the battle-
field.[27] Here Schmitt repeatedly insists that the friend/enemy distinction
is not a "metaphor" but a "concrete, existential" reality, linked to the
possibility of "real physical killing." Reiterating the thesis of *Political
Theology*, he argues that the extreme case of war reveals the core of politics precisely because it is an exception and requires a decision.[28] Politics
is at its core a matter of conflict; law, which attempts to adjudicate conflict, is a form of "civilized" depoliticization and thus the counterpart of
aesthetics. Thus "all genuine political theories"—those of Machiavelli,
Hobbes, and Spinoza, for example—"presuppose man to be evil," inclined to violent conflict and concerned with self-preservation.[29] In light
of this elemental truth of human nature and the existential intensity of
the friend/enemy confrontation, liberal representative democracy and
the notion of the "absolutely autonomous" "aesthetic value judgment"
appear as fundamentally suspect.[30] Political and aesthetic representation are equally condemned. Both in politics and in art, in short, Schmitt
argues for myth and against representation, for decisionism and against
the aesthetic.

Taken together, Schmitt's works from the 1920s and early '30s dramatize his divided attitude toward Hobbes and toward aesthetics. He
praises Hobbes's decisionism and absolutist conception of the sovereign
but criticizes Hobbes's protoliberal, mechanistic understanding of the
state as an artifact. He condemns romantic aesthetics and the aesthetic
dimension of Hobbesian representation; at the same time, however,
there seems to be an aesthetic dimension to Schmitt's preference for
myth.[31] By this, I mean not simply that Schmitt's preference is romantic or subjective (that argument has already been made by Löwith and
others) but that Schmitt is attentive to the power of aesthetic form to
compel the listener or viewer. The best politicians are alert to and can

exploit this power even while exposing it. In Schmitt's account of Mussolini's speech, for example, myth is distinguished from representation
and from metaphor, even as it declares itself to be—or represents itself
as—myth. What Schmitt failed to see is that, by his own account, myth
and representation or myth and technology are not polar opposites but
two sides of the same coin.[32]

Leo Strauss's Critique of Schmitt's Indecision

Schmitt's ambivalence about whether Hobbes was primarily decisionist
or liberal was picked up by the young Leo Strauss in his early commentary on Schmitt's *Concept of the Political*. Strauss sent this commentary
to Schmitt in 1932, and Schmitt later reported to one of his students
that it was the most perceptive critique he received. A year later, when
Strauss was trying to get a fellowship to emigrate from Germany, he
sent Schmitt his as yet unpublished work on Hobbes and asked for a
letter of recommendation to the Rockefeller Foundation. (Schmitt recommended him, and Strauss wrote to thank him from England.) Strauss
then is doubly important here, both for his commentary on Schmitt and
for his credentials as a scholar of Hobbes.[33]

In his "Notes on Carl Schmitt, *The Concept of the Political*," Strauss
performed an immanent critique of Schmitt's critique of liberalism and,
in doing so, drew attention to Schmitt's ambivalence about culture or
poetic self-fashioning. According to Strauss, Schmitt's notion of the political involved "a fundamental critique of . . . the prevailing concept
of culture" as the all-encompassing horizon of various autonomous
spheres of activity.[34] Above all, this notion of the political involved a
critique of culture as a disciplining and civilizing of the human will,
a taming of its bellicose tendencies. Schmitt had argued that Hobbes
was "the author of [this] ideal of civilization" and thus "the founder of
liberalism."[35] Precisely because liberalism had been so successful, subsequent liberal thinkers had forgotten the "unliberal," dangerous, or in
Schmitt's terms "political" nature of man at the foundation of the liberal philosophy of culture. According to Strauss, "Schmitt returns, contrary to liberalism, to its author, Hobbes, in order to strike at the root
of liberalism in Hobbes's express negation of the state of nature." That
is, Hobbes's negation of the state of nature was the ultimate liberal act,
informed by the characteristic liberal belief in the human ability to transcend or rectify human sinfulness. Strauss put the historically different
tasks of Hobbes and Schmitt in the following way: "Whereas Hobbes
in an unliberal world accomplishes the founding of liberalism, Schmitt

in a liberal world undertakes the critique of liberalism."[36] Both in his critique of liberalism and in his affirmation of the irreducibly political nature of man, Schmitt, in Strauss's account, was—or should be—the anti-Hobbes.

According to Strauss, however, Schmitt's notion of the political was fundamentally flawed. We can gloss this by saying Schmitt was undecided about the nature of the political because he was undecided about human nature. Either human beings are fundamentally evil and "need to be ruled" absolutely, or they are not fundamentally evil and thus capable of being educated in a liberal fashion regarding their self-interest.[37] Schmitt's admiration for Hobbes's portrayal of human nature as a matter of amoral animal power blinded him to the ineradicable evil of human nature and made him complicit with Hobbes's own liberal presuppositions regarding individual rights. Schmitt bought the Hobbesian myth of the state of nature, we might say, but failed to see its corrosive liberal underside. For Hobbes's view that individuals have a right to self-preservation and thus a right subjectively to determine when their lives are threatened would eventually undermine the absolutist state.

In Strauss's critique, Schmitt was both aesthetic and liberal. First, he was guilty of an "aesthetic" or purely formal admiration of animal power in the Hobbesian state of nature. Second, in occluding the moral basis of absolute rule—the absolute evil of human nature—Schmitt's decisionism provided no grounds for an affirmation of the political. He was thus reduced to "the affirmation of fighting as such, wholly irrespective of *what* is being fought *for*." He was "neutral" or "tolerant" vis-à-vis the "content" of any particular decision, as long as it involved a decision to fight. This liberal neutrality was equivalent to an aesthetic attitude toward politics.[38]

In Strauss's view, then, Schmitt's "entangle[ment] in the polemic against liberalism" was not "an accidental failure" but a consequence of Schmitt's view that "all spiritual concepts . . . are to be understood only in terms of concrete political existence," as well as his view that all political concepts have a polemical meaning. The first, Strauss implies, is a kind of existentialist historicism, the second a kind of relativism.[39] But these views are incompatible with attaining "a pure and whole knowledge." For that, one needs to move beyond liberalism. Such a radical critique, Strauss asserts, is possible only on the basis of an adequate understanding of Hobbes. Judging from Strauss's own work on Hobbes, this means understanding not only Hobbes's destruction of the political but also his aesthetic construction of the myth of Leviathan.[40]

Hobbes Revisited (1): The Myth of Leviathan

In its reevaluation of Hobbes, Schmitt's 1938 book on *Leviathan* shows the traces of Strauss's critique of *The Concept of the Political*. Here Schmitt presents the seventeenth-century absolutist state as the first product of the age of technology. That is, the early modern state is a man-made artificial product—a creation designed to neutralize the religious conflicts of the early seventeenth century by means of a purely formal or technical conception of the law. In the context of religious wars on the continent, "auctoritas, non veritas, facit legem" had the advantage of sidelining the disputed question of truth in favor of formal equality and "technical-political" neutrality. This is why, Schmitt insists, the Hobbesian maxim "is anything but a slogan of irrational despotism."[41] Irrational despotism was precisely what Hobbes was trying to combat, by proposing a conception of law that was divorced from "religious and metaphysical standards of truth." According to Schmitt, Hobbes thought that an authority that was formal rather than content based was more likely to produce peaceful coexistence, especially if it could be shored up by the biblical myth of the state as Leviathan. So far, this is an account of Hobbes that many modern readers would accept.

But, Schmitt went on to argue, in the long run Hobbes was wrong because "a technically neutral state" can be "intolerant" as well as "tolerant"; because Hobbes's myth of the Leviathan state that terrifies the proud was not enough to counteract Hobbes's other message about the state as a mechanism or artifact, the message that the state was man-made, mortal, and in the service of particular interests; and because, by making a private space for individual conscience within the state, Leviathan internalized the cause of its own downfall.[42] It is true that Hobbes makes room for the destruction of Leviathan from within by the exercise of individual conscience.[43] But the specific point Schmitt wished to make was that the liberal reluctance to infringe on the right of conscience, along with the liberal technological approach to government, amounted to aesthetic indifference to substantive goals—an indifference to the harm that subjective conscience could do to the state. This harm could be catastrophic if one interest group managed to gain access to the efficient mechanism of the state.[44] Here Schmitt was reading *Leviathan* with the fall of the Weimar republic in mind. Hobbes's adversaries had included the indirect power of the Catholic Church, as well as the English Presbyterians and radical sectarians. The modern version of

Hobbes's adversaries were those political parties, social organizations, and trade unions that weakened the power of the Weimar republic and that made it vulnerable to radical fringe interest groups, thus fostering intolerance rather than tolerance.[45]

This analysis of the vulnerability of the liberal Hobbesian state to intolerance has led some readers to see Schmitt's *Leviathan* book as an oblique criticism of the Nazi party. According to John McCormick, Schmitt's description of the vulnerability of the technically neutral liberal state to appropriation by an irrational despot is a "Hobbesian depiction of National Socialism." Nazi mythmaking is not the solution to liberal fragmentation, but rather its perverse fulfillment. Rather than preserving the political in the form of a "qualitative total state" that would exist above society, fascism penetrates every aspect of existence, conflating state and society in a quantitative total state. Instead of observing the liberal quid pro quo of protection for obedience, the Nazi state kills its own citizens.[46] Needless to say, Schmitt's indirect criticism of the Nazis—if it is that—was perfectly compatible with anti-Semitism, which is registered in this text by Schmitt's displacing the historical responsibility for the destruction of the Hobbesian state onto the Jewish people. As part of this argument, it is not Hobbes but "the Jew" Spinoza who makes the state into a technological instrument. Moreover, Schmitt does not change his mind about the superiority of myth to liberal rationality or to the liberal notion of representation.

Ultimately, Hobbes failed to establish an adequate model of state power, according to Schmitt, because he chose the *wrong myth*.[47] Hobbes failed to realize that the image of the Leviathan was ambiguous: in the Bible, Leviathan is a powerful sea monster, but also one hated by the Jews. To Hobbes's contemporaries, Leviathan suggested the evils as well as the instrumental uses of state power; and the evil image of Leviathan in turn summoned the "indirect powers who [were] usually hostile to one another [but] were suddenly in agreement and coalesced to 'catch the huge whale.'" That is, Leviathan summoned up the indirect powers—including, for Schmitt, the stateless Jewish people—interested in obstructing the creation of the secular nation-state. In contrast to Machiavelli, Hobbes failed to understand the power of myth as "a sure combat tool and the weapon of a simple, concrete decision."[48] Instead, Hobbes unwittingly chose to represent his commonwealth by the one mythic figure whose double meaning anticipated the self-destructing artifact of the liberal state. By the end of Schmitt's *Leviathan*, the difference that Schmitt once located between Hobbesian decisionism and

Lockean representative democracy he now locates within Hobbes. This splintering of Hobbes is aesthetic as well as political: Hobbes could not keep his political myth from deteriorating into something like mere representation, and this aesthetic lapse was symptomatic of the triumph of merely formal—"technically neutral" or "mechanical"—representation of interests in the political sphere.

Hobbes Revisited (2): Liberal Representation

If we now turn to Hobbes, we see that the entwinement of myth and representation that Schmitt criticized is not the unintended consequence of the Hobbesian project but rather its very point. Schmitt's antipathy to representation blinded him to the fact that myth and representation are not two separate dimensions of *Leviathan*: instead, the myth of Leviathan is an artificial myth, a technologically produced myth or aesthetic artifact. Moreover, Hobbes is not the decisionist Schmitt made him out to be. This is because the power of the Hobbesian sovereign is a matter as much of legitimacy as of force, and this legitimacy is predicated on the consent of the individual to the political contract and to the mechanisms of political representation. Above all, the person of the Hobbesian sovereign cannot be assimilated to the personalism of *Roman Catholicism and Political Form*, as Schmitt would have seen from the beginning if he had been more attentive to the self-conscious theatricality of Hobbesian representation.

At first glance, it's true, Hobbes's sovereign might seem to be the sort of myth Schmitt approved of. Not only is this a personal sovereign who decides the exception; he is also "the reall Unitie" of the subjects of the commonwealth:

> The only way to erect such a Common Power, as may be able to defend them from the invasion of Forraigners, and the injuries of one another, and thereby to secure them in such sort, as that by their owne industrie, and by the fruites of the Earth, they may nourish themselves and live contentedly; is, to conferre all their power and strength upon one Man, or upon one Assembly of men, that may reduce all their Wills, by plurality of voices, unto one Will: which is as much as to say, to appoint one Man, or Assembly of men, to beare their Person. . . . This is more than Consent, or Concord; it is a reall Unitie of them all, in one and the same Person.[49]

The language of real unity suggests the Catholic notion of real presence. It suggests, in other words, that Hobbes sees the commonwealth as more than simply the numerical aggregate of discrete individuals. But, as Schmitt was well aware, Hobbes was no fan of Catholicism, whose fantasies of transubstantiation and "incorporeal substance" he satirized in books 3 and 4 of *Leviathan*. Accordingly, at the same time that Hobbes elaborates a myth of "reall Unitie," he analyzes the *mechanisms* of authorization and impersonation that allow Leviathan to be constructed in the first place. In contrast to Schmitt's argument that Hobbes's artifice undermines his decisionism, Hobbes tells us that artifice is the basis of decisionism: the sovereign's authority is derived from the people's authorization and what Hobbes calls representation as opposed to mere power. "A person," Hobbes famously writes in chapter 16 of *Leviathan*,

> is he, *whose words or actions are considered, either as his own, or as representing the words or actions of an other man, or of any other thing to whom they are attributed, whether Truly or by Fiction.*
>
> When they are considered as his owne, then is he called a *Naturall Person.* And when they are considered as representing the words and actions of an other, then is he a *Feigned* or *Artificiall person.*

Hobbes then goes on to give the theatrical etymology of the word "person":

> The word Person is latine: instead whereof the Greeks have *prosopon,* which signifies the *Face,* as *Persona* in latine signifies the *disguise,* or *outward appearance* of a man, counterfeited on the Stage; and sometimes more particularly that part of it, which disguiseth the face, as a Mask or Visard: And from the Stage, hath been translated to any Representer of speech and action, as well in Tribunalls, as Theaters. So that a *Person,* is the same that an *Actor* is, both on the Stage and in common Conversation; and to *Personate,* is to *Act* or *Represent* himselfe, or an other; and he that acteth another, is said to beare his Person, or act in his name . . . and is called in diverse occasions, diversely: as a *Representer,* or *Representative,* a *Lieutenant,* a *Vicar,* an *Attorney,* a *Deputy,* a *Procurator,* an *Actor,* and the like.[50]

Like Schmitt, Hobbes conceives of representation in terms of an office. But, in contrast to Schmitt's Catholic representation, Hobbesian representation has nothing to do with tradition, incarnation, or real presence. Instead, Hobbesian representation is essentially theatrical: a person is not someone who has "personal authority," so that "the representative as well as the person represented must maintain a personal dignity."[51] Rather, a person is a theatrical and legal fiction, a disguise or outward appearance, a matter of convention rather than incarnation. In striking contrast to Schmitt's discussion of the vicar of Christ, the Hobbesian "vicar" is an actor, wearing a visard; and the political subject is someone who has consented to this divorce between the author and the agent, between himself and his representative. He has consented to alienate his power to decide the exception to the sovereign, in exchange for the sovereign's protection. In theatrical terms, the subject has consented to be a member of the audience and to watch—as if on a stage—the sovereign play or counterfeit his actions. The important point is that the sovereign's power to decide is inseparable from his power to counterfeit—which, in this case, means his power *not to represent* his subjects' decisions but to decide for them and instead of them. The noncorrespondence of agent and author is the source of the sovereign's power to decide.[52]

As Hobbes instructs us, acting is something that natural persons do, as well as artificial persons. The natural is always already a representation. The great achievement of *Leviathan* is to turn what Schmitt (perhaps thinking of Benjamin) calls Hobbes's "baroque idea of representation"[53] itself into a myth—both in the sense of a means of securing the people's consent and in the sense of a self-declared fiction. But, in contrast to Schmitt, Hobbes views this theatrical notion of representation as a source of political strength rather than weakness. First, the subject's consent to the sovereign's representing or "acting for" the subject becomes the basis of the legitimacy and the *verità effettuale* of state power. Second, the sovereign as representative stands in an allegorical rather than symbolical relation to his subjects: the sovereign is not obliged actually or literally to represent his subjects since, by virtue of delegating their power to him and authorizing his actions, they effectively agree to be identified with him whatever he does (as long as it doesn't threaten their security). In short, the sovereign has the authority to decide the exception because he has been authorized or authored to do so by the subject. Schmitt's inability to see this is part of a more general insensitivity to what we might call—after Schmitt and Benjamin—the baroque dimension of early modern theories of representation.

From Hobbes to Shakespeare

Schmitt's reevaluation of Hobbes in his *Leviathan* book left him without a hero of decisionism and of the existential confrontation with "the political." As we have seen, in comparison with the Hobbes of *Political Theology*, the Hobbes of *Der Leviathan* is a tarnished figure, one who failed to understand the importance of myth and who unwittingly inaugurated the protoliberal, technological vitiation of politics. I now want to suggest that in Schmitt's 1956 work *Hamlet oder Hekuba*, Schmitt turned to Shakespeare in order to elaborate his own countermyth of early modern politics, one designed to counteract the deleterious effect of Hobbes.[54] As in *Leviathan*, however, Schmitt's inattention to aesthetic form mars his interpretation of the workings of the text, even as his reliance on the aesthetic power of *Hamlet* serves to propagate a self-serving myth regarding Schmitt's own tragic political decisions.

Even more than *Leviathan*, *Hamlet* has a long history as the avatar of modernity, particularly in Germany. In Goethe's *Wilhelm Meister*, the title character laments the decline of what Schmitt calls representative publicness and asserts that, in the modern age, "the stage alone can supply" what he requires. The first part he chooses to play is that of Hamlet.[55] Following Goethe's example, Hegel, Schiller, Friedrich Schlegel, and Wilhelm Schlegel all offered interpretations of Hamlet as a symbol of modern self-consciousness divided against itself. Such self-division pointed in two directions. On the one hand, Hamlet represented what Hegel described as the modern subject in his "weakness of irresolution, . . . swithering of reflection, [and] perplexity about the reasons that are to guide decisions."[56] On the other hand, in his romantic intensity of emotion and sublimity of conception, Hamlet served as a synecdoche for all of Shakespeare's plays, which, in their "vigor" and "bold freedom," epitomized what Friedrich Schlegel called "the poetry of the north." In this second interpretation, Shakespeare—and *Hamlet*—begin to seem more decisive than indecisive and more German than English. In a deft move that effectively annexed England to Germany, Schlegel argued that Shakespeare is "most justly acknowledged to be the favorite poet not only of the English, but of all nations of Teutonic origin."[57] A minor German poet named Ferdinand Freilingrath composed a poem before the outbreak of the 1848 revolution in which he lamented Germany's political indecisiveness and asserted, "Germany is Hamlet!" (Schmitt quotes this poem in the introduction to *Hamlet or Hecuba*.) In 1911 Friedrich Gundolf, a member of the Stefan George circle, published his enormously successful *Shakespeare und der deutsche Geist* (Shakespeare and the German Spirit), which argued that Shakespeare contributed in powerful ways to "the formation of the German spirit."[58] During the Nazi period, Shakespeare's plays had an important role to play in the cultural politics of the Third Reich, and Hamlet in particular was seen to represent the Nordic qualities appropriate to an Aryan nation.[59] All of this helps to explain why Schmitt—who was intimately familiar not only with the romantics but also with Nazi cultural politics—turned to *Hamlet* to reflect on the recent history of Germany and on his own decisions.[60]

The immediate occasion of the *Hamlet* book appears to have been a seminar that Schmitt gave at the Volkshochschule in Düsseldorf in 1955. But one broader context for understanding this work must surely be Schmitt's situation in postwar Germany. In 1945 Schmitt was arrested by American soldiers and imprisoned for a year and a half. In 1947 he was finally interrogated to see if he should stand trial at Nuremberg, and although he was quickly freed, he refused to sign a certificate of de-Nazification. In his intellectual biography of Schmitt, Gopal Balakrishnan reads this refusal as a demonstration that Schmitt's "opportunism had limits." At the same time, he goes on to quote an astonishing exchange from the transcript of Schmitt's interrogation by Robert Kempner that dramatizes Schmitt's unlimited capacity for heroic self-aggrandizement. In a wide-ranging discussion of his attitude toward the Nazi regime, Schmitt denied he had any contact with Hitler, but he also described himself as "someone [who] takes a position in such situations. I am an intellectual adventurer." In subsequent reflections on Kempner's interrogation, Schmitt illustrated "the struggle for access to the power holder"—the problem of gaining access to Hitler and affecting domestic and foreign affairs—by reference to Schiller's *Don Carlos*. Referring to the scene in which the King announces that Marquis Posa may in the future be admitted to the royal presence unannounced, Schmitt commented: "After this climax there is a sudden turn to the tragic—the turning point of great drama. The fact that he was successful in gaining access to the power holder proved to be the undoing of the ill-starred Marquis Posa." Here Schmitt was illustrating "the fundamental irreconcilability of the omnipotence of the Führer and the legalizing order of the state," but he was also making it clear that the Nazi period—and perhaps his own failed attempts to advise the Führer—are best conceived of as a genuine tragedy.[61]

In the postwar years, Schmitt kept up this pose of heroic self-dramatization. Although he was prohibited from assuming a regular university post, he received many visitors at his home in rural Sauerland,

and he exerted considerable influence on the postwar conservative academic culture in the German Federal Republic and elsewhere. Critics on the left, such as Norberto Bobbio and Jürgen Habermas, were also interested in Schmitt's work.[62] Still, as his rantings in *Ex captivitate salus* (1950) demonstrate, he felt beleaguered and embattled. The *Hamlet* seminar provided one further occasion for his efforts at self-rehabilitation.

In *Hamlet oder Hekuba*, Schmitt subscribes to the romantic view of Shakespeare as sublimely barbaric, but for reasons that should already be clear, he wants to distinguish his view from the reception of Shakespeare in German romanticism and in Benjamin.[63] This may explain why, at the beginning of the book, Schmitt seems more preoccupied with the faults of literary critics than with politics. He begins his analysis of *Hamlet* by taking issue with a narrow, literary-critical approach to the play, one that focuses on the genius of the author, the psychology of the title character, and the aesthetic autonomy of the work of art. This aesthetic approach might be appropriate to the lyric poet, whose "creative freedom" is unconstrained by external forces, but the dramatist's invention is limited by historical circumstances, a very real audience, and the "public sphere."[64] Accordingly, Schmitt proposes to consider both history and artistic form, or rather the irruption of historical forces within the work of art. *Hamlet* is important for Schmitt because it dramatizes or—in Schmitt's lexicon in *Roman Catholicism*—"represents" the religious conflicts of the Reformation at the moment before these conflicts are resolved by the institution of a nonconfessional nation-state. Shakespeare, that is, antedates the Hobbesian sovereign state, the state that Hegel described as "the realm of objective reason beyond theology whose *ratio* put an end to the heroic age, the age of heroic law and heroic tragedy."[65] In *Hamlet* we find a pre-Hobbesian world—a world before poiesis and aesthetics—in which heroism and tragedy are still possible.

In this reading of *Hamlet*, Schmitt explicitly takes issue with Walter Benjamin's 1928 interpretation of the seventeenth-century *Trauerspiel*, an interpretation that drew on Schmitt's own notion of sovereignty.[66] According to Benjamin, tragedy turns on the decision of an individual character, whereas the baroque play of mourning involves a dislocation of sovereignty and thus of a world in which decisions can take place.[67] This is a world in which character is not unified or consistent, and in which history is no longer the medium of significant action. Instead, the sovereign has become dysfunctional; action has been replaced by

acting; and the temporal disjunction of decision-making has been replaced by spatial dislocation in which everything is exceptional and so
nothing is.[68]

The explanation for this situation, according to Benjamin, is that
the baroque world knows no eschatology.[69] In northern Europe, the
deus absconditus (hidden God) of the Reformation and the Lutheran
critique of works together deprived history of any providential meaning. Quoting Hamlet's "What is a man,/If his chief good and market of
his time/Be but to sleep and feed? A beast, no more," Benjamin comments, "These words of Hamlet contain both the philosophy of Wittenberg and a protest against it."[70] Hamlet's sense of the futility of action
and his desire to fight against this feeling are equally the product of
the newly secularized "empty world," a world of "creaturely life" and
mere "externality," in which the trappings or props of royalty serve only
to allegorize their own artifice rather than symbolizing anything like a
plenitude of power. "The new theatre," Benjamin observes, "has artifice
as its god." As this epigram suggests, part of what Benjamin is tracing is
a shift from a world in which the paradigm of sovereignty is theological to one in which there is a divorce between God and the world of
human action. This divorce is in turn reflected in the heightened sense
of art, understood as artifice and theater. But instead of seeing this shift
in terms of a new autonomy of the human subject, a new capacity for
agency and self-determination, Benjamin sees a new attention to the
incoherence of the subject, manifest in the fragmentation, materialism,
contingency, and "puppet-theatre" of the surrounding world.[71]

At the same time, as Benjamin's remarks about Hamlet's protest
against the philosophy of Wittenberg suggest, the *Trauerspiel* produces
something like an immanent critique of this world. This critique takes
place primarily on the level of form, especially in the critique of the
symbolic conception of art by allegory. According to the classical conception of art as symbol, "the beautiful is supposed to merge with the
divine in an unbroken whole." But this notion of art as "the indivisible
unity of form and content" amounts to a theological, undialectical mys-
tification of both art and social relations.[72] In contrast, the allegorical
qualities of the *Trauerspiel* both represent and critique the reification
of social relations: "in the field of allegorical intuition the image is a
fragment, a rune. . . . The false appearance of totality is extinguished."
This amounts to "a deep-rooted intuition about the problematic character of art" conceived in terms of the symbol. But allegory doesn't just
demystify the transcendental claims of the symbol, it also provides a

model for the critical activity of the reader: "The profound vision of allegory transforms things and works into stirring writing." In a similar way, "criticism means the mortification of works."[73] The critic literally deconstructs works and juxtaposes fragments to produce new insights. As John McCole has commented, "The task of criticism is not to conjure up the appearance of the work 'as it really was,' restoring a false totality to it, but to collaborate with the corrosive effects of the passage of time. Decay is an indispensable ally of the indirection necessary to a philosophical criticism that seeks to avoid transfiguration."[74] As McCole's gloss hints, in his remarks about allegory Benjamin is not simply commenting on the theological-political conditions of early modernity; he is also allegorizing the fragmentary, empty world of late capitalism and the crisis of sovereignty in Weimar Germany.[75]

Although, as we will see, Schmitt subscribes to certain parts of Benjamin's analysis and although he explicitly praises Benjamin's treatment of the allegorical dimension of Shakespeare's play, his characterization of the tragic dimension of *Hamlet* is ultimately incompatible with Benjamin's notion of *Trauerspiel*. In the chapter called "The Source of the Tragic," Schmitt begins his discussion of *Hamlet* as *Trauerspiel* by calling attention to the word *Spiel* or play. He asserts that the essence of theater is play and that in play there is "a fundamental negation of the critical situation [*Ernstfalles*]." Here we can see that the distinction between *Trauerspiel* and tragedy maps onto Schmitt's distinction between aesthetics and politics. Schmitt concedes that Shakespeare's plays are *Trauerspiele* in the self-reflexive, theatrical sense that Benjamin and others found characteristic of baroque drama. He writes, "Men of action in this epoch saw themselves on center stage before spectators and understood themselves and their activities in terms of the theatricality of their roles." But what this meant according to Schmitt is that drama was viewed as inseparable from an already theatricalized life: "the play on stage could appear without artificiality as theater within theater, as a living play within the immediately present play of life. The play on stage could magnify itself as play without detaching itself from the immediate reality of life. Even a double magnification was possible: the play within the play."[76] Perhaps not surprisingly, this emphasis on immediate reality produces a reading of the play very much in contrast to Benjamin's. In particular, Schmitt argues that there is something in *Hamlet* that transcends *Trauerspiel*, that Shakespeare "succeeded in elevating *Trauerspiel* to tragedy."[77]

According to Schmitt, what specifically distinguishes tragedy from other forms of drama is "the objective reality of tragic action itself, . . .

the enigmatic concatenation and entanglement of indisputably real people in the unpredictable course of indisputably real events. This is the basis of the seriousness of tragic action which, *being impossible to fictionalize or relativize*, is also impossible to play."[78] The real events in *Hamlet* have to do with King James's accession to the English throne. James is like Hamlet (or vice versa) in that his father was murdered, and his mother married the murderer. According to Schmitt, this historical reality "breaks into" the play *Hamlet* in two ways. First, in Gertrude's ambiguous guilt, Shakespeare raises the question of the responsibility of James's mother, Mary Queen of Scots, for the death of her husband. By not making her innocent, Shakespeare caters to the Protestant dislike of Catholic Mary. But by not making her guilty, Shakespeare supports (at least in the first quarto) James's bid for the throne—which would have been awkward if Mary was guilty. Second, reality breaks into the play in the distortion or "Hamletization" of the revenge hero: in Hamlet's indecision about the nature of the ghost (is it a real ghost from Catholic Purgatory or a devil disguised as a ghost from Protestant Hell?), Shakespeare figures James I, caught between Catholics and Protestants.[79] In so doing, he gestures toward the wider religious conflicts of the Reformation. As Schmitt remarks, "The philosophizing and theologizing King James embodied . . . the entire conflict of his age, a century of belief and religious civil war."[80]

For Schmitt, these historical facts provide the necessity against which the tragic action defines itself. Or, to put this another way, they limit the poet's invention and in so doing raise *Trauerspiel* to tragedy. Whereas "an invented fate is no fate at all," "the core of tragic action, the source of tragic authenticity, is something so irrevocable that *no mortal can invent it, no genius can produce it out of thin air*."[81] "In tragedy," in other words, "the common public sphere (which in every performance encompasses the author, the actors, and the audience) is not based on the accepted rules of language and play, but upon the living experience of a shared historical reality." This shared historical reality may be a powerful myth or heroic legend (here Schmitt is glossing the classics scholar Wilamowitz-Moellendorff), but can never be a mere literary source or mere historical knowledge. These may produce Schiller's historical dramas but not Shakespeare. What distinguishes tragedy from historical drama and Shakespeare from Schiller, then, is the representation of a historical state of emergency that requires a decision. The greatness of the play *Hamlet*, however, lies not in resolving the historical crisis (as we see from Hamlet's own indecision, and the ambiguity regarding Gertrude's guilt), but rather in making it powerfully real to the audience.[82]

Hamlet may not be decisive, we might say, but *Hamlet* is—not least of all in representing the state of emergency of early seventeenth-century England and the historical necessity of a decision between Catholicism and Protestantism.[83]

We can now detect the outlines of the political myth that Schmitt finds in Shakespeare's tragedy. In his remarks on the tragic, we've seen that Schmitt emphasizes indisputably real events and the necessity of shared historical reality, which he illustrates in terms of myth and legend. If we recall Schmitt's remarks on Sorel's "theory of unmediated real life" in *The Crisis of Parliamentary Democracy*, we can see that, in his reading of *Hamlet*, Schmitt is elaborating his own myth of tragic immediacy.[84] Schmitt explicitly contrasts this myth—and the political decision it invites—to the playacting Hamlet comments on in his famous soliloquy on the traveling theater troupe. Schmitt quotes from the first quarto of 1603, before James had come to the English throne, where the loss of the crown is mentioned (after 1603, according to Schmitt, it was no longer necessary to include this motive): "Why these Players here draw water from eyes:/For Hecuba, why what is Hecuba to him, or he to Hecuba?/What would he do and if he had my losse?/His father murdred, and a Crowne bereft him." In Hamlet's reflection on the difference between himself and the players (we should hear the *Spiel* of *Trauerspiel* in the word "players"), Schmitt finds support for his mythical-tragical reading of *Hamlet*:

> It is inconceivable that Shakespeare intended no more than to make his Hamlet into a Hecuba, that we are meant to weep for Hamlet as the actor wept for the Trojan queen. We would, however, in point of fact weep for Hamlet as for Hecuba if we wished to divorce the reality of our present situation from the play on the stage. Our tears would then become the tears of actors. We would no longer have any purpose or cause and would have sacrificed both to the aesthetic enjoyment of the play. That would be bad, because it would prove that the gods in the theater are different from those in the forum and the pulpit.[85]

Hamlet, in this interpretation, is the anti-Hobbes. In its immediacy and direct relevance to our lives, *Hamlet* is part of a world that is "not yet 'civilized' [*poliziert*]." This means that politics has not been separated off as an autonomous sphere of action (as in the case of liberalism), nor is there yet a corresponding autonomous realm of play or aesthetics. Rather, "the play still belonged to life itself," a "barbaric and elemental" life of "seafarers and adventurers."[86] It is only after Shakespeare that politics (as opposed to the genuinely political) comes into its own with the modern, Hobbesian state—a state concerned with order, peace, and security. In response to the wars of religion, such a state creates a newly rationalized or "a policed existence," which puts "an end to . . . the age of . . . heroic tragedy." Then, in the wake of this policed existence, we find the emergence of Schiller's notion of art as "a realm of autonomous representation," a realm of play that "can be opposed to both seriousness and life." In this way, Schmitt comments, "politics, police and *politesse* become a remarkable troika of modern progress opposed to religious fanaticism and feudal anarchy—in short, to medieval barbarity," which Schmitt sees in *Hamlet* and Tudor England. *Hamlet* and the character Hamlet, in Schmitt's reading, thus stand for the authentic world of politics, whereas Hecuba stands for artifice and aesthetics.[87]

Although, at first glance, Schmitt's reading seems both oddly positivistic and romantic, there is also something sensible about Schmitt's efforts to read Shakespearean tragedy in the context of the historical shift from medieval theology to the secular nation-state. We can also, I think, appreciate Schmitt's efforts to cast the religious struggles of the late sixteenth century and the resulting loss of certainty as themselves the stuff of tragedy and the morally demanding decision. Put that way, of course, Schmitt comes to seem less perverse as a reader of Shakespeare, and more like Franco Moretti or Stephen Greenblatt, not to mention Dover Wilson or Lillian Winstanley (the two critics cited by Schmitt)—until, that is, we remember that all of Schmitt's "historical reality" comes at the price of any serious attention to the language or form of the play.[88]

For what's strange about Schmitt's reading of Hamlet and Hecuba—and the distinction between politics and aesthetics on which it rests—is that it is undermined by the very speech from *Hamlet* to which Schmitt alludes in the title of his book (not to mention by the play as a whole). For most of the play, as Schmitt is well aware, Hamlet is incapable of action or decision, and his own incapacity is the subject of his reflections when he is confronted with the player from the traveling theater troupe who performs the speech about Hecuba. As we've seen, Schmitt quotes from the first quarto of 1603. But in quoting from the first quarto, Schmitt neglects the more reliable second quarto and first folio, where the metaphor of theater is much more pronounced.[89] Here is the speech as it appears in a modern edition, which draws on both the second quarto and the first folio:

O, what a rogue and peasant slave am I!
Is it not monstrous that this player here,
But in a fiction, in a dream of passion,
Could force his soul so to his own conceit
That from her working all his visage wanned,
Tears in his eyes, distraction in his aspect,
A broken voice, and his whole function suiting
With forms to his conceit? And all for nothing!
For Hecuba!
What's Hecuba to him, or he to Hecuba,
That he should weep for her? What would he do
Had he the motive and the cue for passion
That I have? He would drown the stage with tears
And cleave the general ear with horrid speech,
Make mad the guilty and appall the free,
Confound the ignorant, and amaze indeed
The very faculties of eyes and ears.

(2.2.559–76)[90]

In this metatheatrical speech, Hamlet laments that the actors are more capable of action than he is.[91] Schmitt reads the speech as allowing Hamlet to recognize the difference between mere acting and action, between weeping for Hecuba and taking vengeance.[92] Hamlet, that is, recognizes the urgent need for real action. In terms of Schmitt's earlier distinction between myth and invention or mere fiction, we could say that Hecuba, a figure from the world of Greek myth, now appears as a mere literary invention, while Hamlet, Shakespeare's most famous literary invention, rises to the stature of tragic myth. As a result, Schmitt argues, Shakespeare's audience comes to understand the difference between mere aesthetic appreciation of *Hamlet* the play and the necessity of a genuinely tragic decision in the face of a state of emergency.[93]

I want to propose an alternative reading of the metatheatrical dimension of the play. In this reading, Hamlet learns that action and play-acting are not necessarily opposed, as Schmitt seems to think they are. Hamlet's initial response to the speech of the player king is to imagine an even more extravagantly theatrical performance—drowning the stage with tears and cleaving the general ear with horrid speech. He imagines the player king with his own "motive" and "cue for passion"—rather than a simple cue for action, as Schmitt reads the scene. He then reflects ironically on his own hyperbolic response by recasting the conventions of revenge tragedy in terms of farce: "Who calls me villain, breaks my

pate across,/Plucks off my beard, and blows it in my face?" This passionate response to the player then gives Hamlet his plan—or theatrical
cue—for action, which in this case involves putting on a play:

> I have heard that guilty creatures sitting at a play
> Have by the very cunning of the scene
> Been struck so to the soul that presently
> They have proclaimed their malefactions;
> For murder, though it have no tongue, will speak
> With most miraculous organ. I'll have these players
> Play something like the murder of my father
> Before mine uncle. I'll observe his looks,
> I'll tent him to the quick. If a but blench,
> I'll know my course.
>
> (566-75)

Hamlet reasons that, just as he was "struck to the soul" by the player
king's performance, so too will Claudius be by the play within the play,
and his response will provide Hamlet with a "course" of action. If Hamlet has learned to be decisive, it is not in a Schmittian sense. One might
say instead that the sequence of Hamlet's responses to the player king
unsettles any simple distinction between the players and Hamlet. What
Hamlet's speech teaches us is that, in both Elsinore and seventeenth-
century England, theatrical representation is not simply at odds with
political action, though it also can't simply be equated with it. Against
Schmitt's opposition between aesthetic play and political seriousness,[94]
Hamlet's metatheatrical reflections, along with his powerful aesthetic
response to the players, help us see that it is theatrical or aesthetic form
that allows for (but does not guarantee) political action. In the "aesthetic" autonomy of art lies its potential for both ideological closure
and critical power.[95]

Shakespeare, in other words, cannot provide the countermyth or
antidote to Hobbes—at least not the countermyth Schmitt proposes.
As the authors of the two most self-consciously metatheatrical works
of the early modern period, Shakespeare and Hobbes inhabit the same
universe. As we saw in *Leviathan*, even those natural persons acting
for themselves are already implicated in a social and political world
of nonmimetic representation. In *Hamlet*, this insight into baroque
representation—rather than simply the brute historical circumstances
of James's accession—is the stuff of tragedy, of Hamlet's tragic indecision. That is, it's the indecision that's tragic, rather than the facts of the

succession. In *Leviathan*, this same insight into representation becomes the source of comedy, that is, of social and political order.

The important difference between the world of the *Trauerspiel* and Hobbes's *Leviathan* is that in the former theatricality is a problem, whereas in *Leviathan* it is the solution. In *Hamlet*, the title character is incapable of sovereignty; in *Leviathan* the sovereign is monstrously effective. The Hobbesian sovereign (or Hobbes himself as sovereign/plotter) turns all those dysfunctional aspects of the baroque polity to his advantage. Like the creator of a *Trauerspiel*, his goal is to create a world in which "the buffeting of the individual figures in the winds of passion finds its adequate representation in a staging that demonstrates its own artifice," a world in which action has been replaced by acting, and participation by spectatorship.[96] The famous frontispiece to *Leviathan*, in which the figure of the sovereign is made up of tiny figures gazing up at him, represents this theatrical and spectatorial dimension of both action and sovereignty. So does the famous discussion of personification in chapter 16 of *Leviathan*. *Leviathan* is a *Trauerspiel* in which the emphasis is on *Spiel*, the play of representation, rather than on *Trauer* or mourning.

One might go further on the basis of this opposition and argue that Shakespeare does indeed provide the antidote to Hobbes, though not a Schmittian one. Rather than dramatizing a genuinely political barbarism, Shakespeare's self-conscious staging of the homologies between action and acting could be seen as undermining the ideological fiction of absolute sovereignty. Whereas in *Leviathan*, the political subject alienates his capacity for representation and for acting to the absolute sovereign in a manner consistent with the *lex regia* of Roman law, in Shakespeare, by contrast, theatrical self-consciousness buttresses a common law critique of such pretensions to absolutism. This critique may also be evident in the play's foregrounding of election to, rather than inheritance of, the Danish crown.[97] But Schmitt, for all his emphasis on the irruption of historical reality into the world of the play, has nothing to say about the common law or royal election, just as he has little to say about the "public sphere" in which Shakespeare's plays were performed and to which they contributed.[98]

And what about political theology? For Schmitt, as for Benjamin, *Hamlet* ultimately stages the eclipse of the medieval worldview. But the two come to very different conclusions about the religious dimension of the play, as well as its relation to the aesthetic, or to play more generally. At first, Benjamin observes of the seventeenth century, "religious aspirations did not lose their importance: it was just that this century denied them a religious fulfillment, demanding of them, or imposing on them, a secular solution instead." In the *Trauerspiel*'s world of immanence, in which God is a *deus absconditus*, fatality takes the place—or plays the role—of providence. The transcendent is utterly immanent in the form of an ever-present sense of catastrophe, which is less an interruption of the natural order of things than it is "the very estate of man as creature." This creatureliness amounts to "the secularization of the historical in the state of the creation." To put this another way, in a world without eschatology—as Benjamin describes the baroque—history itself is secularized. The creaturely world is no longer subordinated to a providential telos but manifests the historical instead in physical vulnerability or what Hegel called "the extreme embodiment of violability."[99] And this in turn makes the martyr more of a neopagan stoic, confronting the ravages of nature, than a genuinely religious figure: the literary representation of the martyr "has nothing to do with religious conceptions; the perfect martyr is no more released from the sphere of immanence than is the ideal image of the monarch. In the drama of the baroque he is a radical stoic."[100]

And yet, even as Benjamin notices the fragmentary, contingent, material, and allegorical dimension of *Hamlet*, he insists on a quasi-religious element of transcendence in the play.[101] If Hamlet wants to die by some accident, this accident in turn conjures up a world of sacrifice and martyrdom: "Whereas tragedy ends with a decision—however uncertain this may be—there resides in the essence of the *Trauerspiel*, and especially in the death-scene, an appeal of the kind which martyrs utter."[102] Or, as Benjamin later remarks of Hamlet, "His life, the exemplary object of his mourning, points, before its extinction, to the Christian providence in whose bosom his mournful images are transformed into a blessed existence. Only in a princely life such as this is melancholy redeemed, by being confronted with itself. The rest is silence. . . . Only Shakespeare was capable of striking Christian sparks from the baroque rigidity of the melancholic, as un-stoic as it is un-Christian, pseudo-antique as it is pseudo-pietistic." *Hamlet* is "the unique spectacle" in which melancholy and acedia are "overcome in the spirit of Christianity."[103] It's hard to know exactly how to understand this claim. Does Benjamin really think that the play points to Christian redemption? Or is he reading the play in the light of a messianic materialism, which produces a kind of transcendence from within the immanent and material realm of human experience, in the "spirit" of Christianity (echoing, perhaps not incidentally, the title of a work by Hegel and also one by Feuerbach)? Whether literally or figuratively, Benjamin does appear to find a moment of transcendence in the play's conclusion.[104]

By contrast, Schmitt, who is insensitive to the elements of contingency in the play, rejects the theological recuperation of *Hamlet*: "*Hamlet* is not Christian in any specific sense, and even the famous passage concerning providence and the fall of the sparrow (5.2.227–228) that Benjamin invokes does not alter this fact."[105] Although Schmitt sees the play as representing the historical conflict of Catholics and Protestants in early modern England, he does not read this conflict as pointing toward a specifically Christian resolution or even a Christian message. To the contrary, what interests him is the way in which the play depicts the barbarism of political relations before the resolution of the confessional conflict by the early modern state: "Shakespearean drama in general and *Hamlet* in particular is no longer religious in the medieval sense, but neither is it state-centered or political in the concrete sense that the state and politics acquired on the European continent through the development of state sovereignty during the sixteenth and seventeenth centuries." Instead, England avoided "the constricted passage of continental statehood," leaping to "the land appropriation of a New World and . . . the maritime appropriation of the world's oceans."[106]

Schmitt and Benjamin agree, then, that *Hamlet* dramatizes a break with a medieval, theological worldview. In the world of *Hamlet* there is a new divorce between a *deus absconditus* and the world of human action. But whereas Schmitt sees the workings of tragic fate in the play, Benjamin emphasizes fragmentation, materialism, intrigue, and puppetry. This difference of approach produces two different versions of aesthetic play. For Benjamin, the drama of the period is characterized by a heightened sense of art as artifice; for Schmitt, the artifice of theater only brings it closer to the theatricality of "real life." For Benjamin, the distancing effects of artifice are a condition of self-reflection; for Schmitt, artifice is that which needs to be overcome for action to be possible. Hence Schmitt's comment in his appendix on Benjamin's *Trauerspiel* book that "the crux of [*Hamlet*] can't be understood in terms of intellectual or aesthetic categories like the Renaissance and the Baroque." Instead, it must be understood in terms of the "antithesis between the barbaric and the political."[107] And yet at the heart of Schmitt's analysis is an intense reliance on the aesthetic category of tragedy. Why?

The Tragedy of Carl Schmitt

Even more than Schmitt's *Leviathan* book, *Hamlet oder Hekuba* shows that Schmitt realized that Hobbes could not be simply conscripted into his Sorelian myth of the sovereign. As we've seen, Hobbes's notion of the sovereign is much closer to Benjaminian allegory—to what Schmitt himself called "the baroque idea of representation"—than to what Schmitt meant by myth or political theology. Hobbes's myth of the commonwealth is precisely what Schmitt pronounced impossible: an invented myth, which is as much to say an allegory of the loss or illegibility of the theological; a myth designed not to move to action (as Machiavelli's or Mussolini's was) but to elicit consent and contemplation. What remains to be considered is why Schmitt thought Shakespeare was more promising than Hobbes as the locus of the genuinely political.

Here, perhaps, is the place to state the obvious Schmittian interpretation of *Hamlet*, which Schmitt oddly avoids. In this reading, which would draw on Schmitt's definition of the sovereign in *Political Theology* as he who decides the exception, Hamlet's indecisiveness would prefigure the indecisiveness of the liberal state. This interpretation would be in sync with Schmitt's references to the Freilingrath poem of 1848 that declares that "Germany is Hamlet!"—a judgment that Schmitt elsewhere applied to his own historical moment. *Hamlet* would be a modern myth because it dramatizes the fatal indecisiveness of liberal modernity. The tragedy of *Hamlet* would then be the tragedy of the death of "the political," not only for Stuart England but for twentieth-century Germany. But Schmitt conspicuously does not propose this interpretation of the play. One reason for this may be that he has a different and, in an important sense, a more intimate case to make.

In this concluding section, I want to suggest that Schmitt's interpretation of *Hamlet* is a kind of *apologia pro vita sua*, one in which the most modern of early modern tragedies serves as an allegory for Schmitt's own "tragic" decisions. In this light, the "taboo" that "irrupts" in the play is the taboo of Schmitt's own membership in the Nazi party and the works he wrote supporting Hitler's dictatorial power. But Schmitt has to do some fancy footwork to construct this apology. This is because, for most of his career, he was determined to distinguish between myth and artifact, Catholic representation and parliamentary representation, tragedy and *Trauerspiel*. But in *Hamlet oder Hekuba* he also blurs these distinctions by arguing that *Trauerspiel* may be elevated to tragedy. Why? Perhaps the answer goes something as follows: If what Benjamin represented as the *Trauerspiel* par excellence is really a tragedy, if Hamlet's indecisiveness can be recast as *Hamlet*'s decisiveness, if a play can be the basis of sublime barbarism or political theology, then perhaps, Schmitt may imply, his own modern tragedy can be read as heroic rather than romantic. If so—to return to a passage I quoted at the beginning of this chapter—he is not guilty of mistaking the poison gas of Auschwitz for a silk blouse.

To understand this apologia, it is helpful in conclusion to turn from Benjamin to Kierkegaard. As numerous critics have noticed, Schmitt praises Kierkegaard's remarks on the exception in *Political Theology*. In formulating his conception of the political, Schmitt also draws on Kierkegaard's conception of the "teleological suspension of the ethical"—his notion that faith demands an existential decision that can't be conceptualized in terms of preexisting ethical or aesthetic categories.[108] But more directly relevant than either of these, I suggest, are the remarks on ancient and modern tragedy by "A" (Kierkegaard's aesthete) in *Either/Or*. These remarks can help us further understand how Schmitt's assimilation of *Hamlet* to ancient tragedy was crucial to his self-rehabilitation.

A's depiction of modern life in *Either/Or* sounds remarkably like Schmitt's critique of liberalism and modernity. According to A, modern life is made up of discrete individuals, who join together in associations that cannot overcome their isolation. All modern associations "bear the stamp of the arbitrary." "Is not the invisible and spiritual bond lost which held the state together politically; is not the power of religion, which held fast to the invisible, weakened and annihilated?"[109] In contrast to ancient Greek life, where the individual "still rested in the substantial categories of state, family, and destiny," the modern individual is characterized by anxiety, melancholy, and despair.[110] In contrast to ancient Greek tragedy, where the tragic was located in plot and action, modern tragedy places the emphasis on situation and character, "subjective reflection and decision." Thus "Hamlet is deeply tragic [in a modern sense] because he suspects his mother's guilt," whereas Antigone in Sophocles's tragedy "is not at all concerned about her father's unhappy destiny. [Instead] this rests like an impenetrable sorrow over the whole family."[111]

According to A, the modern age, with its emphasis on individual responsibility and individual self-fashioning, is in danger of losing a sense of the tragic altogether—a sense, that is, of something that transcends the individual.[112] "The tragic has in it an infinite gentleness; it is really in the aesthetic sense with regard to human life, what divine love and mercy are." The tragic is like divine love and mercy because it can occur only at the point where free will and necessity or external circumstances intersect, and this means that the individual is not completely responsible for the tragic outcome. Structurally—in its aesthetic form—tragedy forgives the individual, even as it holds him responsible.

Rhetorically—in its aesthetic effect—tragedy elicits what A, after Hegel, calls "true tragic pity": the sympathy with the sufferer that is at the same time an ethical justification because it recognizes the external circumstances affecting the sufferer.[113] Here, in the comparison between tragedy and divine love and mercy (as well as the later discussion of Christ crucified as a tragedy), Kierkegaard calls our attention to the relationship between the aesthetic and the theological.[114] The aesthetic, as Kierkegaard sometimes describes it, is before the ethical (if we think of stages of spiritual development); and the theological is after or beyond the ethical. Neither resides in the realm of absolute human responsibility and human self-fashioning.

Here we can see how Schmitt might confuse the aesthetic and the theological even as he insists on their distinction, and why he might want to. Carl Schmitt, the critic of romanticism, may find in the romantic celebration of Shakespeare's barbaric aesthetic achievement "true tragic pity"—or divine forgiveness—for his own decisions. Schmitt, that is, uses the aesthetic power of Shakespeare to allegorize his own situation in World War II as genuinely—classically—tragic. If Hamlet is tragic in the modern sense because he needs to decide about Gertrude's guilt, *Hamlet* is tragic in a classical sense because it dramatizes an objective religious conflict—and the objective necessity of a decision—with world-historical implications. Just as Shakespeare's *Hamlet* transcends *Trauerspiel* and becomes truly tragic, so—ideally—does Carl Schmitt.

As I have tried to suggest, Schmitt's critique of liberalism and the aesthetic is well worth our attention. But it is worth our attention as much for what it conceals as for what it reveals. For Schmitt, as Heinrich Meier has argued, "moral man longs for tragedy, and he conceives of the world in its image as fate and dispensation."[115] By virtue of its existential seriousness, tragedy is raised above the liberal sphere of culture; no longer an instance of fiction, tragedy instead returns us to a moment before aesthetics, when the political, rather than poiesis, was the dominant mode of conceiving one's relation to the world. But for Shakespeare and Hobbes, poiesis—understood both as poetry and as the essence of their new anthropology—is not antithetical to politics, but its very condition.

2 Sacred Kingship and Political Fiction: Ernst Kantorowicz, Carl Schmitt, Ernst Cassirer, and Walter Benjamin

At about the same time that Schmitt was writing *Hamlet or Hecuba*, the emigré intellectual historian Ernst Kantorowicz was finishing his magnum opus, *The King's Two Bodies: A Study in Medieval Political Theology*. Although the two books are very different in scope and rhetoric, Kantorowicz was in many ways addressing a similar constellation of issues regarding the history of political theology and its relation to the early modern state. And just as Schmitt turned to *Hamlet* to explore the problem of political theology, so Kantorowicz found an eloquent articulation of the theological-political idiom of the king's two bodies in Shakespeare's *Richard II*. Unlike Schmitt, however, for whom the theological crisis in *Hamlet* dramatized the genuinely political and the necessity of a decision, Kantorowicz read *Richard II* as a dismantling of political theology, one that points in the direction of liberal constitutionalism. Buttressing this reading is Kantorowicz's powerful analysis of political theology as a poetic and legal fiction. In Kantorowicz's argument, we could say, political theology is reoccupied by poiesis. This analysis, I argue, can be seen as a response to Schmitt's *Political Theology* on the one hand and Ernst Cassirer's *Myth of the State* on the other. It can also be seen as a reflection on Kantorowicz's own early intellectual allegiances and intellectual trajectory.

Kantorowicz was born into a prosperous, assimilated Jewish family in Posen, in 1895. He served in World War I and then in the Freikorps, a right-wing paramilitary group that fought against the Spartacists in Berlin in 1919. After his military service, he studied at Heidelberg where he came under the influence of the German poet Stefan George. George sought to create a spiritual and cultural elite that would eventually provide the leadership for a new *Kulturnation* and remedy the spiritual impoverishment of Weimar Germany. Although George's followers included several young Jewish academics, George himself and some of his acolytes could be remarkably anti-Semitic (I'll return to this point shortly). Central to George's cultural program was poetry, especially the poetry of Dante and Shakespeare, and what George called the artistic element, "das Künstlerische." George was also partial to Nietzsche's idea of monumental history, the history of great men who would provide examples for the present.[1] In the medieval Hohenstaufen emperor Frederick II, whom Nietzsche had praised in *Beyond Good and Evil*, George found just such an exemplary leader.[2] Kantorowicz's first book, a biography of Frederick (1927), was written under the influence of George, who saw the cosmopolitan ruler as the prefiguration of the new *Kulturnation* that would transcend the bourgeois nation-state.[3]

The biography of Frederick was extraordinarily controversial when it appeared because of the idiom in which it was written. It is hard to know whether contemporary readers of this biography were more shocked by the absence of footnotes or by the prophetic tone, including the comparison of Frederick to both the Messiah and the Antichrist. But perhaps it isn't necessary to choose, since the absence of scholarly apparatus was a symptom of the larger goal of the work to provide "Secret Germany"—the circle around George—with a model for a more integrated and spiritual form of life.[4] Frederick appears as a cosmopolitan emperor and Nietzschean Übermensch, whose *renovatio* of the Roman Empire, it is implied, foreshadowed not only the Renaissance but also George's vision of the "new Reich."[5] Whatever George may have intended by this phrase, it's easy to see how the Frederick biography could have been enthusiastically received by Hitler and Goebbels, who read it as a celebration of German nationalism and of a specifically Germanic heroism. The reception of the Frederick biography, then, was vexed not only because it constituted a powerful, Nietzschean critique of positivist historiography in the 1920s but also because it was perceived as advancing protofascist ideals.[6]

Martin Ruehl has argued that there is more than a grain of truth in the charge of protofascism. In support of this claim, he describes one particularly painful episode in Kantorowicz's dealings with George that illustrates his willingness to submerge his own identity in that of "the Master" and to entertain, at least hypothetically, the idea that Nazi Germany might be the realization of George's ideals. On July 10, 1933, Kantorowicz wrote to George, "'May Germany become as the Master envisioned it.' And if today's events are not just a travesty of that vision, but actually the true path to its realization, then everything may turn out well. . . . If the Fates do not allow one access to the 'Reich'—and as a 'Jewish or coloured person,' as the new twin expression has it, one is necessarily excluded from a state founded on purely racial criteria—then one has to summon up the *amor fati* and make decisions accordingly."[7] Remarks such as these suggest that Kantorowicz was willing to accept anti-Semitism as the price of realizing George's cultural ideal, though he was uncertain whether the Nazi Reich was in fact the Reich George had in mind. By 1938, however, he had made the very different "decision" to emigrate to England. His subsequent comments about the Frederick biography suggest that he regretted some of the political ideals that informed it and the uses to which it was put. As we will see in the conclusion to this chapter, however, Kantorowicz returns to these ideals in his later work, refurbished for his new audience in the United States.

The reception of Kantorowicz's first book appears to have left its mark on *The King's Two Bodies* in more than one way. Published in 1957 after Kantorowicz had emigrated to the United States, *The King's Two Bodies* is a hard—perhaps deliberately hard—book to read. Kantorowicz himself fostered the notion that the book had no argument, writing in his preface something no scholar could get away with today: "Only hesitatingly and rarely did the author find it necessary to draw conclusions or indicate how the various topics discussed in these pages should be . . . [integrated] with each other."[8] Whereas the first edition of the Frederick biography flouted scholarly protocol by ostentatiously omitting all footnotes, *The King's Two Bodies* practically drowns in them, as though to advertise its commitment to disinterested scholarship, even to the study of arcane historical sources for their own sake.

In fact, the book does have an argument, one that is directly relevant to Kantorowicz's earlier work. Beginning in the twelfth century and moving forward to the English civil war, Kantorowicz tracks the appropriation of theological metaphors, above all the ecclesiastical body of the Church and the incarnated body of Christ, for secular political purposes, showing their distinctive use by English common lawyers for the crown. But the argument and central exhibits of *The King's Two Bodies* also seem intended to provide an antidote to the misuse of Kantorowicz's *Frederick II*. First, *The King's Two Bodies* shows how the idea of the two bodies could morph into the distinction between person and office, which in turn played a crucial role in the dethroning of Charles I in 1649. If charisma is one effect of the king's two bodies, the other is—at least in the long run—constitutionalism. Second, myth conspicuously gives way to fiction. By fiction I mean first of all the notion of a legal fiction, which is central to Kantorowicz's historical analysis of the king's two bodies. But by fiction I also mean literature. As we will see, Kantorowicz himself links the idea of a legal fiction to literary fiction, when he frames the argument of *The King's Two Bodies* with a reading of Shakespeare's *Richard II* on one hand and Dante's *Divine Comedy* on the other. Whereas Shakespeare depicts the fatal separation of the king's two bodies and thus anticipates the regicide of Charles I and the English republic, the *Divine Comedy* articulates what the George circle saw as Dante's secular religion of humanity and his vision of a world community. We could then provisionally say that *The King's Two Bodies* presents two arguments or narratives: the first concerns the Christological origin of secular constitutionalism in Shakespeare's England; the second concerns the secular religion of humanity best articulated by Dante.[9] The analysis of legal and literary fictions in these two "literary" chapters in particular responds to the work of Schmitt on the one hand and Cassirer on the other.

We can see this dual response already in the subtitle and preface to *The King's Two Bodies*. The subtitle, "A Study in Medieval Political Theology," almost certainly alludes to Schmitt's *Political Theology*.[10] Moreover, Kantorowicz borrows Schmitt's general argument when he claims that English and continental lawyers used theological concepts to shore up the secular power of the medieval and early modern state. Yet by 1957, when *The King's Two Bodies* was published, Kantorowicz would also have known that Schmitt's political theology had been tarnished by his dealings with the Nazi regime in the 1930s. That Kantorowicz was aware of the Nazi connotations of political theology is signaled by the coy denial that appears in the preface to *The King's Two Bodies*:

> It would go much too far . . . to assume that the author felt tempted to investigate the emergence of some of the idols of modern political religions merely on account of the horrifying experience of our own time in which whole nations, the largest and the smallest, fell prey to the weirdest dogmas and in

which political theologisms became genuine obsessions defying
in many cases the rudiments of human and political reason.[11]

At the same time, Kantorowicz admits in the very next sentence that
he "was not unaware of the later aberrations," which I take it refers to
the Nazi death camps. Kantorowicz then goes on to announce that he
thinks of *The King's Two Bodies* as a contribution to what Ernst Cassirer called "the myth of the state," in a 1946 book by that title written
in response to his experience of Nazi Germany.

At first glance, this lineage seems improbable. Cassirer was a neo-
Kantian philosopher who had elaborated a philosophy of symbolic
forms, in which myth appeared as an early, primitive stage of symbolic
thought. But the political events of World War II, in particular the Nazi
regime, changed Cassirer's thinking on these matters. It was Nazi propaganda that forced Cassirer to recognize that myth had not been historically superseded by rationalism; to the contrary, myth could "be
manufactured in the same sense and according to the same methods
as any other modern weapon—[such] as machine guns or airplanes."[12]
Germany's rearmament, according to Cassirer, had begun not in 1933
but even earlier, with the manufacture of new political myths. Cassirer
presented *The Myth of the State* as a critical analysis of such artificial
mythmaking. "It is beyond the power of philosophy to destroy the political myths. A myth is in a sense invulnerable. It is impervious to rational
arguments; it cannot be refuted by syllogisms. But philosophy can do us
another important service. It can make us understand the adversary."[13]

In the conclusion to *The Myth of the State*, Cassirer tells us that one
specific adversary he had in mind was Heidegger, whose notion of *Ge-
worfenheit*, or existential thrownness into the world, compels us to give
up "all hopes of an active share in the construction and reconstruction of
man's cultural life."[14] Here it's helpful to remember that Heidegger had
engaged Cassirer in a famous philosophical debate in Davos, Switzer-
land, in 1929. The consensus at the time was that the younger Heidegger
had won the debate, and that he had vindicated a historicist philosophy against Cassirer's neo-Kantianism. In the gloss of Peter Eli Gordon,
"Heidegger's philosophical 'victory' over Cassirer's transcendentalism
stands at the origins of the twentieth century's turn towards historicism,
and thus serves as one of the indispensable foundations for intellectual-
historical method today"; "the dispute between Heidegger and Cassirer
represents the ongoing challenge of reconciling hermeneutic-historicist
modes of situated understanding with the transcendentalist, non-
historicist premises of philosophic rationality."[15] From this vantage

point, we can see *The Myth of the State* as challenging Heidegger's historicism with a rational analysis of historical events that does not succumb to existential relativism. So when Kantorowicz writes that *The King's Two Bodies* is a contribution to the project outlined by Cassirer, he signals his own desire not simply to reproduce or advocate political myths (as he did in his *Frederick II*), but to analyze how they worked. Unlike Cassirer, however, Kantorowicz was also interested in redeeming myth—including artificial or manufactured myth—for modernity.

We can begin to recover some of the original impulse and continuing interest of *The King's Two Bodies* if we see Kantorowicz as positioning himself between Schmitt's political theology and Cassirer's critique of existential historicism. From Schmitt he takes the idea of the secular appropriation of theological concepts, as well as the idea of the congruence of theological or metaphysical ideas and political forms within a given historical moment. From Cassirer, he adopts the persona of the rational, secular demystifier of historical and contemporary myth. But unlike either Schmitt (who was hostile to the merely aesthetic) or Cassirer (who was critical of the modern political use of myth), Kantorowicz also defends the positive role of what all three recognized as the manufactured or invented myth in the twentieth century. For Kantorowicz, this kind of myth can be found above all—though not exclusively—in literature. In prefacing his historical analysis of the king's two bodies with Shakespeare, Kantorowicz challenges—through literature—Schmitt's critique of liberal ideas of representation. In concluding with Dante, who represents a secular religion of humanity and world community, Kantorowicz attempts to answer Cassirer's fears about the irrational role of myth in the twentieth century. In neither case does literature simply function as yet another source of historical evidence. Instead, as I hope to show, Kantorowicz finds in literature an exemplary self-consciousness about the symbolic dimension of human experience, about the human capacity to make and unmake symbolic forms. In modern terms, we might say that, in Kantorowicz's reading of Shakespeare and Dante, literature reveals its capacity both for ideological critique and for enabling fictions of human community. It can serve as an antidote to political theology of the Schmittian sort, even as it authorizes a new vision—a new "secular 'political theology,'" to borrow Kantorowicz's phrase—of the human community.[16]

Legal and Literary Fiction

As a jurist, Schmitt was intimately familiar with the long history of thinking about legal fictions, and this history shaped his own political thought. As we saw in chapter 1, Schmitt criticized the liberal idea of representation and defended a Catholic understanding of political form as representing the "concrete" human community.[17] By his own account, this notion of Catholic form was indebted to Roman legal thinking about juristic persons.

> The Church also is a 'juridical person,' though not in the same sense as a joint-stock company. . . . The typical product of the age of production is a method of accounting, whereas the Church is a concrete personal representation of a concrete personality. All knowledgeable witnesses have conceded that the Church is the consummate agency of the juridical spirit and the true heir of Roman jurisprudence. Therein—in its capacity to assume juridical form—lies one of its sociological secrets. But it has the power to assume this or any other form only because it has the power of representation. [The Church] represents the *civitas humana*, it presents at every instant the historical connection with Christ's becoming-human and sacrific[ing himself] on the cross; it represents Christ himself, in person, God become Man in historical reality. In this representative dimension resides its superiority over an age of economic thinking.[18]

Yet, while Schmitt clearly accepted the scholarly consensus that Roman law was the model for canon law notions of the Church as a juridical person, he also went out of his way to distinguish between the Roman idea of the corporation and the Church as the corporate body of the faithful.[19] Whereas the idea of the corporation involves merely an abstract legal fiction, the Catholic juristic person needs to be a genuine representative. Schmitt went on to assert that "the world of representations has its own hierarchy of values and its own humanity. It is home to the political idea of Catholicism and its capacity to embody the great trinity of form: the aesthetic form of art; the juridical form of law; finally, the glorious achievement of a world-historical form of power."[20] Significantly, Schmitt here allied Catholic form with aesthetic form, though he also distinguished such form from the merely aesthetic productions of the eighteenth and nineteenth centuries. Aesthetics correctly understood takes up the task of representing the concrete political idea of the Catholic *civitas humana*. Thus Schmitt praised the medieval Church for being "the mother of poets no less than saints, Dante no less than St. Dominic." "Today," however, in contrast to the earlier Church's understanding of the spiritual and political significance of poetic form,

"the bond between the Church and the creative arts has been broken."
Modernity has only a superficial, vitiated understanding of "beautiful
externals," which Schmitt equates with "aesthetics" in the Kantian and
romantic senses of the term.[21]

The similarities and differences between Schmitt and Kantorowicz
are striking. Kantorowicz also tells the story of the appropriation of
theological concepts for political purposes. Like *Political Theology* and
Roman Catholicism and Political Form, *The King's Two Bodies* sketches
a history of representation in the political sphere, in which the relationship of person and office has a crucial role to play. And, like Schmitt,
Kantorowicz is deeply concerned with what the Church called the *civitas humana*. But the differences are even more striking. In particular,
Schmitt and Kantorowicz differ on their interpretations of juridical per-
sonhood and political theology—interpretations that depended on the
(for Kantorowicz) related notions of legal fiction and literary form.

Kantorowicz's understanding of the juristic person is key to understanding his idea of political theology. Rather than adopting Schmitt's
interpretation of the juristic person as excluding the notion of the
corporation, Kantorowicz deliberately equates them. That is, where
Schmitt insists on a Catholic, personalist notion of representation,
which he clearly distinguishes from a joint stock company, Kantorowicz argues that the Roman-canon juristic person is compatible with
the legal notion of a corporation. This in turn means that Kantorowicz
sees the juridical person or corporation as an enabling fiction rather
than a "real being."[22] Kantorowicz then suggests that juristic fictions
may have some relation to nominalist intellectual fictions. And he goes
on to argue that the fact "that this corporate person was a fictitious
person detracted nothing from its value, especially its heuristic value.
. . . Aquinas, actually following Augustine, could define 'fiction' in a
signally positive sense as *figura veritatis* [figure of truth]. And Baldus,
elaborating glosses of Accursius and Bartolus, finally declared, with a
slight twist of an Aristotelian tenet: '*Fiction imitates nature*. Therefore,
fiction has a place only where truth can have a place.'" And, in a fascinating footnote, Kantorowicz anticipates later legal work on legal and
poetic fiction by noting the overlap between these two concepts in the
Aristotelian tradition.[23]

The thrust of this analysis is to account for what we might call the
fictionalizing of the crown, which in turn eventually helped to undermine the crown's claims to divinity. Thus, in a section of *The King's
Two Bodies* entitled "The Crown as Fiction," Kantorowicz shows how

medieval glossators used the Roman law of inheritance—specifically the "fiction of Law" that guaranteed the continuity of predecessor and successor—to explain the continuity of temporal authority.[24] In the same period, Pope Innocent III tried to strengthen the power of the papacy in relation to the empire by sharply rejecting the idea of a "Christ-like or Christ-centered kingship."[25] In particular, Innocent elaborated a distinction between person and crown that influenced later English political thought by implying that the crown could not simply be identified with the king but stood instead for something more like "the body politic": "Briefly, as opposed to the pure *physis* of the king and to the pure *physis* of the territory, the word 'Crown,' when added, indicated the political *metaphysis* in which both *rex* and *regnum* shared." Gradually, "the notion of the Crown, introduced in England during the twelfth century mainly in fiscal and legal matters, began to gain new momentum under the impact of Canon Law concepts and to assume constitutional connotations which it did not have before."[26] In time, the separation between person and crown made it possible to imagine the demise of monarchy.[27]

Kantorowicz's reading of *Richard II* has sometimes been glossed as a lament for the loss of charismatic political authority, and the tone of his analysis at times appears to support this interpretation. Dismissing the pertinence of Shakespeare's familiarity with legal cases, Kantorowicz observes, "It seems all very trivial and irrelevant, since the image of the twinned nature of a king, or even of man in general, was most genuinely Shakespeare's own and proper vision." And he goes on to assert that "*The Tragedy of King Richard II* is the tragedy of the King's Two Bodies," as though to suggest that not just Richard but also Shakespeare mourned the loss of this theological-political idiom.[28] It is all the more important, then, to recognize that Kantorowicz attributes the awareness of the connection between nominalism and the crown as fiction to Richard himself. Commenting on Richard's speech in the opening of act 2, scene 3, Kantorowicz writes: "A curious change in Richard's attitude—as it were, a metamorphosis from 'Realism' to 'Nominalism'—now takes place. The Universal called 'Kingship' begins to disintegrate; its transcendental 'Reality,' its objective truth and god-like existence, so brilliant shortly before, pales into a nothing, a *nomen*." And a little later he notes, "The fiction of the oneness of the double body breaks apart. Godhead and manhead of the King's Two Bodies . . . stand in contrast to each other."[29] The fictive Richard II, that is, comes to understand kingship itself as a fiction that can be dismantled:

Now mark me how I will undo myself:
I give this heavy weight from off my head,
And this unwieldy sceptre from my hand,
The pride of kingly sway from out my heart;
With mine own tears I wash away my balm,
With mine own hands I give away my crown,
With mine own tongue deny my sacred state,
With mine own breath release all duteous oaths:
All pomp and majesty do I foreswear.[30]

When, at a later moment, Richard represents himself as a traitor to "the pompous body of a king," Kantorowicz observes, "It is as though Richard's self-indictment of treason anticipated the charge of 1649, the charge of high treason committed by the *king* against the *King*."[31] "The demise of Richard" is at the same time "the rise of a new body natural," not only that of his successor, Henry IV, but the corporate body of the people themselves.

Kantorowicz could have found this insight in Edmund Plowden, the sixteenth-century common lawyer who is Kantorowicz's main source for the language of the king's two bodies. As Lorna Hutson has shown, Plowden cites legal discussions of the king's two bodies only to show that they were for the most part rejected by the common lawyers.[32] But Kantorowicz appears more interested in the way Shakespeare imaginatively anticipated the unraveling of the fiction of the king's two bodies than in reading Plowden closely. In fact, he seems to attribute to literature—or at least to Shakespeare—a unique ability to effect such unraveling, to reveal the "fiction" of the king's two bodies as just that.[33] "It was ... the live essence of [Shakespeare's] art," he writes, "to reveal the numerous planes active in any human being, to play them off against each other, to confuse them, or to preserve their equilibrium, depending all upon the pattern of life he bore in mind and wished to create anew."[34] A page later, Kantorowicz refers to the "'duplications' which Shakespeare . . . unfolded in the three bewildering central scenes of *Richard II*. The duplications [are] . . . all one, and all simultaneously active in Richard— 'Thus play I in one person, many people' (5.5.31). . . . Moreover, in each one of those three scenes we encounter the same cascading: from divine kingship to kingship's 'Name,' and from the name to the naked misery of man."[35] As Kantorowicz notes, Shakespeare's contemporaries recognized the extraordinary power of this metafictive moment. In response to a performance of *Richard II* staged shortly before Essex's rebellion, Queen Elizabeth famously remarked, "I am Richard, know ye

not that?" Some fifty years later, in a scene Kantorowicz neglects, King
Charles I imagined himself as Shakespeare's Richard during his trial for
treason to the English people.[36]

With this exploration of literary fiction, we might seem to have wan-
dered very far from the legal fiction of the king's two bodies. But for
Kantorowicz, a legal fiction is distinguished from a literary fiction only
by its institutional home. Thus, in his later essay "The Sovereignty of
the Artist," he writes:

> "Art imitates Nature" was, of course, an Aristotelian maxim. It
> became generally known after the *Physics* had been translated,
> some time before 1200, and the likewise relevant *Poetics*, around
> 1250. There were, however, other literary channels accessible to
> the Middle Ages through which knowledge of these doctrines
> could have been transmitted in a more indirect fashion. One
> of these channels, which was quite independent of the normal
> literary currents, was Roman law. While harking back to early
> Roman jurists of the first and second centuries, Justinian's *In-
> stitutes* and *Digest* reproduced, and medieval jurists therefore
> began to interpret, the essence of the Aristotelian maxim. To be
> sure, in the legal jargon the famous principle did not refer to
> visual arts or artistic vocation at all, but referred to art only in
> a very special sense, far removed from painting or sculpture. It
> was quoted for a rather prosaic and sober purpose, that is, to
> clarify a central point of the law of adoption. "It is the opinion
> that a younger person cannot adopt an older one; for adoption
> imitates nature, and it would be monstrous if the son were older
> than the father." That is to say, Jurisprudence, commonly de-
> fined as an art (*ius est ars boni et aequi*), "imitated nature" just
> as every other art was supposed to do, and imitated it, in the
> case of adoption, by means of an artistic fiction.[37]

Kantorowicz goes on to show how, in time, the idea of the legislator
shifted from the imitator of nature to the creator of new laws ex ni-
hilo—like God and the sovereign. This notion of the sovereign's power
of creation was in turn extended to the artist himself: the equating of
"poet and emperor or king—that is, of the poet and the highest office
representing sovereignty—began as early as Dante," who saw Apollo's
laurel as the reward of "a Caesar or a poet" (*Paradiso* 1.29).[38] I will
return to the importance of this line from Dante toward the end of this
chapter. For now it's clear that for Kantorowicz a legal fiction is just a

particular kind of artistic fiction, which helps to explain why artistic fictions can shed so much light on the working of fiction in the law.[39] And this in turn suggests that political theology is not so much a methodological and existential postulate of "the political," as it is for Schmitt, as what Hans Blumenberg would call a metaphorology, an analysis of the dominant metaphors that inform our social, legal, and political arrangements.[40]

Poetry and Political Theology

I think we can press this analysis even further: *Richard II* doesn't simply lay bare the fiction of the king's two bodies; it also attributes to Richard a skepticism about his own theological-political rhetoric from the outset. In the very first scene of the play, Richard dramatizes his own awareness of the weak fiction of royal absolutism:

> We were not born to sue, but to command;
> Which since we cannot do to make you friends,
> Be ready, as your lives shall answer it.
> At Coventry upon Saint Lambert's day.
> There shall your swords and lances arbitrate
> The swelling difference of your settled hate:
> Since we cannot atone you, we shall see
> Justice design the victor's chivalry.
>
> (1.2.196–203)

In this speech, Richard admits he cannot command Bolingbroke and Mowbray to cease their quarrel. As a result, he gives over the determination of justice to trial by sword, while attempting to disguise this concession as a command. Moreover, even when Richard seems most invested in the fiction of divine kingship, he is sufficiently realistic to attend to the "supplement" of force. We see this realism in the conclusion of Richard's famous speech in act 3 about the balm of an anointed king:

> Not all the water in the rough rude sea
> Can wash the balm off from an anointed king;
> The breath of worldly men cannot depose
> The deputy elected by the Lord.
> For every man that Bolingbroke hath pressed
> To lift shrewd steel against our golden crown,
> God for his Richard hath in heavenly pay

> A glorious angel; then, if angels fight,
> Weak men must fall, for heaven still guards the right.
>   [Enter Salisbury]
> Welcome, my lord. How far off lies your power?
>   (3.2.54-63)

Here too heavenly angels must be supplemented by earthly power, specifically, the power Richard expects from Salisbury's troops. Yet this
power is not forthcoming, despite Richard's assertion that he is "the
deputy elected by the Lord." In an ironic twist on his own speech, Richard learns that "the breath of worldly men"—in the form of rumor—
has more power than he thinks. Salisbury replies that the rumor of
the king's death has prompted men to abandon his cause: "For all the
Welshmen, hearing thou wert dead,/Are gone to Bolingbroke, dispersed
and fled" (3.2.73-74).

In Kantorowicz's reading of the play, as we've seen, *Richard II* is
the tragedy of the king's two bodies, the tragedy of a king who suffers
the loss of his royal body and the humiliation of his physical body. But,
as with *Hamlet*, the term tragedy seems less appropriate to the self-
dramatizing protagonist than does Benjamin's notion of the *Trauerspiel*,
in which self-conscious theatricality is joined with "the creaturely exposure of the person."[41] Like the dysfunctional sovereign of a *Trauerspiel*,
Richard mournfully and theatrically narrates his own downfall, decking
it with allegorical emblems:

> For God's sake let us sit upon the ground
> And tell sad stories of the death of kings:
> Some haunted by the ghosts they have deposed,
> Some poisoned by their wives, some sleeping killed,
> All murdered—for within that hollow crown
> That rounds the mortal temples of a king
> Keeps Death his court, and there the antic sits,
> Scoffing his state and grinning at his pomp,
> Allowing him a breath, a little scene,
> To monarchize, be feared, and kill with looks,
> Infusing him with self and vain conceit,
> As if this flesh which walls about our life
> Were brass impregnable; and, humored thus,
> Comes at the last, and with a little pin
> Bores thorough his castle wall, and farewell king!
>   (3.2.155-70)

Just as the *Trauerspiel* is characterized by allegory and plays within the play, so here Richard imagines the allegorical figure of Death as the true monarch, who briefly allows him "a little scene" to play the role of monarch.[42] Richard's pomp is like that of "the kings and princes" of the *Trauerspiel*, who "appear with their crowns of gilt paper, very melancholy and mournful."[43] In contrast to (in Benjamin's account) the silent hero of Greek tragedy, Richard speaks at length, and his speeches are filled with lamentation. His emotions take the place of action. Confronted with Bolingbroke's rebellion, he seems less attentive to the political emergency than to the "state of emergency in [his] soul, the rule of the emotions."[44] Thus the Bishop of Carlisle rebukes him, "My lord, wise men ne'er sit and wail their woes/But presently prevent the ways to wail" (3.2.178–79). But Richard, true to the logic of the *Trauerspiel*, describes the transformation of the sovereign into a martyr, at the same time that he calls attention to the artificiality of his comparison:

> What must the King do now? Must he submit?
> The King shall do it. Must he be deposed?
> The King shall be contented. Must he lose
> The name of king? a God's name, let it go.
> I'll give my jewels for a set of beads;
> My gorgeous palace for a hermitage;
> My gay apparel for an almsman's gown;
> My figured goblets for a dish of wood;
> My scepter for a palmer's walking staff;
> My subjects for a pair of carvèd saints;
> And my large kingdom for a little grave,
> A little, little grave, an obscure grave.
> (3.2.142–53)

Here, as elsewhere, Richard is acutely attuned to the "props" his role demands. These props can make a sovereign, just as their absence can unmake him: the difference between king and holy beggar is a matter of exchanging jewels for a set of beads. A little further on, Richard tries to recoup some of his royal charisma by explicitly asserting the connection between his own deposition and the martyrdom of Christ, but his awkward rhetorical multiplication of "Pilates" invites us to see that the comparison is excessive and unconvincing: "Though some of you, with Pilate, wash your hands,/Showing an outward pity: yet you Pilates/Have here delivered me to my sour cross,/And water cannot wash away your sin" (4.1.238–41). Here, as in the earlier passage where Richard divests

himself of the trappings of royalty, his rhetoric undoes itself, revealing
the willfulness of his comparisons, rather than their persuasiveness.

Richard's remarks in the deposition scene enact the complicated relationship between poetry and political theology. From one perspective,
they capture the logic of the sovereign turned aesthetician and martyr.
As Lutz Koepnik has remarked, "stumbling over the cobblestones of
secularized politics," the *Trauerspiel* monarchs become indecisive and
"flee into poetic self-representations; they refurbish their court as a sen-
timental stage rather than present themselves as utilitarian engineers
of power."[45] But such poetic self-representations can themselves be an
instrument of manipulation, and Richard plays them to the hilt, hoping
to turn martyrdom into a new form of power.[46] In act 4, scene 1, his
theatrical self-consciousness allows him to stage-manage the usurpation that Bolingbroke is trying to conceal. Richard is brought before
Bolingbroke, lamenting his fate and professing ignorance of the reason
he has been called:

> *Richard.* God save the King! Will no man say "Amen"?
> Am I both priest and clerk? Well, then, amen.
> God save the King, although I be not he;
> And yet amen, if heaven do think him me.
> To do what service am I sent for hither?
>   *York.* To do that office of thine own good will,
> Which tired majesty did make thee offer:
> The resignation of thy state and crown
> To Henry Bolingbroke.
>   *Richard.*   Give me the crown.
> Here, cousin, seize the crown.
>
>   (4.1.172–81)

In the couplet "God save the King, although I be not he;/And yet amen,
if heaven do think him me," Richard exposes the paradox that divine
right is consistent with de facto political power. The highest principle of
legitimation is also a justification of mere possession, and this holds out
the hope, however briefly, that Richard may yet retain his crown. But
the real theatrical coup here occurs when Richard extends the actual
crown to Bolingbroke, requiring him to "seize" it and thus to enact his
usurpation before all those present. In this way, Richard reduces the
metaphorical crown to a mere physical crown, a stage prop, as though
to say that what Bolingbroke's usurpation reveals—or produces—is a
view of kingship as a matter of entirely human artifacts. This, too, is

characteristic of the play of mourning. *Trauerspiel*, as Benjamin wrote, is characterized by a "loyalty to the world of things": "Crown, royal purple, sceptre are indeed ultimately properties, in the sense of the drama of fate."[47] At times, as here in act 4, scene 1, Richard's focus on props seems Machiavellian, designed literally to force Bolingbroke's hand. Elsewhere, Richard's melancholy contemplation of the theatrical nature of kingship seems to imply some genuine self-recognition: "I wasted Time, and now does Time waste me" (5.5.49).

J. Dover Wilson (in the edition Kantorowicz used) called *Richard II* "a Tudor passion play," and Kenneth Muir has argued that Shakespeare went out of the way to stress Bolingbroke's sin against the divine right of kings by inserting the Bishop of Carlisle's prophecy of civil war right before the deposition.[48] But the play doesn't simply support divine right, as though it were a political pamphlet by, say, James VI of Scotland; instead, it repeatedly stages and repeatedly undermines this claim. Benjamin's model of the *Trauerspiel* is relevant here precisely because of the theatricality with which every figure, including Richard, manipulates this theological-political idiom. In this light, it's arguable that Richard's final speech, "I have been studying how I may compare/This prison where I live unto the world," is just the final example of the activity of comparison that underlies all political fictions, including the political theology of divine right, just as it is the final example of the exposure of the creaturely, mortal body of Richard, whom no comparison can satisfy: "Thus play I in one person many people,/And none contented; sometimes am I king,/Then treasons make me wish myself a beggar,/ And so I am" (5.5.31–34). These treasons include, of course, not only Bolingbroke's usurpation but also Richard's own treasons against himself. As he remarks in the deposition scene, "Nay, if I turn mine eyes upon myself,/I find myself a traitor with the rest" (4.1.246–47). In the end, Richard is a traitor to himself in demystifying and failing to believe his own theological-political rhetoric. This demystification ultimately allies Richard's theatrical and poetic self-consciousness with the critique of political theology.

Cassirer and the Myth of the State

As Kantorowicz makes clear in the conclusion of his book, one goal of *The King's Two Bodies* was to show that English common law was not as isolated from continental legal thought as had sometimes been assumed. But I think the import of this claim has often been misunderstood. In his reading of the legal and literary fiction of *Richard II*, and of

English legal thought more generally, Kantorowicz exposed what Alain Boureau has called the liberating function of Roman law, "its power to create fictions that allow man to escape from the direct influence of nature, force, and the group." And Kantorowicz did so in order to bring out the constitutionalist implications of royal charisma.[49] Thus, while the corporation could take the form of the "corporation sole" of the king, in time it comes to be equated with the corporate body of the people. (Here we could say that Kantorowicz would have agreed with William Blackstone, who called corporations "little republics.")[50] Kantorowicz's reading of Shakespeare is in keeping with this line of argument. Where Schmitt conceived of Shakespearean tragedy as resisting both an aesthetic notion of art and a liberal conception of the state, Kantorowicz conspicuously allies Shakespearean tragedy with Anglo-American constitutionalism.[51] At the same time, however, Kantorowicz does not simply abandon Schmitt's notion of Catholic political theology and the *civitas humana*. Instead, he reconfigures them in a way that is diametrically opposed to Schmitt. Rather than seeing the state as constituted by the friend-enemy distinction, Kantorowicz imagines a cosmopolitan empire—what we might call a global order. In so doing, he submerges the genre and metaphysics of tragedy into a new divine comedy.

This is why, I think, *The King's Two Bodies* concludes with a chapter on Dante. Given his participation in the Stefan George circle, it's not surprising that Kantorowicz saw literature as the prime instantiation of what Schmitt called the Catholic *civitas humana*. Unlike Schmitt's "Catholic political form," however, Kantorowicz's political form requires a self-conscious act of mythmaking, involving the deliberate appropriation and manipulation of signs and symbols, including in literature. Kantorowicz's Dante chapter thus constitutes an aggressive rewriting of Schmitt, not only in the pride of place it gives to literature but also in its vision of the *civitas humana*. As such, it also constitutes a response to Cassirer, whose vision of myth in the modern age seemed to be only negative.

Before we can fully understand the role of Dante in *The King's Two Bodies*, then, we need to return to Cassirer. In the 1920s, when Kantorowicz was writing his biography of Frederick II, Cassirer was completing his monumental *Philosophy of Symbolic Forms*, a three-volume study of language, myth, and art that Kantorowicz probably knew.[52] In the volume on myth in *The Philosophy of Symbolic Forms*, Cassirer rejected both idealist and empirical or genetic accounts of myth, focusing instead on the internal logic of myth, including the relationship between sign and signified. At the same time, he cautioned against confusing myth with other symbolic or semiotic modes of expression. Myth for Cassirer is an early stage of symbolic thought and is the product of a community rather than an individual. In Cassirer's teleological account of the development of symbolic forms, myth is followed by language and then finally by art. With art,

> for the first time the world of the image becomes a self-contained cosmos with its own center of gravity. And only now can the spirit enter into a truly free relation with it. Measured by empirical, realistic criteria, the aesthetic world becomes a world of appearance; but in severing its bond with immediate reality, with the material existence and efficacy which constitute the world of magic and myth, it embodies a new step toward the truth. Thus, although myth, language, and art interpenetrate one another in their concrete historical manifestations, the relation between them reveals a definite systematic gradation, an ideal progression towards a point where the spirit not only is and lives in its own creations, its self-created symbols, but also knows them for what they are.[53]

This is a Hegelian vision, in which art's self-knowledge is ultimately surpassed by that of science, which recognizes even more than art the role of symbolic form in mediating the truth: "For what distinguishes science from the other forms of cultural life is not that it requires no mediation of signs and symbols and confronts the unveiled truth of 'things in themselves,' but that, differently and more profoundly than is possible for the other forms, it knows that the symbols it employs *are* symbols and comprehends them as such."[54] For Cassirer, art has a role in man's coming to self-consciousness, but it is ultimately superseded by scientific rationalism.

If Kantorowicz knew Cassirer's work on symbolic form, he must have been struck by Cassirer's very different approach. For, unlike Kantorowicz, Cassirer focused on problems of epistemology and remained remarkably uninterested in politics. Cassirer's 1927 book *The Individual and the Cosmos in Renaissance Philosophy* (contemporaneous with the *Philosophy of Symbolic Forms*) provides a good example of this blind spot. Even as Cassirer struggled to reconcile a Kantian emphasis on a priori logical categories of understanding with the contingency of historical events, he had little to say about the Italian city-state, the rise of the nation-state, or early modern political thought. Instead, Cassirer argued for the new "primacy of form in Renaissance life and thought" and asserted that this notion of form embraced both artistic and scientific pursuits, but not politics. "Thus it has been said of humanism," Cassirer commented, "that its deepest root, and the common bond that joined all humanists, was neither individualism nor politics, neither philosophy nor common religious ideas, but simply artistic sensibility."[55] This is the context in which Cassirer discusses the Florentine humanist Pico della Mirandola's oration on the dignity of man. The *Oration* famously includes a fable about the creation of man in the image and likeness of God, with divinely given capacities for free will and self-transformation. In Cassirer's gloss on Pico, "the being of man follows from his doing; and this doing is not only limited to the energy of the will, but rather encompasses the whole of his creative powers. For all true creativity implies more than mere action upon the world. It presupposes that the actor distinguishes himself from that which is acted upon, i.e. that the subject consciously stands opposed to the object." What the Renaissance discovers, in other words, is a new relation of "the Ego to the world," where ego and world are both polar opposites and mutually constitutive.[56] The individual subject comes to self-consciousness by working on and transforming the world. In Cassirer's account, there is thus a historical dimension to the development of self-consciousness both in the life of the individual and in the sense that the Renaissance understanding of *homo faber* represented a decisive advance over the Middle Ages.[57] Here Cassirer adopted a Hegelian confidence in the teleological march of history. As he wrote in the later *Essay on Man*, a synopsis of his philosophy of symbolic forms, "History as well as poetry is an organon of our self-knowledge," and "Human culture taken as a whole may be described as the process of man's progressive self-liberation."[58] But if art is an important part of man's progressive self-liberation, decisive proof of the forward march of history is provided, above all, by the scientific revolution.

It was not until the last years of Cassirer's life, when he was in exile in the United States, that he turned his scholarly attention to contemporary politics.[59] The impetus seems to have been twofold: the request of friends that he speak about recent political events and Cassirer's own sense of indebtedness to his adopted country for saving him from war-torn Europe. Nazi Germany forced Cassirer to revise his ideas about the progress of reason in history and the obsolescence of myth. But he did not entirely abandon his ideas about the irrationalism of myth. We see this in particular in Cassirer's worry over the reception of Machiavelli, who figured prominently in his account of the gradual secularization of political theory in the early modern period. According to

Cassirer, Machiavelli's myth of Fortuna was designed to help the prince manage the inevitable contingency and unpredictability of human action and was thus in the service of human rationality. In the long run, however, Machiavelli's insights were taken over by post-Enlightenment or nineteenth-century romantic thinkers such as Schelling and Hegel, whose "metaphysical spiritualism . . . paved the way for the most uncouth and uncompromising materialism in political life."[60] It is easy to see how this view fits with Cassirer's intervention in the philosophical debates of his own time, above all his exchange with Heidegger. The problem, for Cassirer, was how to shore up a secular conception of agency, without falling prey to historicism and relativism. Here, in an odd chiasmus of influence, Cassirer turned to Kantorowicz.

Cassirer admits that Machiavelli was not the first person in history to think of the state as secular. He was preceded by, among others, the medieval emperor Frederick II:

> One of the earliest examples of a complete secularization of political life is the state founded by Frederick II in the south of Italy; and this state had been created three hundred years before Machiavelli wrote his book. It was an absolute monarchy in the modern sense; it had emancipated itself from any influence of the Church. The officials of this state were not clerics but laymen. Christians, Jews, Saracens had an equal share in the administration; nobody was excluded for merely religious reasons. At the court of Frederick II a discrimination between sects, between nations or races was unknown. The paramount interest was that of the secular, the "earthly" state.[61]

Cassirer goes on to note that it was paradoxically Frederick's claim of "a personal relation to God" that emancipated him from ecclesiastical influence and allowed him to erect secular reason in the place of church authority. This explains Dante's admiration for Frederick, even though he put him in the circle of heretics in the *Inferno*. Cassirer then credits this view of Frederick to "his biographer," Kantorowicz. In this way, Cassirer himself almost seems to suggest that Frederick's notion of political theology—that is, theology in the service of a secular vision of the state—is a better version of Machiavelli and a better model for modern times than the Machiavelli who had been absorbed into the at once idealist and historicist vision of Hegel and his contemporaries.

If we now return to Kantorowicz, we can see that his claim to be continuing the work of Cassirer is somewhat ironic. Cassirer was a late-comer to the analysis of the myth of the state. In contrast, if there is one thing that is constant in Kantorowicz's work—from the Frederick II biography to *The King's Two Bodies*—it's a preoccupation with the political dimension of symbolic forms, and the contribution of the manufactured myth to political power. When Kantorowicz claims to be continuing the work of Cassirer, we are meant to understand that Kantorowicz shared Cassirer's postwar concern about the harmful effects of myth on politics. I believe, however, that his chief interest was not in condemning the myth of the state but in redeeming the power of manufactured myth for politics. This, for Kantorowicz, is the interest of Dante.

Dante

As we've seen, both Kantorowicz and Schmitt emphasized the distinction between person and office in their analyses of political theology. But Kantorowicz, in his gloss on Dante, also stressed the division between ecclesiastical and political power, the papacy and the empire, the spiritual and the terrestrial paradise. He did so, in part, by arguing along with Dante that the emperor derived his power directly from God, without the mediation of the Church (*De Monarchia*, bk. 3). But the pope and the emperor did not simply stand for separate institutions or separate spheres. Equally important for Dante and Kantorowicz was the claim that the emperor represented the distinctively human ethical community, and that he did so by appropriating the symbolism of the Church for secular purposes. Here's Kantorowicz:

> It was . . . the major premise of . . . [*On*] *Monarchy* that Dante, inspired by Aristotle, attributed to the human community a moral-ethical goal which was a "goal in itself." [It] was para-ecclesiastical, and therefore independent of a Church which had its own goal. . . . Dante, in order to justify the self-sufficiency and sovereignty of the *universitas generis humani* [corporate body of humanity] appropriated, like the jurists, theological language and ecclesiastical thought for expressing his views concerning the secular body politic; and thereby he arrived at the construction of "a secularized imitation of the religious notion of the Church," while endowing his creation even with a blessedness of its own: the terrestrial paradise.[62]

Kantorowicz stressed that "Dante did not turn *humanitas* against *Christianitas*, but thoroughly separated one from the other; he took the human out of the Christian compound and isolated it as a value in its own right—perhaps Dante's most original accomplishment in the field of political theology." In his separation of being human from being Christian, Dante effectively envisioned a cosmopolitan world community made up of Jews, Muslims, and pagans as well as Christians. Here, we might say, was an imaginary "solution" to the Jewish Question avant la lettre, a revision of his earlier account of Frederick II, and perhaps also a subliminal apology for his letter to Stefan George of 1933.[63]

Dante also provided a new model of the sovereign subject. According to Kantorowicz, when Virgil crowns Dante in *Purgatorio* 27 and pronounces the words "I crown and mitre you over yourself" (a scene Kantorowicz also mentions in his essay "The Sovereignty of the Artist"), he invests Dante as an individual man with the *dignitas*, or office, of man, "which 'never dies.'" Kantorowicz uses the phrase "dignity of man" explicitly to suggest that Dante anticipates Pico's *Oration*. But in Kantorowicz's genealogy of the dignity of man, dignity refers less to the individual's intrinsic nobility than to an office, a notion of representation, whereby the individual comes to stand for the mystical body of mankind. Kantorowicz concedes that medieval jurists and political theorists imagined the two bodies of the "two-natured God, . . . Justice and Law . . . [or the] People and Polity. . . . It remained, however, to the poet to visualize the very tension of the 'Two Bodies' in man himself, to make *humanitas* . . . the sovereign of *homo* and to find for all those intricate cross-relations and interrelations the most complex, terse, and simple, because most human, formula: [Virgil's] 'I crown and mitre you over yourself.'"[64] By quoting Dante's Virgil, who authorizes Dante's own career by crowning him with laurels, Kantorowicz points to the role of literature in creating the notion of the sovereign subject and restoring the dignity of man.[65] In particular, Virgil enacts a minicoronation that grants to the poet of the *Commedia* a personal autonomy and poetic authority that, to Kantorowicz's modern readers, sounds very much like a liberal notion of autonomy. In one and the same literary moment—Dante's crowning of Virgil—we have both a coronation and its constitutionalist revision, thereby dramatizing Kantorowicz's conviction that the idea of *dignitas*, or office, works historically both to authorize and to undermine the notion of divine kingship. In a similar way, we could say that the idea of *dignitas* functions in Kantorowicz's own book, in methodological terms, both to underwrite a Foucauldian analysis of the theatrical effects of power (the New Historicist reading of Kantorowicz) and to permit the recovery of a humanist, even protoliberal ideal of human autonomy that was central to Kantorowicz's response to Schmitt's political theology.[66]

The Dante chapter doesn't simply revise Schmitt; it also replies to Cassirer's concerns about the irrational use of myth. In Dante's scene of coronation, we find the powerful sense of human agency that Cassirer thought was missing in Heidegger and perverted in Nazi mythmaking. As with the implicit rejoinder to Schmitt, here too a crucial part of this reply has to do with the literary dimension of Kantorowicz's argument. Just as Shakespeare comments on and, according to Kantorowicz, dramatizes the real significance of Plowden's legal reports, so Dante's *Commedia* appears as the necessary supplement to his *De Monarchia* and the legal treatises of the late Middle Ages. Dante, that is, figures prominently in Kantorowicz's argument not only because he was an important historical commentator on the investiture controversy but also because he was a poet who envisioned in the manufactured myth of the *Commedia* a new notion of human autonomy and community. Moreover, Dante explicitly linked this idea of the human to the work of literature, in the scene in which Virgil crowns Dante with the laurel wreath. Kantorowicz (who knew of Stefan George's fondness for dressing up as Dante, complete with laurels) must certainly have been aware of the metapoetic dimension of this scene of coronation. Here, we could say, Kantorowicz reveals the essential literariness of his idea of making (both cultural and political), just as, in his reading of *Richard II*, he reveals the literariness of his idea of unmaking. At the same time, he may be telling us that the constitutionalist vision implicit in *Richard II* needs to be complemented by the theological authority Dante appropriates for his own poetic project, if it is not to be vulnerable to Schmitt's critique of liberalism as mere formal neutrality—as illustrating in the political sphere the formalism of the Kantian notion of aesthetics. We might wonder, then, whether this celebration of Dante also responds to Cassirer's description of Enlightenment philosophy: "This philosophy believes . . . in an original spontaneity of thought; it attributes to thought not merely an imitative function but the power and the task of shaping life itself."[67] This is a power and task that Cassirer attributed above all to reason and science, but that Kantorowicz ascribes to literature, juristic fictions, and myth.

Kantorowicz's reading of Dante draws near in some respects to Auerbach's famous chapter in *Mimesis*, a book whose defense of the Western literary tradition and of philology was explicitly conceived in exile from Nazi persecution.[68] For Auerbach, philology was an appropriate task for men in dark times, and not the least of its burdens was an account of the emergence of a secular concept of literature. Ironically, one of the best examples of Auerbach's celebration of secular literature is the chapter on Dante. In a close reading of canto 10 of Dante's *Inferno*, Auerbach explores the paradox of Dante's Christian realism, the fact that the long dead Farinata and Cavalcante seem more real than ever, "as passionately interested in the present state of things on earth" as they were in life. According to Auerbach, this paradoxical realism can be explained by Dante's figural view of history: his belief that the events of the Old Testament prefigure the events of the New Testament, and that earthly events prefigure events in the afterlife. This figural conception of history "is the foundation for Dante's realism, this realism projected into changeless eternity." Although Farinata's and Cavalcante's lives are over, their unchanging nature reveals their historical preoccupations all the more intensely, and thus the basis for God's judgment: "earthly existence remains manifest [in the afterlife], for it is always the basis of God's judgment and hence of the eternal condition of the soul." In this way, Auerbach argues, Dante took "earthly historicity" into the "beyond."[69]

Significantly for our purposes, Auerbach is not content with this conclusion. He goes on to argue that Dante's characters burst out of the theological frame in which they appear. Dante produced the effect of human individuality with such power and intensity "that he opened the way for that aspiration toward autonomy which possesses all earthly existence. In the very heart of the other world, he created a world of earthly beings and passions so powerful that it breaks bounds and proclaims its independence. Figure surpasses fulfillment, or more properly: the fulfillment serves to bring out the figure in still more impressive relief. We cannot but admire Farinata and weep with Cavalcante. What actually moves us is not that God has damned them, but that the one is unbroken and the other mourns so heart-rendingly for his son and the sweetness of the light." Dante turns the "beyond" into "a stage for human beings and human passions"; "within the figural pattern, [he] brings to life the whole historical world." And our response to this world is not constrained by the theological assumptions that govern it.[70]

In Auerbach's interpretation, then, the *Commedia* performs an immanent critique of Dante's theology: "by virtue of this immediate and admiring sympathy with man, the principle, rooted in the divine order, of the indestructibility of the whole historical and individual man turns *against* that order. . . . The image of man eclipses the image of God. Dante's work made man's Christian-figural being a reality, and de-

stroyed it in the very process of realizing it." "In this fulfillment, the figure becomes independent: even in Hell there are great souls, and certain
souls in Purgatory can for a moment forget the path of purification for
the sweetness of a poem, the work of human frailty."[71] With these comments, Auerbach invites us to read Dante—whatever Dante himself may
have intended—as an allegory of the production of secular literature.[72]

Similarly, in the conclusion to *The King's Two Bodies*, Kantorowicz
may be suggesting that the advantage of Dante over Frederick II (both
the emperor and Kantorowicz's book by that title) is that, whereas Frederick stands for the manipulation of myth, the *Commedia* (like *Richard II*) stands for literature or fiction that knows itself as such. The
Dante chapter thus amounts to a revision of Schmitt's idea of Catholic
political form, in line with Stefan George's elevation of literature to
the highest form of culture. It also amounts to a revision of Cassirer's
idea of symbolic form, which progresses teleologically from myth, to
art, to science. Whereas Cassirer elevated science over art because science "knows that the symbols it employs *are* symbols and comprehends
them as such," Kantorowicz reserved this self-consciousness for art and,
especially, literature. But if the conclusion of *The King's Two Bodies* is
about the role of art in bringing about a new, secular cosmopolitanism,
such secular cosmopolitanism is not the teleological result of reason in
history. To the contrary, it is always vulnerable to the upsurge of the irrational forces of myth.

Here we may finally be in a position to address the odd reverse chro-
nology of *The King's Two Bodies*, that is, the fact that the book opens
with Shakespeare and concludes with Dante. In designing his book in
this way, Kantorowicz may be inviting us to question traditional narratives of secularization, which chart the decline or demystification of
religion and the rise of rationalism. Such narratives tell a story of progress from the benighted age of myth to one of enlightenment. Kantorowicz, by contrast, appears to think, with Dante, that the secular sphere
depends on the religious sphere for definition; he may even think, like
Dante, that both the notion of "the human" and the creative powers of
the poet depend on the invocation of the higher authority of God or
some divine authorizing principle.[73]

As we've seen, in *The King's Two Bodies* Kantorowicz uses the resources of the legal and literary traditions to reimagine the relationship
between politics and theology and the idea of the secular state. And he
does so in a way that differs from the narratives of Schmitt or Cassirer.
Schmitt's account of the emergence of the liberal state involved a declen-
sion from a genuine idea of the political; Cassirer told the story of the

rational legitimation of the modern state and its subsequent dismantling by Nazi mythmaking, even as he advocated a return to the principles of rationality. In contrast, Kantorowicz's model is not narratological or teleological at all, but what we might call tropological or chiastic.[74] Theology, for Kantorowicz, is always already about representational fictions, which is one of the reasons we can use legal and literary fictions as resources for reconceiving the relationship between politics and theology. Kantorowicz develops a new model that insists on both the theological contribution to secularism and the constitutional implications of absolutism. But against Schmitt, he favors Anglo-American constitutionalism; against Cassirer, he advances what we might call a political theology or myth of human rationalism, one capable of reinvigorating the notion of liberal constitutionalism. Moreover, if we think back to the preface of *The King's Two Bodies*, where Kantorowicz alludes to the political theology of fascism, we can say that in Dante he finds a model of the relationship between religion and secular life that is in principle antifascist. It is antifascist in part because it is antinationalist. But it is antifascist as well because it insists on a liberal notion of individual autonomy, even while acknowledging its mythical status.[75]

Here, in conclusion, we may see the ongoing relevance of Kantorowicz's argument about the king's two bodies for modern discussions of political theology. In an essay entitled "The Permanence of the Theological-Political?," which I criticized in the introduction to this book, Claude Lefort argues that religion is an essential or permanent part of the symbolic dimension of the political, even though modern rational thought tends to define politics over against theology.[76] Tellingly, however, Lefort goes on to identify religion with the work of the imagination: "What philosophy discovers in religion is a mode of portraying or dramatizing the relations that human beings establish with something that goes beyond empirical time and space within which they establish relations with one another. This work of the imagination stages a different time, a different space." A little further on, Lefort makes the equation between religion and the imagination even more explicit: "Modern philosophy cannot ignore its debt to modern religion; it can no longer distance itself from the work of the imagination or appropriate it as a pure object of knowledge." Although Lefort goes on to claim that "any society which forgets its religious basis is laboring under the illusion of pure self-immanence and thus obliterates the locus of philosophy," this "religious basis" proves to be a metaphor for the gap between the symbolic and the real.[77] Thus, in a defense of democracy as that political form that preserves a sense of the contingency of political institutions and political power, Lefort writes:

> Of all the regimes of which we know, [democracy] is the only one to have represented power in such a way as to show that power is an *empty place* and to have thereby maintained a gap between the symbolic and the real. It does so by virtue of a discourse which reveals that power belongs to no one; that those who exercise power do not possess it; that they do not, indeed, embody it; that the exercise of power requires a periodic and repeated contest; that the authority of those vested with power is created and re-created as a result of the manifestation of the will of the people.[78]

Strikingly, in Kantorowicz's history of the king's two bodies, the body falls away to be replaced, ultimately, by fiction or, in Lefort's terms, by the distinction between symbolic and real power. Whereas fascism and religious fundamentalism attempt to give society a body, the usefulness of the category of fiction is that it complicates any attempt to locate power in one particular body or one particular place.[79] This displacement of the body is, ironically, the message of *The King's Two Bodies*, which, in pointing us to the role of legal fiction in bringing about the emergence of the constitutional state, may be thought of as a secular version of negative theology or as the tragedy of political theology averted.

3 Machiavelli and Modernity: Leo Strauss, Carl Schmitt, and Ernst Cassirer

In Machiavelli's time, the chief representative of political theology and the most influential person in Florentine politics was the Dominican priest Fra Girolamo Savonarola. Invited to Florence by Lorenzo de' Medici in the last years of his reign, Savonarola rose to power after Lorenzo's death by preaching a message of political, religious, and social reform, and by claiming that "it is not I, but God, who says these things."[1] An astute and self-promoting politician, Savonarola won the hearts and minds of the Florentines by speaking in a language they could understand: a language we might call prophetic republicanism. Although the best form of government was rule by one man, Florence, he argued, had always been a republic established by God (*mandato da Dio*). In fact, God had been especially concerned with Florence in recent years, going so far as to give them an imperfect government so as to exercise the citizens' intellect and free will, and encourage the practice of the "culto divino." In time, Savonarola prophesied, the Florentine republic would become so religious that it would be a paradise on earth.[2]

Needless to say, Savonarola did not succeed in his efforts to reestablish a divinely ordered republic in Florence. His critique of the papacy irritated the pope, just as his critique of the Florentine oligarchy alienated his original Medici supporters and their friends. In 1497 Alexander VI excommunicated Savonarola, and in 1498 he was burned at the stake by the Florentine government for being a "schismatic and a heretic."[3] In his letters, Machiavelli expressed his amazement that the Florentine followers of Savonarola had been as gullible as they had, and in the *Discourses on Livy* he condemned Savonarola for his "ambitious and partisan spirit."[4] Later, in *The First Decennale*, Machiavelli commented sardonically that to prevent Savonarola's prophetic teaching from ruining Florence, his divine light had either to increase or be "extinguished with a greater fire."[5] Despite these ironic jabs, Machiavelli was sympathetic to at least some of Savonarola's republican reforms, just as he recognized the usefulness of religion in the realm of politics. Where he differed from Savonarola was in advancing a civil religion, rather than a political theology, a religion that was subordinate to the state rather than the model for it.

This chapter explores Machiavelli's civil religion as an alternative paradigm for thinking about the relationship between politics and theology. For both Schmitt and Strauss, as we've seen, political theology stands in an antithetical relationship to the development of liberalism in the seventeenth century: this is because liberalism claimed to have solved the theological-political problem by relegating religion to the private sphere and by positing the realm of politics as a realm of equality before the law, without respect to persons or religious beliefs. In elaborating this argument, both Schmitt and Strauss turned to the moment before liberalism proper, which they identified with Machiavelli. For Schmitt, Machiavelli was antiliberal in the sense that he recognized the fundamental evil of human nature and the necessity of an autonomous realm of politics, constituted by the conflict between friend and enemy. For Strauss, Machiavelli's vision of human nature was already complicit with liberalism, because it elaborated an anthropology of the lowest common denominator and bracketed philosophical questions of ultimate value.

In the following pages, I draw on both Schmitt and Strauss to arrive at a conclusion radically different from either of theirs. My argument is that Machiavelli's view of religion elaborates a political theology in the specific sense that it makes religion a contested political instrument: theology in this sense is relevant only to the extent that it is politically useful or has political consequences. But Machiavelli is divided about the effects of civil religion. While he sometimes presents this religion as a positive bond that ties political communities together, he also presents religion as a political instrument of manipulation and oppression, one that saps the people's *virtù*. Thus Machiavelli offers a diagnosis and critique of the tyrannical uses of religion, but he also offers a radical interpretation of religion as man's indirect self-consciousness of his own agency, including his own creative and poetic powers to make or shape his own experience. The phrase "indirect self-consciousness" gestures toward Feuerbach's analysis of religion, but as we'll see, for Machiavelli the source of this analysis is Lucretius, the classical Roman poet who was well known in the Renaissance as a critic of religious superstition as well as a defender of the positive use of poetic fictions. In demystifying belief as a function of the founder's art and the people's imagination, Machiavelli gives a priority to art that puts him radically at odds with both Schmitt and Strauss. Political theology, to use the typology elaborated by the Roman writer Varro, is always at the same time poetic theology. At the same time, Machiavelli implies, with Schmitt, that the source of value or belief cannot be a transcendent good but must be grounded in the concrete order of a given political community, an order that, contra Schmitt, will always be contested.

Machiavelli and Modernity

In the early twentieth century, Machiavelli was a flashpoint for discussions of secular modernity. In his great work on Machiavellism, Friedrich Meinecke described Machiavelli as a "heathen," who "broke . . . with the dualistic and onesidedly spiritualizing ethic of Christianity, which depreciated the natural impulses of the senses. Although indeed he retained some of the structural ideas about the difference between good and evil, he strove principally for a new naturalistic ethic which would follow the dictates of nature impartially and resolutely."[6] As a result of this break with medieval political theology, "it was now possible for the modern State, following its own inmost vital impulse, to free itself from all the spiritual fetters that had constrained it." While recognizing certain constant features or tendencies of human nature, Machiavelli held that there is no transcendent standard of truth, that truth is relative to history, and that human nature is malleable. Thus, instead of focusing on a timeless model of the ideal state, Machiavelli recommended "a form of reconnoitring and judgment, which was already closely related to modern historical judgment." For Meinecke, such practical judgment was a form of historicism in that it involved the analysis of existing historical conditions and the particular, historically contingent interests of the state. In Meinecke's account of Machiavelli and his influence, historicist thinking emerges as one of the great achievements of Western political thought, a subtle combination of *kratos* and *ethos* that acknowledges the facts of human nature while also crediting our highest aspirations for the common good.[7]

In the conclusion to *Machiavellism*, however, Meinecke expressed concern about the fate of Machiavellian reason of state in the twentieth century. He worried about the effects of unfettered Machiavellism under the new conditions of modernity, including nationalism, militarism, and capitalism. In particular, even as he insisted on "the permanent undeniable discoveries of historicism," he worried about what he called its "relativizing consequences." In response, he declared, "the belief that there does exist an Absolute, capable of being recovered, is both a theoretical and a practical need." For "modern Man," this Absolute lies "in the pure moral law on the one hand, and in the supreme achievements of art on the other." Despite these uplifting remarks, however, the final words of the book capture Meinecke's fears that such an absolute is a slender bulwark against "barbarism": "the executive statesman . . . should always carry State and God together in his heart, if he is not to let himself be overpowered by the daemon (which he is still not quite capable of shaking off completely)."[8]

Meinecke's worst fears were borne out by the rise of fascism and totalitarianism in the 1930s and '40s. Ironically, however, these political developments were associated with a new, distinctively modern political theology.[9] Even more ironically, given Meinecke's view of Machiavelli as a pagan, contemporaries strikingly linked this revival of political theology to the legacy of Machiavelli. Although in *Dictatorship* (1921), Carl Schmitt interpreted Machiavelli as a theorist of political technique, divorced from substantive or moral considerations, in *The Concept of the Political* of 1932, Schmitt referred to Machiavelli to support his view that "all genuine political theories presuppose man to be evil."[10] In his analysis of National Socialism, *Behemoth* (1942), the sociologist and legal historian Franz Neumann argued that National Socialism had revived the techniques of Machiavelli, at the same time that he also described the Nazis as advancing their own political theology.[11] And, as we've seen, in his postwar genealogy of Nazi Germany, *The Myth of the State* (1946), Ernst Cassirer read Machiavelli as a secular analyst of political power while criticizing the Hegelian historicist and romantic appropriation of Machiavelli described by Meinecke, which "paved the way for the most uncouth and uncompromising materialism in political life," by which Cassirer clearly meant the Nazi "myth" or political theology.[12] Leo Strauss, who wrote his dissertation under Cassirer, later reviewed *The Myth of the State* and noted with approval what he called

Cassirer's "proof of the inadequacy of the current historicist interpretation of Machiavelli's teaching," an interpretation that sees Machiavelli's meaning as constrained by its historical context.[13] (Strauss, as we'll see, disagreed not so much with this interpretation as with the usual account of its consequences.) At the same time, Strauss implied that Cassirer was naive to think that his critique of Hegelianism and his exposure of "the myth of the state" could provide a bulwark against more extreme forms of tyranny such as Nazi Germany and the Soviet Union. A decade later Strauss composed *On Tyranny* and *Thoughts on Machiavelli*, both of which traced the modern inability to recognize and condemn Nazi and Soviet tyranny to Machiavelli's conflation of the prince and the tyrant in *The Prince*. For Strauss, this conflation was the result of Machiavelli's historicism and relativism, which broke decisively with medieval political theology and inaugurated what Strauss would later describe as an aesthetic conception of modernity.[14] Taking my cue from Strauss, I want to focus on Machiavelli as the origin of this conception of modernity, as well as of a specifically modern critique of political theology. I think Strauss was right to see Machiavelli as the origin of a modern approach to both politics and political theology. Unlike Strauss, however, I'll argue that we should take Machiavelli's approach to political theology as exemplary for our own time.

Strauss's Machiavelli

Like other readers of Machiavelli (beginning, one might say, with Machiavelli himself), Strauss sees in Machiavelli the beginning of modern political thought. In particular, Strauss argues, Machiavelli's conflation of the prince and the tyrant lies at the origin of a distinctively modern, instrumental approach to politics. But Strauss doesn't see Machiavelli's instrumental reasoning as the origin only of modern *political* thought. He also argues that Machiavelli—rather than, say, Descartes—is the beginning of modern *philosophy*.[15] In short, Strauss is interested in Machiavelli because he sees him as contributing to the crisis of modernity, a crisis that was brought about by the break with premodern notions of rationality. This crisis is invisible from the other side of the break— whence the necessity of reconstructing how Machiavelli must have looked to his contemporaries before he was assimilated to a republican tradition of political thought. What he looked like, according to Strauss, was not a republican or defender of tyrants, but rather a teacher of evil, from both a Christian and a classical perspective.

First, according to Strauss, Machiavelli must be seen as attacking

Christianity, with its emphasis on the sinfulness of human nature. In *Leviathan* Hobbes satirized the church's "kingdom of darkness" in order to inaugurate a state in which the question of revelation was foreclosed. According to Strauss, Machiavelli aimed indirectly to do much the same thing. He did so by putting his criticism of Christianity in the mouth of Livy, by making it clear that Livy (as construed by Machiavelli) should take the place of the Bible, and by implying that the moderns should use Christianity the way the ancients used the Roman religion.[16] But the secret, even more radical message of both *The Prince* and the *Discourses* is that the power of Scripture, of the Church, and of Christianity in general needs to be destroyed. In place of a view of humankind that stressed both human sinfulness and the possibility of salvation, Machiavelli substituted a conception of human nature as incapable of perfection, even with the assistance of God.

According to Strauss, although Machiavelli elevates Livy above Christianity, he also uses Livy as a stalking horse to criticize antiquity. Whereas Livy was a critic of ancient Rome, Machiavelli is a critic of both Roman and Greek antiquity. First, Machiavelli shows that Rome was not simply the opposite of Christianity but also prepared the way for Christianity: "Machiavelli shows that it was in the last analysis the Roman republic which destroyed freedom for many centuries in the West. . . . Hence it remains true that the Roman republic, the greatest republic or the most political community that ever was, prepared the Western world for Asiatic obedience and for the suppression of the supremacy of political or public life. The Roman republic is on the one hand the direct opposite of the Christian republic, and on the other hand a cause of the latter, or even the model for it." But, even more problematic for Strauss, Machiavelli was a critic of Greek antiquity because he abandoned the ancients' "teleological understanding of nature."[17] This is because, although Machiavelli appears to return to an ancient idea of virtue, he rejects the classical ideas of the good and the true. Instead of measuring human beings against a transcendent standard of perfection, Machiavelli begins with human beings as they really are. Instead of the soul, man's highest faculty, Machiavelli focuses on the lowest common denominator of human beings—the passions. And instead of seeing man—as the ancients did—as limited by and defined over against the totality of the cosmos (what Strauss calls "the whole"), Machiavelli stresses the almost infinite malleability of human beings and of their desires. For all these reasons, Machiavelli must be read as attacking not only the Bible but also classical philosophy, which asserted the superiority of theoretical to practical reason, and the natural limits of human nature. In the guise of returning to the ancients, Machiavelli paves the way for the modern emphasis on praxis.

In Strauss's view, Machiavelli's "realistic" portrayal of human nature is in the service of redefining political science in practical rather than theoretical terms. The goal of Machiavelli's political science is to seek not the best state but one that is realizable on earth; not to seek the perfection of human nature but to cater to existing needs and desires. Strauss suggests that, to the extent that Machiavelli's political science is concerned with the "relief of man's estate" rather than theoretical contemplation, this political science might be seen as an offshoot of "biblical charity."[18] As we've seen, however, Machiavelli must be read as attacking not only classical philosophy, which asserts the superiority of theoretical to practical reason, and the natural limits of human nature. He must also be seen as attacking Christianity, with its emphasis on the sinfulness of human nature. According to Strauss, Machiavelli rejects this view of human sinfulness and is instead blasphemously optimistic about the poetic capacities of mankind, the capacity to make or shape the experience of fortune. In the end, Strauss argues, Machiavelli's anthropology and his refusal of any transcendent criterion of judgment lead to Hegel's historicism; just as his privileging of instrumental reason inaugurates the modern separation of fact and value, and thus relativism. For all these reasons, in Strauss's view, Machiavelli helps to produce the crisis—both philosophical and political—that is modernity.[19]

In Strauss's own life, as we've seen, this crisis found its fullest expression in World War II. Strauss argues that, for all of Machiavelli's demystification of religion, Machiavelli contributed to the destructive modern political theologies we know as fascism or totalitarianism. This is because Machiavelli's historicism undermined the classical philosophical notion of reason, including its sense of the limits of or restraints on human reason. It is also because, in lowering his estimate of human nature, Machiavelli aggrandized the claims of political theory to realize its design of mastering nature or contingency. The modern consequences of this critique of theoretical reason and aggrandizement of practical reason have been devastating, according to Strauss. Just as the modern demotion of theoretical reason produced a kind of political decisionism based on the irrational, existential confrontation of friend and enemy, so the modern project of the technological mastery of nature found its demonic realization in the concentration camp. Moreover, when faced with the twin tyrannies of fascism and totalitarianism, the allies were unable to recognize the threat because they too were suffering from the loss of standards that resulted from the purely instrumental conception of reason with its separation of fact and value. The dominance of scientific positivism was responsible for the allies' inability to rationally defend the superiority of democratic liberalism to fascism or totalitarianism.

For students of political theology, Strauss's argument is an important and challenging one. Against Schmitt, Strauss challenges us to take seriously the ancient conception of reason, at the same time that Strauss cautions us that philosophy is incapable of rationally refuting the claims of revelation (how seriously is the subject of considerable debate among his readers).[20] But Strauss's argument is also important for students of modernity because he challenges us to think anew about the legitimacy of the modern age—the legitimacy, we might say, of Machiavelli. This means that Strauss also challenges us to think about whether his own criterion of classical reason (or even Blumenberg's notion of legitimacy) is the right framework in which to think about Machiavelli's positive contribution to modernity. Strauss repeatedly said that the claim to understand a thinker better than he understood himself was a pernicious and condescending form of historicism. So what happens to Strauss's argument when we try to understand Machiavelli's project in Machiavelli's own terms rather than Strauss's? I'll suggest that irrational decisionism is not the only alternative to theoretical reason in Machiavelli's universe; the other option is what Machiavelli calls *virtù*, which can emerge only in the conflictual space of politics and which is dependent in important ways on what Blumenberg called poiesis and what Machiavelli called imagination (*fantasia*). This other option has consequences for the relationship between politics and religion and, by extension, for the question of political theology.

A Poetics of Political Autonomy

In the remainder of this chapter, I propose a reading of Machiavelli that attends both to his self-conscious reflection on the uses of the imagination and to his account of politics as a realm of conflict, in which negotiation or the give-and-take of competing interests cannot be trumped by the appeal to theoretical reason or religious faith. This means that religion is not a special case for Machiavelli in the way that it is for the liberal settlement of seventeenth-century Europe. Rather, religion is one tool among many for creating political allegiance, and like other tools it can be used well or badly. In seeing religion as a tool, Machiavelli treats religion from "the perspective of art," where art is construed as "any activity concerned with *making*." The phrase "perspective of art" is taken from an essay by Charles Singleton on Machiavelli. But Singleton's insight into the role of art in Machiavelli's work probably derives from a famous chapter in Jacob Burckhardt's *The Civilization of the Renaissance in Italy*, on the "state as a work of art," in which Machiavelli figures prominently.[21] Hannah Arendt also attributed the perspective of art to Machiavelli in her essay "What Is Authority?" where she argued that Machiavelli "understood the act of founding entirely in the image of making." And she went on to observe that Machiavelli's justification of violence followed from this paradigm of making: "You cannot make a table without killing trees, you cannot make an omelette without breaking eggs, and you cannot make a republic without killing people."[22] Treating religion from the perspective of art helps explain why Machiavelli's treatment of religion seems, well, so irreligious. But it also helps us to see that the reemergence of a secular way of thinking about politics in the early modern period is part and parcel of the history of art in the sense of poiesis, construction, or making.

As we'll see, making in Machiavelli sometimes means devising a strategic fiction or untruth to mislead the masses. It sometimes refers to the artifactual, the process of imposing form on matter in order to create an artifact understood as a new state of affairs. And it sometimes refers to a communal endeavor, to the process of constructing the common good, construed as a state of freedom and autonomy. Making in this sense is not so different from Arendt's notion of acting in concert. Yet, contrary to Arendt's fears that poiesis is a bad model for politics because it involves instrumental reasoning and imposes a predetermined end upon "the uncertainty of ordinary opinion," Machiavelli's idea of making emphasizes the ability to respond to contingency, individually or jointly, with an ever-flexible art of invention and to discover from within contingency the values of freedom and autonomy.[23]

The question about religion that Machiavelli must ultimately confront is whether Christianity can ever be interpreted in a way that strengthens the state or whether Christianity is intrinsically hostile to politics. That is, does Christianity inevitably encourage passivity on the part of the people and corruption on the part of the Church when the Church intervenes in the secular realm to which it is in theory opposed? If this is the case, then the Roman religion of civic *virtù* will turn out to be preferable, but on the grounds not of its greater truthfulness but of its greater effectiveness. This question is both political and metapoetic for Machiavelli: that is, it is a question about the nature and right use of fictions in the realm of politics. To the extent that Machiavelli calls attention to this metapoetic dimension of human experience, he gives us a more robust defense of human capacities than, for example, Hobbes does. These capacities include freedom and the imagination, interpretation and deliberation, four capacities that cannot be simply reduced to instrumental reason as Strauss claims.[24] The real conflict here is not between classical reason and modern instrumental reason, or between an absolute notion of truth and the relativism of modernity. To the contrary, as Strauss himself at times acknowledged, the real conflict is between philosophy and poiesis. Whereas Strauss advocates the former, Machiavelli calls for the latter. In both *The Prince* and the *Discourses* Machiavelli's critique of religion is inseparable from a meditation on the creative power of art and the imagination.

A few words about *The Prince* are in order before turning to Machiavelli's fuller discussion of these issues in the *Discourses*. In chapter 18, Machiavelli famously argues that "[i]t is good to appear merciful, truthful, humane, sincere, and religious; it is good to be so in reality. But you must keep your mind so disposed that, in case of need, you can turn to the exact contrary."[25] Such advice lends support to the view that Machiavellian *virtù* is a matter of instrumental reasoning. But Machiavelli's ultimate view of politics transcends the technical calculation of means and ends. Both in chapter 18 and elsewhere, Machiavelli compares *virtù* to the activity of poiesis; moreover, he makes it clear that poiesis is intimately related to the goal of self-sufficiency. A prince should be able to use or feign religion, but he should also be able not to: he should be independent of external criteria of action and external sources of support (e.g., mercenary armies), and the model for such independence is art.

We see this most clearly in Machiavelli's treatment of Moses in chapter 6 of *The Prince*. Machiavelli's treatment was shocking to contemporary Christian readers both because he treated Moses as a mythical—or literary—figure, like Cyrus, Romulus, and Theseus, and because Machiavelli only pretended that Moses was in a special category by virtue of the fact that he was divinely inspired:

> Turning to those who have become princes by their own powers [*virtù*] and not by accident [*fortuna*], I would say that the most notable were Moses, Cyrus, Romulus, Theseus, and a few others. And though we should not consider Moses, because he was simply an agent sent by God to do certain things, he still should be admired, if only for the grace which made him worthy of talking with God.

We know this is ironic because Machiavelli proceeds to discuss not only Cyrus but also Moses as a Machiavellian founder, one who encountered the people in a state that he could shape to his own ends:

> But let us turn to Cyrus and the others who acquired or founded kingdoms. You will find them all deserving of admiration; and if you consider their individual actions and decrees, they will be found not much different from those of Moses, who had such a great teacher. When we look into their actions and their lives, we will find that fortune provided nothing for them but an opportunity; that gave them material [*materia*], on which they could impose whatever form [*forma*] they chose. Without the opportunity, their strength [*virtù*] of mind would have been vain, and without that strength [*virtù*] the opportunity would have been lost. Hence it was necessary for Moses to find the children of Israel in Egypt, enslaved and oppressed by the Egyptians, so that they should be disposed to follow him, in order to escape from servitude.[26]

In emphasizing the similarity between Moses's poetic activity of imposing form on matter and that of Cyrus, Romulus, and Theseus, Machiavelli suggests poiesis implies an ethos of self-sufficiency, in contrast to dependence on God. One might even say Moses, for Machiavelli, represents the reclaiming of this creative capacity from the misguided view that it derives ultimately from God. And this ethos of autonomy is apparent in the effects of Moses's activity as well: his liberation of the children of Israel from Egyptian servitude.[27]

In case we missed the point about the creative use of civil religion, Machiavelli repeats this lesson in the final chapter of *The Prince*, where he instructs the Medici in the political uses of religious rhetoric, not least of all by referring to his earlier discussion of Moses and the other mythical figures in chapter 6. The irony is particularly salient in Machiavelli's address to Lorenzo de' Medici: "there is no figure presently in sight in whom [Italy] can better place her trust than your illustrious house, which, with its *fortuna* and *virtù*, favored by God and the Church of which it is now the head, can take the lead in this process of redemption."[28] In the parallel construction, God is implicitly conflated with *fortuna*; just as being favored by God is implicitly equated with the advantage you give yourself by gaining control of the Church. The Medici, Machiavelli implies, are in a better position than they have been in a long time since they now control the papacy. This is an example that illustrates the use of religion, in this case to stir up the Medici to unify Italy. Religion, Machiavelli suggests, is not merely a tool of deception; it can also be used to foster autonomy and liberate Italy from the barbarians.

In the *Discourses*, Machiavelli offers a fuller analysis of the poetic dimension and political uses of religion. The first thing to note is that Machiavelli identifies his own modernity with Christianity just as Strauss does, but not for the same reasons.[29] Both see Christianity as undermining ancient virtue. But Strauss sees Christianity, with its emphasis on charity, its egalitarian ethos, and its attempt to reconcile theology and philosophy, as contributing to the death of philosophy. By contrast, Machiavelli sees Christianity as contributing to the death of politics, especially in Italy, the home of the Catholic Church. First, the institution of the Church is corrupt, and this in turn sets a bad example for the rest of Italy. Second, the Church is responsible for the current weakness of Italy because, as a political power, the Church is too weak to unify Italy while being strong enough to create havoc by calling in foreign powers to support its interests. Third, the Church has weakened Italy because its interpretation of Christianity is at odds with the *virtù* necessary to acquire and maintain a state. In other words, modern Christianity has sapped the political energies of the masses. Hence the necessity of imitating the ancients, especially the ancient practice of religion.

Modern critics are divided about Machiavelli's attitude toward religion. Some argue that Machiavelli's criticism of religion is absolute and that he rejects all appeals to the divine, however disingenuous or politically motivated.[30] Others argue that Machiavelli is an atheist who has a purely instrumental or political view of religion. This Machiavelli thinks that Roman religion is superior to Christianity on practical grounds.[31] Still others argue that Machiavelli is a believer who thinks Christianity has been misinterpreted and that it can be made compatible with militant republicanism if it looks to the example of ancient Rome.[32] I incline to the view that Machiavelli thinks of religion in instrumental terms—or as what I would call a useful fiction. But, in contrast to existing interpretations, I want to stress the metapoetic dimension of Machiavelli's reflections on religion, which amount to a reflection on the human capacity to make or shape experience tout court. Machiavelli signals his interest in this metapoetic dimension in the preface to book 1 of the *Discourses*, which in turn frames his discussion of Roman religion.

In the preface to book 1 of the *Discourses* Machiavelli ostentatiously asserts his modernity by claiming to have entered "upon a path not yet trodden by anyone."[33] As scholars have long recognized, Machiavelli is alluding to the Roman poet Lucretius who, in book 1 of *De rerum natura*, claimed to be "blazing a trail through pathless tracks of the Muses' Pierian realm, where no foot has ever trod before."[34] (Machiavelli knew Lucretius well, having transcribed *De rerum natura* in 1497, whether for himself or for someone else, we don't know.)[35] Lucretius, of course, was writing a philosophical poem, one that was explicitly hostile to political engagement, whereas Machiavelli was advancing a new account of politics. What they shared was a naturalistic account of human nature, including human passions and desires; an emphasis on the importance of chance and free will in human affairs; and an interest in the uses of poetic fiction for purposes of deception and/or enlightenment. Chief among these fictions was religion.

In Machiavelli's time as now, Lucretius was famous for his argument that religion originated in fear and ignorance of the natural world.[36] Fear and ignorance generated the superstitious belief in gods who control the universe and who actively punish or reward human beings. For Lucretius, the gods are thus both an effect of fear and the further cause of it in humans (cf. *De rerum natura* 1.102–12). Lucretius's main goal was to rid his readers of such fears and superstitions by revealing the constitution of the universe and the natural "causes of things."[37]

This revelation of the causes of things paradoxically allowed for a degree of voluntarism in Lucretius's universe. Although the world was made up of atoms or material particles, and governed by strict laws (the "naturae . . . ratio"), Lucretius also insisted that the "swerve of atoms" made room for free will and contingency in an otherwise determined universe. (Machiavelli singled out this passage for special comment in the margins of his transcription of Lucretius.)[38] Once the nature of things was understood, Lucretius believed, people would also see that the gods had no interest in humans, but they would also see that this divine disinterestedness dictated a new ethical attitude—calm of mind—and a new kind of ethical responsibility among humans.[39] In the Renaissance, this ethical dimension of Lucretius was well recognized. Even though *De rerum natura* was banned by the Florentine synod in 1516 as "a lascivious and wicked work, in which every effort is made to demonstrate the mortality of the soul," the number of manuscripts of *De rerum natura* increased fiftyfold in the fifteenth century, and the text received serious and appreciative commentary by some of the century's best-known humanists.[40]

Renaissance readers of *De rerum natura* recognized that Lucretius's criticism of superstition and his claim for individual agency were bound up with his reflections on poetry. One such reader was Marcello Virgilio Adriani, a humanist who may have been Machiavelli's teacher and who later employed Machiavelli in the chancery before the arrival of Piero Soderini. As Alison Brown has shown in a fascinating recent book, even before he transcribed the text of Lucretius, Machiavelli would have been familiar with Adriani's lectures on Lucretius. In Adriani's inaugural lecture as professor of poetry and oratory in Florence, Brown tells us, he "used Lucretius to defend the 'utility and pleasure' of poetry against critics like Plato (as well as Savonarola)."[41] In particular, Adriani quoted the famous passage in book 1 (ll. 936–48), where Lucretius shows how the honey of poetry can sweeten a bitter doctrine and make it acceptable to a recalcitrant reader. Although the passage about honey equates poetry with pleasing deception, Lucretius makes it clear in this passage and elsewhere in *De rerum natura* that he thought of poetry as a form of enlightenment, able to counter the effects of religious superstition. In Lucretius's words, the reader, "although deceived, [is] not betrayed but rather in this way refreshed and helped to grow strong" (1.941–42).

This was not a politically neutral argument. In choosing to speak about the poet Lucretius and in showing that Lucretius himself defended the use of poetry, Adriani was offering a defense of humanistic studies against the contemporary criticism of Savonarola and others.[42] In his *Apologeticus de ratione poeticae artis*, Savonarola had explicitly attacked secular poetry, arguing that there was "an infinite distance between the gentile poets and our prophets: in the former the great trap of the devil lies hidden." According to Savonarola, secular poets are interested in superficial eloquence, whereas prophets are concerned only with "the truth."[43] In later sermons, Savonarola went out of his way to condemn the racy poetry of Luigi Pulci and the erotic works of Ovid, Tibullus, Catullus, and Terence (all favorites of Machiavelli, among others). And he complained that the poets studied in grammar schools were purveyors of mere fables and that students should be so warned: "E dove voi maestri, trovate in quelli vostri libri di poesie Iove, Plutone ecc., dite loro:—Figliuoli miei: queste sono favole."[44] While Cicero and Virgil were allowed, it was crucial to keep in mind the distinction between sacred and secular works. Accordingly, Savonarola rejected the claims of "certain poets and grammarians who say that their branch of knowledge is theology."[45] Pagan history, in particular, has none of the predictive power of Scripture: "look at the example of Livy," Savonarola urged: the Roman historian wrote not to predict the future but merely to describe the past.[46] In fact, Livy seems to have been a particular thorn in the side of Savonarola: in his *Prediche sopra Ezekiele*, he praised Gregory the Great for having burned Livy's works.[47] Adriani's defense of poetry needs to be seen as a response to Savonarola's attack on the prestige of secular literature, an attack that in time produced his notorious bonfires of the vanities.

But Adriani's specific attention to Lucretius also suggests an attack on Savonarola's idea of religion. Savonarola's attack on "poetic theology" was in the service of his own political theology, his argument for the spiritual basis of the Florentine republic. As Savonarola wrote in his treatise on the government of Florence, the fear of God was necessary for the perfecting of the new republic. Once this republic is established, "the city will become so religious as to be a terrestrial Paradise and live in rejoicing, songs, and psalms; and the children will be like angels, and they will live together nourished in Christian and civil life."[48] But Adriani, like his predecessor in the chancery, Bartolomeo Scala, was resolutely secular. Hence the usefulness of Lucretius. As Brown has shown, Lucretius deconstructed Savonarola avant la lettre by arguing that religious believers falsely hope to allay their fears by creating "figures of power" whom they can propitiate with prayers, but in doing so they "only increase [their] fear and servitude."[49] Like Lucretius, Adriani also, if implicitly, presented the constructive uses of poetry as a counter to the religious superstitions and illusions, including those advanced by Savonarola. I suggest that this opposition between the constructive fictions of poetry and the oppressive illusions of superstition governs Machiavelli's double-edged analysis of religion in the *Discourses*. Machiavelli sometimes portrays religion as an oppressive superstition, as Lucretius does. But, unlike Lucretius, he also recommends the political use of religion, understood—at least by some—as a poetic fiction. The person who understands the "causes of things" is not only a critic of superstition but a mythmaker as well. In a passage that seems to allude to *De rerum natura*, Machiavelli writes in *Discourses* 1.12: "It is the duty, then, of the rulers of a republic or a kingdom to preserve the foundations of the religion they hold. . . . And so much the more they are going to do it as they are more prudent and as they have better understanding of natural things [*cose naturali*]."[50]

Before turning to specific examples, it is important to see that, like Adriani's, Machiavelli's use of Lucretius was politically charged. As Carlo Dionisotti showed long ago, in the fifteenth century the Medici had sponsored—and politically tamed—the "Hellenizing philological-philosophical avant-garde" of Poliziano and Marsilio Ficino. Although both showed interest in Lucretius in their youth, their mature work was Neoplatonic, Greek, and idealizing, rather than naturalistic, Roman, and pragmatic.[51] For Ficino, poets were the first theologians, and this conception of poetic theology continued to inform his conception of poetry. Despite his differences with Ficino, Poliziano also saw the poet as inspired by "poeticus furor," and poetry as a civilizing force. But neither had stressed the political uses of poetry; instead, they studiously avoided "any practical political engagement." Thus the Hellenizing literary program initially produced political quiescence. Dionisotti comments, "This attitude must have instinctively repelled the young Machiavelli. . . . [W]ith the passage of time Machiavelli could not help but realize that the Hellenizing direction taken by Florentine humanism under Poliziano's patronage was incompatible with the 'Roman' orientation, civic and military, which seemed to him ever more clearly necessary."[52] In the late 1490s, Machiavelli's sense of urgency was further aggravated by the new political turn taken by Neoplatonism, specifically the political alliance between Ficino, Pico della Mirandola, and Savonarola. In 1494, Adriani had responded to the crisis of the French invasion by reasserting the traditional link between humanist rhetoric and republican freedom and praising "teachers who understood that, in reading Livy, what mattered most was not 'the prettiness of the style but the substance of Roman power and *virtus*.'"[53] Like Adriani, Machiavelli aspired to make his own mark on the literary and political culture of contemporary Florence by turning it in the direction of ancient republican Rome—a turn that would amount to a new, practical direction for both literature and politics.[54] Hence the choice to write a commentary on Livy. But Lucretius, as a Roman poet who was also a critic of religious superstition, also fit the bill. And he could be politicized, by inserting him into the text of Livy.[55]

The *Discourses* is filled with positive examples of the instrumental use of religion in ancient Rome, beginning with Numa who feigned conversation with a nymph in order to convince the Romans that his "new and unwonted laws" were divinely inspired.[56] This fiction or pretense was necessary, Machiavelli tells us, "because many good things are known to a prudent man that are not in themselves so plainly rational that others can be persuaded of them. Therefore wise men, who wish to remove this difficulty, have recourse to God." Livy described Numa as dedicating the grove in which he spoke to the nymph to the "Camenae," which John Najemy glosses as "fountain nymphs who had the gift of prophecy (crucial both for the pagan and the Christian religions) and whom the Roman poets identified with the Muses, and thus, metonymically, with poetry itself." This suggests that Numa's fiction is, in Najemy's words, "the kind of deception that emerges from the garden of poetry."[57] In striking contrast to Savonarola's prophecies, which served only to weaken the Florentines, Numa's poetic "recourse to God" was responsible for the strength and good fortune of the Roman people: "the religion introduced by Numa was among the chief reasons for the prosperity of that city. Because religion caused good laws; good laws make good fortune; and from good fortune came the happy results of the city's endeavors." Machiavelli then goes on to consider how the absence of religion gives rise to the rule of a tyrant, thereby implicitly allying religion with his republican views: "And as the observance of religious teaching brings about the greatness of states, so contempt for it brings about their ruin. Because, where fear of God is lacking, it is necessary either that a kingdom fall or that it be sustained by fear of a prince, which alone atones for what is missing in religion." But such a state will not last because "princes are short-lived" and unlikely to pass their vigor on to their offspring. Here Machiavelli paraphrases Dante's *Purgatorio* (7.121–23), to the effect that, because probity is only rarely inherited, we know it comes from God. But, whereas Dante is concerned with human sin and divine salvation, Machiavelli is preoccupied with the structural, purely human salvation (*salute*) of the state.[58] The best ruler is one who "will so organize [the state] that even after he dies it can be maintained." For all these reasons, Numa is the anti-Savonarola and the prime example of the strategic use of religion as a political fiction to strengthen the people. The people, in Lucretius's words, "although deceived, are not betrayed but rather in this way refreshed and helped to grow strong."[59]

Machiavelli, however, is acutely aware of the problem that religion can be used to weaken the people as well as to strengthen them. In commenting on the example of Numa, Machiavelli first observes that it is easier to foist the pretense of divine inspiration on a rude and uncultured people, just as it is easier for a sculptor to make a good sculpture from unhewn rock rather than one that has already been touched. But then Machiavelli reminds his readers of Savonarola:

> though rude men are more easily won over to a new order or opinion, it is still not for that reason impossible to win over to it also cultured men and those who assume they are not rude. The people of Florence do not suppose themselves either ignorant or rude; nevertheless they were persuaded by Brother Girolamo Savonarola that he spoke with God. I do not intend to decide whether it was true or not, because so great a man ought to be spoken of with reverence, but I do say that countless numbers

believed him without having seen anything extraordinary to make them believe him, because his life, his teaching, the affairs he dealt with were enough to make them lend him faith.[60]

This example is complicated because Machiavelli's attitude toward Savonarola is as ambivalent as his attitude toward religion. On the one hand, in the *Discourses* and elsewhere, Machiavelli makes it clear that he was impressed by Savonarola's ability to manipulate the Florentine people with his rhetoric, including his representation of himself as a new Moses and his insistence on Moses's exemplary use of violence to maintain political power; on the other hand, in *The Prince* Machiavelli condemns Savonarola as a mere rhetorician, an unarmed prophet who not only failed to introduce lasting laws in Florence, but also failed to preserve himself from being burned at the stake in 1498.[61] Echoing his own comments about Moses in chapter 6 of *The Prince* ("And though we should not consider Moses, because he was simply an agent sent by God to do certain things, he still should be admired, if only for that grace which made him worthy of talking with God"), Machiavelli pretends not to judge Savonarola "because so great a man ought to be spoken of with reverence." But he then goes on to imply that the Florentines were simply duped by the Dominican friar, who failed to do "anything extraordinary to make them believe him." Machiavelli's half skeptical, half admiring comment makes it clear that Savonarola's success depends not on the divine truth of his claims but rather on Savonarola's purely human rhetoric—"his teaching, the affairs he dealt with"—and the credulousness of the Florentines. Savonarola's success from this perspective is not only a prime example of how, in the realm of politics, it's not so much truth as persuasion or the *verità effettuale* that matters; it is also an example of how religion is part of the realm of politics rather than hovering above it. In this realm of competing interests, the use of religion will always be contested—as Machiavelli does here by suggesting that Savonarola's claim to be inspired by God had the unintended effect of disempowering the people. If the Florentines had been less credulous, Machiavelli implies, they might have been better able to sustain Savonarola's republican program by themselves rather than passively "depending on the *virtù* of one man alone."[62]

This lesson receives a further gloss in Machiavelli's discussion of the Roman practice of auspices. Here again the examples are two-sided, offering advice to both the ruler and the people. Machiavelli first tells us that the prudent Roman leaders, who had a "better understanding of natural things" (*più conoscitori delle cose naturali*), knew how to use apparent miracles and auguries, "even though they think [them] false," to manipulate the people and the army and strengthen the state.[63] In the example of the Roman consul Papirius, Machiavelli further shows that it's fine to manipulate the auspices, but you have to do so prudently, by making it seem as though you are really obeying them. When Papirius was about to fight an important battle with the Samnites, he consulted the *pullarii*, the augurs who read signs from the behavior of chickens. The chief of the *pullarii*, seeing that the soldiers were eager for combat, told the consul that the omen was good, even though the chickens had refused to eat. When the soldiers later learned the truth, Papirius told them that their duty was to fight, and if the *pullarius* had told lies, he would suffer the consequences. And, Machiavelli writes, "that the result might correspond to the prophecy (*prognostico*) [that is, Papirius's own prophecy], he ordered the legates to put the *pullarii* in the very front of the combat."[64] As they advanced, the chief *pullarius* was killed by the dart of a Roman soldier. What impresses Machiavelli at this point is Papirius's skillful interpretation of the event as a religious sign: "When he heard this, the Consul said everything was going well and with the favor of the gods, because by the death of that liar the army was purged of every fault and of all the wrath that they had conceived against it. And thus, by knowing well how to fit his plans to the auspices, [Papirius] made his decision to engage in combat without the army's perceiving that in any respect he had neglected the rules of their religion." As John Najemy comments, "Among religious leaders, it is these skillful handlers—whether of chickens, of oaths, or of conversations with God— that Machiavelli admires, not because they subvert or mock religion but because they recognize its power and know how to harness it."[65]

But in line with Lucretius's critique of the harmful effects of religion (e.g., 1.80–130), Machiavelli also gives examples of auspices and signs being used to dispossess the people of their agency. For example, Machiavelli tells us that when the people elected tribunes who were almost all plebeian, the nobility defeated the people's bid for more power by arguing that the recent pestilence and famine were providential signs that the gods were angry that Rome "had used badly the majesty of her power." Confronted with this interpretation, the people ceased to support their own tribunes. Something similar happened when the tribune Terentillus proposed to codify the laws that limited the power of the consuls, in order to empower the people. In response, the Senate interpreted the Sibylline books as showing that the popular unrest made Rome vulnerable to attack from her enemies.[66] Unlike Livy, who writes that the tribunes merely "swore the prophecies were a fake,"[67] Machiavelli tells us that this fabrication was "exposed by the Tribunes"; but he goes on to observe that "this prediction still put so much fear into the breasts of the plebeians that their ardor for following the Tribunes was cooled." When the tribunes persisted in proposing the Terentillian law, one of the senators argued that the people were bound by an oath they had sworn to one of the consuls that trumped any allegiance to the tribunes and any further discussion of the new law. As Machiavelli notes, in commenting on this episode Livy praises the people's religiosity: "Not yet this neglect of the gods, that now possesses the age, had come to pass; nor that each man should make for himself laws suited to interpreting his oath."[68] By contrast, in Machiavelli's Lucretian rendition, the practice of augury and oaths serves to disempower the people, using their faithfulness and religious sense of obligation against their own interests. Machiavelli's point here seems to be twofold: the patricians' manipulation of the plebeians' religious beliefs was effective, even overcoming the tribunes' exposure of this manipulation; and the people should be wary of such manipulation. Machiavelli may even imply that the people should adopt an attitude of strategic distance from their own beliefs, of the sort Machiavelli recommends in chapter 18 of *The Prince*: "It is good to appear merciful, truthful, humane, sincere, and religious [*relligioso*]; it is good to be so in reality. But you must keep your mind so disposed that, in case of need, you can turn to the exact contrary." In the *Discourses*, such distance need not be equated with manipulation of the people by the prince. It could instead by equated with an ironic self-consciousness about the myths the citizens live by.

Machiavelli presents a similarly two-sided view of religion in his discussion of the Roman war with the Samnites. He writes that the Samnites strengthened the resolve of their soldiers by having them swear an oath to fight the Romans unto the death, and by savagely murdering those who refused to swear. Concerned that this news would terrify his own army, the Roman consul Papirius roused his soldiers by mocking the Samnite oath. He told his soldiers that the oath "moved [the Samnites] to fear and not to fortitude, because they were obliged to be at the same time in terror of [their own fellow] citizens, gods, and enemies." Here Machiavelli puts Lucretius's critique of religion in the mouth of Papirius, who articulates the notion that fear and ignorance are the cause of the Samnite religion, which in turn saps the free will of the individual soldier. Machiavelli then tells us that, in the battle that followed, the Samnites fought bravely but were still defeated because "Roman *virtù* and the fear derived from past defeats" overcame "the *virtù* of [Samnite] religion and the oath [the Samnites] had taken."[69] As he often does, Machiavelli dismantles conventional assumptions about virtue by punning on the Italian word *virtù*, opposing the active *virtù* of Rome to the passive virtue of the Samnite religion. Machiavelli suggests both that religion was well used (*bene usata* [Ital., 173]) by the Samnite general to motivate his soldiers, and that what really seems to have motivated the Samnites was not so much fear of their God as fear of Roman *virtù*. Machiavelli's celebration of Roman *virtù* is entirely consistent with his comment in his poem *Asino* that "[t]o believe that without effort on your part God fights for you, while you are idle and on your knees, has ruined many kingdoms and many states."[70] For the Samnites, religion is necessary but, finally, insufficient for military success. In a similar way, from a Roman perspective, it's not the positive appeal to Roman religion but rather the demystification of the Samnite religion that strengthens the *virtù* of the Roman soldiers, which, in turn, terrifies the Samnites.

The contrast between the *virtù* of the Romans and that of the Samnites is replayed in book 2, chapter 2 of the *Discourses* in the famous concluding opposition between Roman religion and Christianity. In this chapter, Machiavelli elaborates a comparison between the people's love of free government and their hatred of tyranny.[71] He argues that republics are great because they promote the common good, while tyrannies are internally weak because the tyrant cannot afford to make the people strong, out of fear they will overthrow him. Machiavelli goes on to cite the example of Hieronymus from Livy as support for the claim that the people naturally love liberty. But in doing so, he substantially revises Livy's account to give even more agency to the people, thereby undercutting Livy's aristocratic prejudices. At the same time, Machiavelli also undercuts the claim of contemporary figures such as Savonarola that Christianity, understood as the "truth and the true way," is the best support for the republican ambitions of Florence.

In book 24 of his history, Livy describes the aftermath of the assassination of Hieronymus, grandson of Hiero of Syracuse. Livy is particularly interested in what happened after the death of two conspirators who subsequently plotted to take over the government. After their deaths, the mob called for the execution of their wives as well, believing that "no member of the family of tyrants ought to survive." It's at this point that Livy comments, "Indeed, that is the nature of crowds: the mob is either a humble slave or a cruel master. As for the middle way of liberty, the mob can neither take it nor keep it with any respect for moderation or law."[72]

In Machiavelli's account, when Hieronymus was killed, the army "began to riot and to take arms against his murderers, but when they heard that in Syracuse there was a proclamation of freedom, being attracted by that name, they entirely quieted down, laid aside their anger against the tyrannicides, and considered how in that city they could organize a free government." Livy wrote that when the army heard the phrase "liberty restored," "hopes grew of substantial benefits out of the dead king's money and of the chance of service under better commanders"[73] In contrast to Livy, Machiavelli emphasizes the army's deliberation about how "they could organize a free government," and he conspicuously makes no mention of the mob as a humble slave or a cruel master.[74] Instead, he goes on to ponder "why it can be that in those ancient times people were greater lovers of freedom than in these." He concludes that "it came from the same cause that makes men now less hardy. That I believe is the difference between our religion [i.e., Christianity] and the ancient. Ours, because it shows us the truth and the true way, makes us esteem less the honor of the world; whereas the pagans, greatly esteeming such honor and believing it their greatest good, were fiercer in their actions." In these remarks, Machiavelli ironically juxtaposes "the true way" that makes moderns weaker to the "honor" that makes the ancients stronger.[75] In doing so, he makes it clear that it's not the truth of Christianity that matters as much as its effectiveness, which is weak in comparison with the religion of ancient Rome. Conversely, Roman religion is strong to the extent that it encourages the autonomy of the Roman people, their love of free government.

In this passage, we can almost hear Machiavelli not only criticizing Christianity but also cautioning us that there is not just one true antiquity and not just one true way. To Strauss's emphasis on the classical philosopher's theoretical contemplation of the truth, Machiavelli opposes the Roman republic's practical love of liberty. Here the Christian preoccupation with a transcendent truth is not so different from Strauss's preoccupation with a philosophic truth (with the result that Strauss turns out to be a mirror image of what he rejects): both distract from the *verità effettuale* of politics. Concern with this effectual truth will sometimes dictate the exposure of religion; at other times it will dictate the use of religion. What is admirable about the Roman use of religion, in contrast to both Straussian philosophy and Christianity, is the way it has contributed to strengthening the resolve of its soldiers and the commitment of its citizens to the common good.

Despite his praise of Roman religion, however, it's clear that Machiavelli was impressed with the strength of Christianity—a strength derived not so much from arms as from a distinctive set of fictions regarding the divine legitimation of political power and the promise of the afterlife. Though Machiavelli was critical of Savonarola, he clearly appreciated the way Savonarola used his considerable rhetorical skills to persuade the Florentines to join his cause. Machiavelli undoubtedly also perceived the striking parallels between his own situation and Savonarola's (not to mention Christ's) as an "unarmed prophet" (see chapter 6 of *The Prince*). Though Savonarola's lack of arms eventually led to his downfall, according to Machiavelli, Christianity, we might say, triumphed over Rome historically by virtue of a uniquely persuasive set of fictions. Machiavelli can't deny this as much as he would like to; he can only point to the way that Christianity has sapped genuinely political *virtù*. To the extent that Machiavelli sees Christianity as the religious idiom of his time that any savvy politician will need to deal with, Machiavelli's goal, in both *The Prince* and the *Discourses*, is to supplant the view of Christianity as "the true way" and return Christianity to the status of a useful fiction, a fiction, moreover, whose uses will always be contested in the uncertain realm of politics.[76] Thus the end of *The Prince*, where Machiavelli invites the Medici to save Italy in ostentatiously religious rhetoric, can be read as both a parody of Savonarola's sermons and an example of the right use of religion for political ends. Religious rhetoric is removed from Savonarola's register of truth and recast in the register of what Machiavelli called imagination or *fantasia*.[77] For Machiavelli, imagination thus joins critical analysis and productive manipulation: the critical dismantling of superstition is the first step to being able to manipulate the "appearance" of religion and render it more "effective."

Good and Bad Fictions

But here a question emerges: how do we distinguish between good and bad uses of religion, or good and bad fictions, if we can't refer to some standard of truth? And wasn't this Strauss's question all along? Machiavelli's answer always takes into account "effectiveness," but he does not simply equate the political good with what is effective or with instrumental reason. Instead, Machiavelli is interested in the affective commitments that produce a binding sense of community. We could call this affective commitment *virtù*, even when it does not produce success.[78] And this distinction returns us to Machiavelli's own affective commitment to ancient Rome, despite its decline and the subsequent rise of Christianity.

Ultimately, then, Machiavelli's understanding of Roman religion has more positive connotations that the notion of manipulation might suggest. In *Discourses* 1.55, Machiavelli discusses "how much goodness and how much religion" the Romans possessed during the period of Camillus's campaign against the Veientes; and he goes on to observe, "In Germany this goodness and this religion are still important among the people. These qualities enable many republics to exist there in freedom and to observe their laws so well that nobody outside or inside the cities dares try to master them."[79] Similarly, Machiavelli's repeated injunctions to bring citizens back to the mark, by reenacting the founding violence of their communities, may also be read as a revision of Epicurus and Lucretius, who had used the word *sign* to refer to natural law, in contrast to religion.[80] By contrast, Machiavelli used *segno* to refer both to the realm of appearances and to his ultimate target: the creation of the affective and political bonds that will strengthen the state. For example, in the preface to book 1 of the *Discourses*, Machiavelli laments that there is no sign of ancient virtue (*di quella antica virtú non ci è rimasta alcun segno*).[81] His remedy for this is the imitation of the ancient Roman practice of exemplary acts of violence that remind the citizens of the founding political moment (*gli uomini ritirare verso il segno*) and recall them to their civil commitments.[82] Strikingly, here too Machiavelli uses the word *segno*, as though to suggest that the signs that produce true opinions and political commitments are not the maxims of natural law (Epicurus's signs) but the artificially constructed signs or interventions of human rulers: the examples Machiavelli gives of bringing citizens back to the mark include the death of Brutus's sons. Such acts of violence may be what Machiavelli had in mind when he wrote in *The Prince* that it is necessary to be able to coerce belief.[83] But *Discourses* 3.1 also suggests that Roman civil religion was a vehicle of human agency as well as an obstacle to it. If this is the case, poetry or fiction should not be thought of simply as demystified religion; religion—at least in Machiavelli's sense—is instead encompassed by the analysis of the human capacity for poiesis.

Accordingly, not all examples of religion in the *Discourses* involve manipulation of the people by a superior. In book 1, chapter 12, Machiavelli describes how the soldiers who were sacking Veii entered the temple of Juno to remove the statue of the goddess. When one of the soldiers asked (Livy writes "whether divinely inspired or merely [as] a young man's joke"), "Do you wish to come to Rome?," "one thought he saw [the statue of Juno] nod and another that she said 'Yes.'"[84] Livy comments skeptically on this story, even as he indulges in personification of the statue: "In any case—fables apart—[the statue] was moved from her place with only the slightest application of mechanical power, and was light and easy to transport—almost as if she came of her own free will—and was taken undamaged to her eternal dwelling-place on the Aventine" (5.22).[85] In contrast to Livy's skepticism, what interests Machiavelli is the relationship of the soldiers to this event:

> Because, since these men were full of religion [*ripieni di religione*] (which Livy makes plain because, on entering the temple, they entered it without disorder, all devout and full of reverence), they seemed to hear the answer to their question which perhaps they expected. Camillus and the other chief men of the city in every way favored and magnified this opinion and belief.[86]

Religion here indirectly authorizes and empowers the soldiers' desires and actions; in this case, the voice of the god really is the voice of the people. In contrast to Livy (5.20), who emphasizes Camillus's religious preparations for the destruction of Veii, Camillus's role here is merely to reinforce the soldiers' "opinion and credulity." Machiavelli then turns this positive lesson about the soldiers' religious empowerment into a lesson for his own times: "If religion of this sort had been kept up among the princes of Christendom, in the form in which its giver founded it, Christian states and republics would be more united, much more happy than they are. Nor can a better estimate of its decline be made than by seeing that those peoples who are nearest to the Roman Church, the head of our religion, have least religion." And he concludes by blaming the papacy for the current political crisis in Italy: "through the bad examples of that court this land has lost all piety and religion."[87]

And yet it's not so clear that the example of the soldiers at Veii can be reproduced in Machiavelli's Italy. In the very same chapter in which he discusses Veii, Machiavelli raises the crucial question of whether Christianity can be interpreted in a politically empowering way. Noting that religions too need to be renewed by being brought back to their first principles, Machiavelli adduces the examples of Saint Francis and Saint Dominic:

> They with their poverty and with the example of Christ's life brought it [Christianity] back into the minds of men when it had disappeared from them. The power of their new orders is the reason why the improbity of the prelates and the heads of our religion does not ruin it; for still living in poverty and having great influence with the people because of hearing confessions and preaching, they give them to understand that it is evil

to speak evil of what is evil, and it is good to live under the prelates' control and, if prelates make errors, to leave them to God
for punishment. So the prelates do the worst they can, because
they do not fear that punishment which they do not see and
do not believe in. This renewal, then, has maintained and still
maintains our religion.[88]

In an extraordinary display of self-restraint, Machiavelli makes no direct comment on this example, as though it were yet another instance of
the kind of renewal he has been describing in ancient Rome. Yet it's clear
that reform here has the effect of bolstering the status quo: it reinforces
political passivity by reminding Christians of their otherworldly voca-
tion and of the doctrine that judgment is the prerogative of God. Given
that this is an example of returning Christianity to its first principles, it's
not clear that Machiavelli thinks Christianity *can* be interpreted (as opposed to simply used or manipulated) in a way that would be consistent
with Machiavellian *virtù*.

Machiavelli, then, doesn't respond to the question of how to tell
good fictions from bad, at least not in Strauss's terms. Nor does he
throw the question back, as it were, to Strauss, by asking how we could
distinguish between good and bad philosophy. He shifts the terms of
the question, rejecting the exclusive opposition between philosophical
reason and mere poetry, advancing instead a political art of the exact
imagination. Drawing on Bacon and Leibniz's art of invention (*ars inve-
niendi*), Theodor Adorno once described exact imagination as "the demand to answer the questions of a pre-given reality each time, through a
fantasy which rearranges the elements of the question."[89] Adorno might
also have adduced Machiavelli, who in his "Ghiribizzi" (Fantasies) of
September 1506 wrote to Giovan Battista Soderini that men must learn
how to change their imaginations.[90] Machiavelli's prince or founder
also tries to answer the questions of a pregiven reality through an art of
invention, a fantasy or imagination that rearranges the elements of the
question. If we think of the question as how to acquire and maintain
power in the realm of politics, Machiavelli's rearrangement turns necessity into an occasion for *virtù* and good fortune into the product of such
political invention. And just as Machiavelli puns on the Christian and
classical ideas of *virtù* to construct a fundamentally new political capacity, so he plays with the Roman and Christian meanings of *religione*
to absorb the transcendent claims of Christianity into the immanence
of civil religion. This art of the exact imagination is Machiavelli's own
artistic achievement in the *Discourses*.

Machiavelli glosses this achievement in *Discourses* 1.10, where he argues that writers too can be founders.[91] He writes, "Among all famous men those are most famous who have been heads and organizers of religion. Next after them are those who have founded either republics or kingdoms. After these, they are famous who, when set over armies, have enlarged their own dominion or that of their native land. Next to these are put men of letters [*uomini literati*]. And because these are of many kinds, they are celebrated, each one of them, according to his rank."[92] Machiavelli is just such a literary man who uses his art to construct a new discourse of politics. The *Discourses* itself outlines the new myth that Machiavelli aims to substitute for the less effective myth of Christianity. This is the myth not of Livy's Rome but of the Rome Machiavelli constructs through his reading of Livy: a Rome whose greatness was owing not to *fortuna* but to the *virtù* of its citizens. Recalling Machiavelli's allusion to Lucretius at the outset of the *Discourses*, we could say that this myth reimagines the Lucretian gods who inspire fear as the malleable occasions of fortune and in the process recovers the Lucretian swerve of human agency, which Machiavelli called *virtù*. This is a better myth to live by than Christianity, Machiavelli suggests, because it is empowering rather than debilitating, even as or precisely because we recognize that we have made it ourselves.

Strauss and Schmitt Revisited

In conclusion, I'd like to suggest that, while Machiavelli rejects Strauss's preoccupation with philosophy, Strauss found some common ground with Machiavelli's view of the role of religion in the political sphere. For all his criticism of Machiavelli, Strauss actually agreed both with Machiavelli's implicit critique of religion's claim to supernatural knowledge, and with Machiavelli's views about the positive uses of civil religion. Early in *Thoughts on Machiavelli* Strauss contrasts what he describes as the modern indifference to religion or the modern nostalgia for lost faith to Machiavelli's serious critique: Strauss asks, "Are not these [modern] kinds of unbelief much more insulting to belief than is an unbelief, like Machiavelli's, which takes seriously the claim to truth of revealed religion by regarding the question of its truth as all-important and which therefore is not, at any rate, a lukewarm unbelief?"[93] I think it's doubtful Machiavelli took the truth claim of revelation seriously. But perhaps Strauss meant only that Machiavelli took it seriously enough to combat it, not least of all by arguing against the putative Christian emphasis on love, and by returning us to the terror inherent in man's situation. Machiavelli also engaged Christianity, according to Strauss, by making it clear that, of all tyrants, the most dangerous tyrant is the biblical God.[94] This is both because biblical religion unmans citizens and makes them vulnerable to tyranny, including the indirect tyrannical rule of priests, and because Christianity in particular presupposes a tyrannical God, a God who like an earthly tyrant deprives the people of their agency.[95] According to Strauss, this is because "the Biblical command is revealed; its acceptance is based not on reason but on authority; [and] authority will not be accepted in the long run and by many people if it cannot use compulsion 'in order to keep firm those who already believe and to make the unbelievers believe.'"[96] Human beings, according to Christian doctrine, must be punished or coerced because of their sinful human nature. In contrast to the Christian view of human nature, Strauss writes, "Machiavelli teaches that man's nature is not bad, originally or as a consequence of sin; men are often corrupt; yet this corruption can be counteracted."[97] Thus to the authority of revelation, Machiavelli counterposes the agency of human *virtù*.

In these remarks of Strauss, especially about "an unbelief . . . which takes seriously the claim to truth of revealed religion," Strauss seems to be describing himself as well as Machiavelli. Strauss's lesson—which he attributes to Machiavelli—is that we need to take seriously the claim to truth of revealed religion, not ignore it. For Strauss, to take it seriously means to defend the critical enterprise of philosophy or secular thinking over against the authority of revelation. But it also means to recognize the importance of civil religion in helping to enforce obedience to the laws and thus preserving the state.

If I'm right that Strauss agreed with Machiavelli about the civil or political uses of religion, then Strauss's difference with Machiavelli was not over Machiavelli's account of civil religion but over the fact that he made this account public. He did so, in Strauss's view, because he had no interest in the esoteric wisdom of philosophy; instead Machiavelli was interested in the democratizing project of enlightenment. And this means that, for Strauss, Machiavelli repressed the theological-political problem as Strauss understood it, but less because he was uninterested in revelation than because he was not concerned with the permanent philosophical questions that engaged Strauss. Because Machiavelli was not concerned with the higher philosophical questions, he did not need to make a distinction between the philosophic elite (who had privileged knowledge of philosophy and of the political function of religion) and the common man. The common reader is invited to understand the political uses of religion just as the philosopher is.

This, of course, has been one of the standard defenses of Machiavelli since the sixteenth century: according to his defenders, Machiavelli doesn't so much recommend tyrannical behavior as reveal the tyrant's secrets of state to the people he oppresses, thereby enabling their resistance. It would be more accurate, however, to say that Machiavelli both recommends tyrannical actions and exposes their limitations, in the form of the tyrant's ultimate dependence on the people. Similarly, we can say that Machiavelli recognizes the uses of religion to strengthen the state, at the same time that he dissects the ways in which the appeal to religion can be used to weaken the people. If we think of poetry or fiction as a useful deception, then Strauss and Machiavelli are agreed that religion is a useful fiction. But if we think of poetry as the truth that we know only what we make or construct ourselves, then Strauss is a critic of poetry and Machiavelli is its defender. If this is the case, then Machiavelli's relation to the philosophical tradition is not simply a matter of bracketing what Strauss would call the permanent philosophical problems. Instead, in ignoring the distinction between the philosopher and the common man, between theoretical contemplation and practical politics, Machiavelli helps poetry—construed as the human power of feigning and creative interpretation—win its age-old quarrel with philosophy.[98]

Why revisit this debate now? I want to suggest that the confrontation of Strauss and Machiavelli helps to clarify the issues and options facing us today. Against critics of liberalism who call for a "return to religion," as many are doing in the United States, Strauss advocates a return to classical reason for the philosopher while stressing the ongoing necessity of something like civil religion for the masses.[99] In contrast, Machiavelli offers a different account: one that stresses the usefulness of religion—interpreted correctly—for civic virtue, while also warning about the tyranny of religion as the repression of human agency and human creativity. At times it seems that Machiavelli might have preferred to do away with Christianity entirely and simply substitute love of Florence, as he famously did in his letter to Francesco Vettori in which he pronounced that he loved his country more than his soul.[100] But, in the end, Machiavelli was too much of a political realist not to accept the existence of Christianity and to try to reinterpret it in a way that was conducive to civic virtue. Thus we can say that Machiavelli rejects political theology if by this we understand the view that "there is a permanent social order that mirrors the will of God."[101] But he also accepts the political usefulness of religion, even as or precisely because he understands it as a human artifact or fiction. Religion so conceived is a means of reminding citizens of their commitment to the communal project that is the state. But the ultimate logic of religion conceived from the perspective of art is the secular project of self-assertion whose lineaments Machiavelli traced to ancient Rome.

And what about Carl Schmitt? One conclusion we can draw from a reading of Machiavelli is that Schmitt's famous maxim—that "all significant concepts of the modern theory of the state are secularized theological concepts"—is simply wrong. This is because Schmitt's history of the political begins with Christianity. But Machiavelli begins with pagan antiquity, the period that gave us such nontheological concepts as *politeia* and *stasis*, *salus populi* and *res publica*. It was only after antiquity that some of these political concepts were theologized by the Catholic Church. Rather than thinking of "all significant" modern concepts of the state as secularized theological concepts, then, we might think of at least some modern concepts of the state as repaganized.[102] In this light, we could say that Machiavelli challenges us to question the assumption that politics needs a theological foundation rather than simply being the product of the will and of our purely human capacities of negotiation and fabrication. A second conclusion is that there are ways in which Machiavelli anticipates what is best in Schmitt, while avoiding what is least palatable. For Schmitt, the political is the realm of existential conflict. In this realm, decisions cannot simply be referred to—and thus canceled out by—appeal to some higher, objective norm. Strauss undoubtedly thought of his return to classical reason as an antidote to Carl Schmitt's existential political theology. By contrast, Machiavelli's own antidote to the abuse of political theology is much closer to Schmitt's concept of the political than to anything we might find in Strauss. For both, every decision then implies a *parti pris*, which can be justified only by reference to a "concrete order" of life. Moreover, what constitutes a concrete order is itself subject to a political battle. As William Rasch has argued, politics, by this definition, cannot compensate for the lack of a transcendent norm, "but rather, by being its effect, *guarantees* this lack. It does not repress violence in the name of the good life; it structures and limits it."[103] This does not mean that our decisions are arbitrary. As Rasch comments, "We do in fact make distinctions. We do decide that *this* war was fought for the right reasons, and *that* one for the wrong ones . . . but we do not really *know* whether we are correct or not. Barring revelation, which remains incommunicable, we have no ultimate or transcendental assurance that our decisions are valid for all times and all places. . . . These decisions we make are political decisions; and what Schmitt fears most of all, one might say, is the loss of our ability to make political decisions once their contingency is masked by a façade of necessity."[104] Rasch goes on to point out the irony that Schmitt's support of the Nazi state effectively obliterated any possibility of domestic politics, even as he insisted on "the political" between nation-states. By contrast, we can say that Machiavelli was far more concerned with preserving the space of the political within his own contemporary Florence. As we've seen, while Strauss was preoccupied with the competing claims of philosophy and politics, philosophy and poetry, Machiavelli ignores both the claims of philosophy and the absolute claims of religion. The sphere of politics translates all absolutes into competing claims, even competing strategic fictions. This means that theology, in Machiavelli's view of politics, is political theology only if by this we understand the subordination of theology to politics, the realm of disunion and conflict.

4 Spinoza and Liberal Culture: Leo Strauss, Carl Schmitt, and Hannah Arendt

In the 1920s and '30s there was a remarkable revival of interest in Spinoza on the part of German intellectuals, including Carl Schmitt and Leo Strauss. For some, Spinoza's pantheism—his famous equation of God and nature—provided an alternative to the early twentieth-century "crisis theology" of Karl Barth and Friedrich Gogarten.[1] For others, Spinoza was important as an early modern political theorist who contributed to the liberal settlement between religion and the state. Schmitt and Strauss were sensitive to both dimensions of Spinoza's relevance, but it was particularly Spinoza at the dawn of liberalism who interested them. Writing in the charged interwar years, they returned to Spinoza's *Theological-Political Treatise* to diagnose the crisis of the Weimar state. For both, Spinoza was synonymous with the Jewish Question, the fate of liberalism, and the problem of liberal culture. For Strauss, Spinoza also raised the question of historicism and its compatibility with philosophy. Taking a cue from Strauss, I argue that returning to Spinoza can help us rethink the contemporary debate about political theology. But, unlike Strauss, I will argue that Spinoza's treatise offers an exemplary critique of political theology, as well as a defense of democracy and of the liberal idea of culture that is worth recovering today.

Finally, I'll suggest that, in ways Spinoza could not have anticipated, this defense draws near to our modern idea of literature.

In his book on Hobbes's *Leviathan* (1938), Schmitt argued that Spinoza drew out the radical implications of Hobbes's distinction between a believer's faith and his outward confession and, in doing so, dismantled Hobbes's authoritarian account of the state. According to Hobbes, the individual may believe whatever he wants privately, "but as soon as it comes to public confession of faith, private judgment ceases and the sovereign decides about the true and the false."[2] Schmitt then commented that this distinction "contained the seed of death that destroyed the mighty leviathan from within and brought about the death of the mortal god. Only a few years after the appearance of the *Leviathan*, a liberal Jew noticed the barely visible crack in the theoretical justification of the sovereign state." This liberal Jew was of course Spinoza, who expanded Hobbes's account of the individual sphere of conscience or piety "into a universal principle of freedom of thought, perception, and expression." In contrast to Hobbes, who "focused on public peace and the right of sovereign power" as the essential matters, Spinoza emphasized instead "individual freedom of thought" as "the form-giving principle" and treated the right of sovereign power as a secondary matter, or as what Schmitt called a "mere proviso." Here Schmitt seems to be referring to the fact that, as a Jew, Spinoza approached the religion of the state as an outsider, someone for whom state power must always be external and contingent. In this way, Schmitt added, "a small intellectual switch emanating from the nature of Jewish life accomplished . . . the decisive turn in the fate of the leviathan."[3] This turn was decisive not only for thinking about democratic politics but also, I'll suggest, for thinking about the role of poiesis and specifically of literature as we confront modern arguments for the persistence of political theology.[4]

In *Spinoza's Critique of Religion* (1930), Strauss, too, was fascinated by Spinoza's relation to Hobbes, but, unlike Schmitt, he saw Hobbes as the more radical of the two. Whereas Spinoza developed his critique from within the theological tradition, Hobbes asserted "that the political allegiance of all subjects of the state is a bond whose origin lies in reason alone." In this way, Hobbes's critique of religion "once more takes on the archetypal originality, the integral breadth and depth . . . of Epicurus and Lucretius."[5] In *Hobbes's Critique of Religion* (1933–34), Strauss argued that Hobbes's dismantling of revelation was the necessary precondition of his political science, and he went on to assert the importance of art—or what I have been calling poiesis—for Hobbes's political theory: "It is not the fact of nature as a comprehensible order that lies, for Hobbes, at the basis of every possible orientation in the world but the fact of *art*. . . . By 'art,' in the context of his critique of religion, Hobbes understands nothing but the human capacity to bring about useful effects on the basis of reflection." Strauss went on to clarify that once nature is deemed unknowable in itself, the meaning of art changes as well, so that for Hobbes, in contrast to an ancient figure like Aristotle, "art can no longer be the imitation of nature; art loses its natural model; it turns into a model-less, sovereign invention."[6] This early modern notion of art, as Strauss made clear in his 1936 book on Hobbes, went hand in hand with Hobbes's liberation from "the spell of theological tradition."[7]

Whereas Strauss in 1930 emphasized Spinoza's relation to Hobbes, by the early 1960s Strauss was equally fascinated by Spinoza's relation to Machiavelli. In his 1962 preface to *Spinoza's Critique of Religion*, Strauss described Spinoza's account of the relationship between politics and theology as Machiavellianism raised to "theological heights."[8] By this Strauss seems to have meant that, just as Machiavelli suspended traditional ethical distinctions in the realm of politics, which he conceived of as a relation of forces, so Spinoza conceived of God as the power of nature, without reference to merely human ideas of good and evil. In *Spinoza's Critique of Religion*, Strauss argued that Spinoza was influenced by Machiavelli's instrumental account of religion, just as he learned from the Renaissance revival of Epicureanism and Averroism.

Like Schmitt in his reading of Hobbes and Spinoza, Strauss read the relationship of Machiavelli and Spinoza through the lens of the Jewish Question. In particular, Strauss was grappling with the interpretation of the German Jewish neo-Kantian Hermann Cohen, whose magisterial presence hovered over Spinoza scholarship in the early decades of the twentieth century. Cohen famously interpreted Spinoza as a traitor to his religion, a Jew who, banned from the synagogue for his heterodox views, took revenge by criticizing Judaism. Strauss writes in the preface to *Spinoza's Critique of Religion* that "Cohen is justly perplexed by the fact that 'the center of the whole [theological-political] treatise' is the disparagement of Moses and the idealization of Jesus, although the purpose of the work is to secure the freedom of philosophizing. . . . Why then does Spinoza treat Judaism and Christianity differently? Why does he take the side of Christianity in the conflict between Judaism and Christianity, in a conflict of no concern to him as a philosopher?"[9] He answers Cohen by declaring that Spinoza's apparent preference for Christianity was utterly strategic and "Machiavellian." Spinoza was not "the 'God-intoxicated' philosopher but the hard-headed, not to say hard-hearted pupil of Machiavelli and the philologic-historical critic of the Bible." But precisely for this reason Spinoza posed in the most urgent terms the question of political theology: "Orthodoxy could be returned to only if Spinoza was wrong in every respect."[10]

Strauss's Spinoza

The question of orthodoxy was the motive for Strauss's engagement with Spinoza in the 1920s. Early in the preface to *Spinoza's Critique of Religion* Strauss describes himself at the time of its writing as "a young Jew born and raised in Germany who found himself in the grip of the Theological-political predicament."[11] Here the theological-political problem refers to the problem of the relationship between religion and politics, and specifically to the failure of liberalism to solve the Jewish Question in Weimar Germany. Liberalism had claimed to solve the Jewish Question by making religion a personal matter and treating Jews as equals under the law. But such formal equality, Strauss argued, could not address the ongoing problem of discrimination in the private sphere. Political Zionism was a response to this failure of liberalism to deal with anti-Semitism, but—according to cultural Zionists—political Zionism also failed to solve the Jewish Question because it neglected the sources of political affiliation: Jewish history and culture. Yet even cultural Zionism, with its view of Jewish culture as a product of the human mind or "national genius," was a diluted form of Judaism, a religion that claims, after all, to be founded on divine revelation. Jewish faith "must regard as blasphemous the notion of a human solution to the Jewish problem," Strauss wrote. And he continued, "the foundation, the authoritative layer, of the Jewish heritage presents itself, not as a product of the human mind, but as a divine gift, a divine revelation. Did not one completely distort the meaning of the heritage to which one claimed to be loyal by interpreting it as a culture like any other high culture?"[12] In this analysis, Strauss did not object to liberalism simply because the public/private distinction could not guarantee freedom from anti-Semitism. Rather, his objection to liberalism was even more fundamental: in his view, Judaism was a political theology and was thus incompatible with the liberal, Enlightenment idea of culture, that is, with a celebration of "product[s] of the human mind" or a belief in "human solutions" to human problems—with what I have been calling poiesis.[13]

Such an objection might suggest that Strauss was sympathetic to modern critics of Enlightenment reason and culture, such as Heidegger, Karl Barth, and Franz Rosenzweig. And in the late 1920s, when he was writing *Spinoza's Critique of Religion*, he was. We know that Strauss was deeply impressed by Heidegger's lectures at Freiburg and that he thought of Heidegger as the most important philosopher of the twentieth century.[14] Strauss also admired Barth's 1919 commentary on Romans, in which Barth emphasized the power of religion to disturb existing social relations and cultural norms: "Religion," Barth wrote, "though it come disguised as the most intimate friend of men, be they Greeks or barbarians, is nevertheless the adversary. Religion is the KRISIS of culture and barbarism."[15] Against the political theology of German nationalists as well as the cultural relativism of liberal theology, Barth asserted the radical otherness of God, his "utter transcendence of the things of this world." The encounter with God's otherness required an existential decision, a turning toward God and away from social and political conformism.[16] The Jewish theologian Franz Rosenzweig similarly stressed the existential encounter with God. Reacting against the rationalism of the Hegelian tradition and against Cohen's idea of Judaism as a religion of reason, Rosenzweig argued that a "new thinking" (*neues Denken*) was necessary to encompass the experience of the divine. Although Strauss wrote that he found Rosenzweig difficult to understand, he was sufficiently impressed to dedicate *Spinoza's Critique of Religion* to him.[17]

Yet, in the 1962 preface, when Strauss revisited *Spinoza's Critique of Religion*, he was critical of Heidegger, and he used the term "political theology" to refer pejoratively to the secularization of Christian concepts in the work of both Heidegger and Rosenzweig.[18] Heidegger and Rosenzweig, he argued, had rejected Greek philosophy's criterion of reason in favor of an existential experience of a divine call or "being-towards-death." But, according to Strauss, this merely amounted to "a secularized version of the Biblical faith as interpreted by Christian theology." Heidegger wanted to "expel from philosophy the last relics of Christian theology like the notions of 'eternal truths' and 'the idealized absolute subject,'" but he ended up reinterpreting human existence in terms of concepts derived from Christianity, such as "anguish," "conscience," and "guilt."[19] Although Strauss doesn't mention Schmitt in the preface to *Spinoza's Critique of Religion*, Schmitt too might be said to belong in this existentialist camp. For Strauss, all such existentialist "new thinking" was in fact simply old relativism dressed up in new clothes.

Strauss goes on in the preface to imagine the consequences of this intellectual desert for the modern Jew. Confronted with the failure of both liberalism and modern thinking, the modern Jew (aka Strauss) questions whether a return to orthodoxy might be the best course. In attempting this return, however, he discovers that the way is blocked by Spinoza. That is, any Jew who wants to return to orthodoxy needs to confront Spinoza's critique of orthodoxy in his *Theological-Political Treatise* of 1670. This was the task that Strauss set himself in his 1930 book. Spinoza had argued that the Bible provides no evidence for the belief in miracles or, indeed, for a transcendent deity. Instead, the Bible presents moral truths in the form of stories that will inculcate obedience among the uneducated. Spinoza's stated goal was to show that philosophy posed no threat to religious belief—or vice versa—because philosophy and theology occupied entirely separate spheres. But Spinoza's unstated goal, according to Strauss, was to undermine the authority of Scripture altogether by showing that the Bible was a merely human book, with a complicated textual history involving compilation and corruption. According to Strauss, in criticizing political theology and reducing God to nature, Spinoza founded a new church "not based on any positive revelation," "a Church whose rulers were not priests or pastors but philosophers and artists . . . whose flock were [people of] culture and property. . . . The new Church would transform Jews and Christians into human beings . . . of a certain kind: cultured human beings, . . . who because they possessed Science and Art did not need religion in addition."[20] Such cultured and assimilated secular Jews would be Enlightenment critics—possessors of science and art—rather than benighted believers in religion. It is almost as if Strauss were conflating Spinoza with Bruno Bauer on the Jewish Question, only to point out the fallacy of this reasoning.

In Strauss's view, Spinoza's effort to refute belief and found a new "church" of culture failed. This is because belief by definition cannot be refuted by modern philosophical reason. Strauss writes in the preface to *Spinoza's Critique of Religion*: "If orthodoxy claims to *know* that the Bible is divinely revealed, that every word of the Bible is divinely inspired, that Moses was the writer of the Pentateuch, that the miracles recorded in the Bible have happened . . . , Spinoza has refuted orthodoxy. But the case is entirely different if orthodoxy limits itself to asserting that it [merely] *believes* the aforementioned things, i.e. that they [that is, miracles and other supernatural events] cannot claim to possess the binding power peculiar to the known. For all assertions of orthodoxy rest on the irrefutable premise that the omnipotent God whose will is unfathomable . . . may exist." But, Strauss goes on to argue, modern philosophy by this argument is *also* based on belief, specifically the belief in reason: Strauss writes, "philosophy, the quest for evident and necessary knowledge, rests itself on an unevident decision, on an act of will, just as faith does."[21] This means that Spinoza's philosophical critique has the same cognitive status as belief. It also means that modern atheism is what Strauss, following Nietzsche, calls an "atheism out of intellectual probity." Such atheism is both the moral descendant of biblical morality and a modern version of the "will to power."[22] In other words, the rational assertion of the impossibility of a transcendent, inscrutable God is as much a matter of belief as the most devout profession of faith.[23]

Two years later, in 1932, when Strauss wrote his commentary on Schmitt's *Concept of the Political*, he had already moved beyond the critique of reason he articulated in his Spinoza book. We might even say that his commentary amounts to an autocritique in the guise of a critique of Schmitt's existentialism and subjectivism. At the same time, Strauss pursued his critique of culture. As we saw in chapter 1, Schmitt's *Concept of the Political* developed the argument adumbrated in *Political Theology* that liberalism goes hand in hand with a new idea of culture. First and most simply, the liberal assumption that human beings first exist in a prepolitical, amoral state of nature gives rise to the idea that humans can be educated to become cultured or civilized. The assumption here is that individuals fashion themselves just as they artificially form the state. This view was anathema to Schmitt, who held that human beings were dangerous or evil by nature, that this evil provided the moral basis of absolute rule, and that politics was a matter not of self-fashioning but of intense existential conflict between friend and enemy, understood as communities rather than individuals. But equally distasteful to Schmitt was the fact that the whole goal of liberalism was to mitigate the existential or religious intensity of politics by turning politics into one activity among others that an individual might engage in—including law, economics, art, and entertainment. According to Schmitt, culture is another name for this fragmentation of spheres of activity, a fragmentation that obscures the primacy of the political. Instead of a "politically united people," liberalism breaks down this political unity into "a culturally interested public" on the one hand, and a mass of workers and consumers on the other hand.[24]

As we've seen in earlier chapters, Strauss agreed with this association of liberalism with a certain liberal idea of culture.[25] But Strauss accused Schmitt of still working within this idea of culture and so vitiating his own analysis of the political. In particular, in *The Concept of the Political* Schmitt unwittingly endorsed the new protoliberal political anthropology of Hobbes, Spinoza, and Pufendorf, an anthropology that gave rise to the liberal idea that humans could be fashioned by culture.[26] But because the liberal idea of culture that Schmitt unwittingly endorsed was not based on a notion of natural or fundamental right, it turned all human preoccupations into matters of merely subjective preference.[27] For this reason, Strauss claimed, Schmitt needed to move beyond the liberal, individualistic conception of morality and find a new basis on which to affirm the political.[28]

Strauss's critique of Schmitt's entanglement in the liberal idea of culture was also a critique of Schmitt's political theology. In fact, Strauss implied that Schmitt's conception of political theology was merely a continuation of the notion of culture Schmitt attacks. Specifically, Strauss criticized Schmitt for describing "the thesis of [man's] dangerousness as a *'supposition,'* as an 'anthropological confession of *faith.'*" This faith cannot be the basis of the political for Strauss. According to Strauss, "[i]f man's dangerousness is *only supposed or believed in, not genuinely known*, the opposite too can be regarded as possible, and the attempt to eliminate man's dangerousness . . . can be put into practice. If man's dangerousness is *only believed in*, it is in principle *threatened*, and therewith the political is threatened also." And this in turn means that, although Schmitt wants to affirm the political, he can offer no argument for doing so.[29] In Strauss's view, then, liberal culture and Schmittian political theology are mirror images of each other, because each is vulnerable to the charge of irrationalism. In the case of liberalism, irrationalism takes the form of historicism and relativism; in Schmitt's political theology, irrationalism takes the form of relativism and existentialism. Against the subjectivism of Schmitt's political theology, Strauss insists that reason rather than faith is necessary to ground the political.

Strauss's critique of Schmitt thus looks forward to Strauss's later work, specifically Strauss's recuperation of classical philosophy. In this later work, Strauss rejected his own 1930 analysis of Spinoza because it framed the problem of political theology in terms of the conflict of modern reason and revelation, while neglecting the classical notion of reason. As he remarked in his 1962 preface to *Spinoza's Critique of Religion*, the 1930 book was "based on the premise, sanctioned by powerful prejudice, that a return to pre-modern philosophy is impossible. . . . As a consequence of this, I now read the *Theologico-political Treatise* differently than I read it when I was young."[30] Although it is hard to know how to interpret this cryptic last sentence, one possibility is that Strauss came to see that his own project of reclaiming some aspects of classical reason was anticipated by Spinoza.[31] This recognition of the possibility of returning to premodern philosophy already underlies

Strauss's comments on Schmitt's *Concept of the Political*. But it is fully developed in Strauss's later work.[32]

In this later work, even as Strauss developed his defense of premodern reason, Spinoza remained a symptom of the failure of modern rationality. In *Philosophy and Law* (1935), Strauss contrasted medieval rationalism to "the world created by the Enlightenment and its heirs, the world of 'modern culture.'"[33] Alluding to Spinoza, he went on to say that, in its critique of religious orthodoxy, the Enlightenment failed to prove the impossibility of miracles and succeeded only in showing their "unknowability."[34] In an endnote, Strauss added, "If 'religion' and 'politics' are *the* facts that transcend 'culture,' or, to speak more precisely, the *original* facts, then the radical critique of the concept of 'culture' is possible only in the form of a 'Theological-political treatise,'—which of course, if it is not to lead back again to the foundation of 'culture,' must take exactly the opposite direction from the Theological-political treatises of the seventeenth century, especially those of Hobbes and Spinoza. The first condition for this would be, of course, that these seventeenth-century works no longer be understood, as they almost always have been up to now, within the horizon of the philosophy of culture."[35] That is, Hobbes and Spinoza should not be understood from within the liberal set of presuppositions they worked to establish. Rather, they should be understood in relation to the theological-political predicament that their works aimed to solve, however unsuccessfully. Really to address the problem of political theology, Strauss suggests, one needs to take it seriously, not assume it has disappeared. But such a theological-political treatise would not be a work in the style of Schmitt. To the contrary, it would look like the later work of Strauss.

In one of those later works, *Persecution and the Art of Writing* (1952), Strauss returned to Spinoza's *Theological-Political Treatise*.[36] Now the problem is not that Spinoza has failed to prove the impossibility of miracles or to rationally refute the belief in miracles. The problem is, instead, that Spinoza's historicism has unintentionally infected his own defense of reason. In Strauss's view, the *Theological-Political Treatise* is "*the* classic document of the 'rationalist' or 'secularist' attack on the belief in revelation."[37] But the historicist protocols of interpretation that Spinoza elaborates in the *Treatise* make him vulnerable to similar protocols of interpretation and thus undermine his claim to philosophical truth. In particular, Strauss argues that Spinoza's progressive idea of knowledge—the idea that knowledge develops gradually in history—is at odds with his ambition to reveal what Strauss calls the "whole," or the truth. As a result of this focus on progress, Strauss argues, "the history of human thought . . . now takes the place formerly occupied by philosophy or, in other words, philosophy transforms itself into [the] history of human thought. . . . Once this state has been reached, the original meaning of philosophy is accessible only through recollection of what philosophy meant in the past, i.e., for all practical purposes, only through the reading of old books."[38] While Strauss turns to old books to resuscitate an ancient idea of philosophy, he implies that Spinoza has turned the *Theological-Political Treatise* into a different kind of "old book," a mere product of its historical moment or specific culture, which we can evaluate but cannot adopt as our own. We can evaluate the work, or in Strauss's words (borrowed from Schleiermacher), claim to understand it better than the author understood it himself, because our historical distance gives us a superior perspective on the works of the past; but, by the same token, our historicist vision makes it impossible for us to accept an earlier work as the truth. It is for this reason, according to Strauss, that Spinoza's effort to found a new church of culture must fail. To put this another way, culture is the name of this failure.

Spinoza's Enlightenment

I now want to turn to Spinoza to see what kind of resistance the *Theological-Political Treatise* offers to Strauss's reading. Strauss is certainly right that Spinoza's meditation on the relationship between Judaism and the state is an early modern version of the Jewish Question, just as he is right to call attention—in a way that few other readers have done—to the important role of culture in Spinoza's view of the liberal state. As Steven Smith has argued, "The *Theological-Political Treatise* was the first book to treat the persistence of a distinctive Jewish identity as emblematic of the obstacles to the creation of a state in which the individual, not the group, was the fundamental political unit." The goal of the *Theological-Political Treatise* was, accordingly, "to turn Judaism from an authoritative body of revealed law into a modern secular identity."[39] Spinoza did so by turning Jewish history against the theocratic claims of Judaism, smashing the idol of authority in order to release reason from its bondage to superstition. In the process, Spinoza also helped to define a new secular space of culture for the liberal democratic state.

Where I differ from Strauss is in my positive assessment of that liberal, Enlightenment ideal. I'm thinking here of the Enlightenment project as the effort to combine a recognition of the historicity of culture with the transcendence of reason.[40] The task of the Enlightenment is to acknowledge the historical conditions of prejudice while also asking how reason can emancipate itself from the shackles of prejudice and custom. Two common answers have been that reason unfolds itself teleologically through the historical development of culture (a position associated with Hegel) or that culture makes available a space for the cultivation of reason (a position advanced by Habermas). Spinoza, as we'll see, offers a different defense of the liberal state as a space that preserves the tension between reason and culture or the irreducibility of one to the other. The state is not the representative of culture, in Schmitt's and Strauss's pejorative understanding of culture as a space of conflicting interests; nor is the state simply an instrument of reason. Instead, it's the function of the state to protect both the space of culture and the very different activity of philosophy.[41] In a similar way, it's the function of the *Theological-Political Treatise* to mediate between culture and reason, or what Strauss would have called history and reason.[42]

Spinoza's explicit goal in the *Treatise* is to defend the freedom to philosophize and to argue that this freedom is best preserved by republics that grant toleration to different faiths. He does so by arguing that religion and philosophy occupy separate spheres, which means that philosophy poses no threat to religion, but also that religion has no purchase on philosophy. Spinoza makes his argument by elaborating a scriptural hermeneutics, which in turn underwrites a critique of theocracy. Read correctly, the Hebrew Bible demonstrates not only that the prophets have no particular claim to divine inspiration but also that miracles are impossible. This means that the essence of religion is simply a set of basic moral doctrines rather than a matter of supernatural revelation. This "elimination of supernatural agency" from Scripture and from the natural world in turn underwrites Spinoza's critique of theocracy.[43] The theocratic Hebrew state is revealed to be the result of the purely human decision to transfer one's rights to a sovereign, just as in any other state (19.240). Once the essence of religion is revealed to be a set of basic moral doctrines rather than a matter of supernatural revelation, the power of superstition is undercut and, along with this, the power of crafty priests to manipulate the superstitious multitude.

Spinoza supports his rational critique of theocracy with arguments from Jewish history. First, he describes the destruction of the Hebrew state from within, owing to the increasing power of the priesthood (17.228–29). He also argues that it is no longer possible to imitate the ancient Hebrew state because covenants with God are no longer made in ink or stone but "written on the heart by the spirit of God" (18.230). As religion is internalized and universalized by this divine writing on the heart (19.241), it becomes possible to distinguish between internal faith and outward observance. The latter becomes the purview of the state, which, in Hobbesian and Erastian fashion, firmly subordinates all churches to secular control, but also grants toleration to individuals of different faiths as long as they obey the laws of the state.

From the very beginning of the *Treatise*, then, it is clear that, in contrast to Strauss, Spinoza does not think that "religion and politics are *the* facts that transcend culture." To the contrary, along with philosophy, religion and politics are the creations of culture. In Spinoza, the critique of political theology, understood here as a politics based on the claim to revelation, thus goes hand in hand with an elaboration of something like a proto-Enlightenment idea of culture as the historically specific set of beliefs, assumptions, and artifacts produced by a given people.[44] How does this work?

First, the *Theological-Political Treatise* presents scriptural hermeneutics as a process of reading that turns sacred Scripture into stories and religion into culture. Spinoza describes this process as a kind of immanent critique. Against the Dutch Collegiants, Spinoza rejects the view that the interpretation of Scripture requires a supernatural faculty; and against Maimonides, he rejects the view that Scripture must be judged by the criterion of reason.[45] Instead, Spinoza proposes to interpret the Bible according to the Bible itself. Rather than assuming the truth of Scripture at the outset, Spinoza tells us with revolutionary common sense that the truth of Scripture is what needs to be ascertained through reading. This in turn produces a distinction between meaning and truth, and dictates the reader's focus on the explicit meaning of the text rather than its correspondence to some a priori doctrine.[46] Scripture, traditionally construed as divinely authored truth, becomes instead narrative, parable, and other vividly imagined ways of telling the history of the Jews. Prophecy has no particular claim to divine revelation; instead, the prophets are simply men with unusually vivid imaginations (2.27). Thus, in chapter 2 of the *Treatise*, Spinoza describes the different imaginations of the prophets: "For Isaiah saw seraphim with seven wings each, while Ezekiel saw beasts with four wings each; Isaiah saw God clothed and seated on a royal throne, while Ezekiel saw him as a fire. Each undoubtedly saw God as he was accustomed to imagine him" (2.32). Unlike Maimonides, who thought that passages in Scripture that conflicted with reason needed to be interpreted metaphorically, Spinoza doesn't simply subject the prophet's imaginations to translation by reason. Instead, Spinoza argues, the Bible itself makes clear that prophecy should be accepted as the imaginative rendering of the divine. By accepting these imaginations at face value as imaginative, Spinoza disables their claim to theoretical truth. The implication of this analysis is that religion is not in principle different from any other cultural artifact. What is required to understand Scripture apart from the knowledge of biblical Hebrew is simply an understanding of the operation of metaphor, narrative, and allegory, as well as an understanding of the vagaries of textual transmission.

While Spinoza describes prophecy as a function of the imagination, he doesn't simply condemn the imagination as a source of illusion. He also focuses on the positive or constitutive function of the imagination. Here it's important to remember that, by imagination, Spinoza means, first, "all thought, including sense perception." But he also construes "imagination in the more limited and usual sense of the mind's propensity to form ideas of absent objects. Depending on circumstances and the conclusions drawn, this propensity can be viewed as either a power or a defect of the mind."[47] Spinoza argues that precisely because prophecy is a function of the imagination rather than of reason, the prophets' certainty was "not mathematical certainty but moral certainty" (2.28). But he then claims that this moral certainty has a *positive* role to play in the development of ethics: "the reason why [the prophets] are so highly praised and commended was not for the sublimity and excellence of their intellects but for their piety and constancy" (3.35). This means, in the gloss of Yirmiyahu Yovel, that Spinoza "does not envisage a radical, one-time revolution but a gradual growth of rationality from within the domain of [the imagination]."[48]

Spinoza also elaborates a positive role for culture in his analysis of both reason and divine law. In chapter 16 of the *Theological-Political Treatise* he tells us that most individuals in the state of nature are governed not by reason but by "desire and power" (16.196), and that reason is something that needs to be "cultivated" (16.197: the Latin is "Rationis cultu"). The same is true of religion and politics. The state of nature, Spinoza tells us, is "prior to religion both by nature, and in time. No one knows from nature that he is bound by obedience towards God" (16.205).[49] And he goes on to observe that "if men were bound by nature to the divine law, or if the divine law were a law of nature, it would be superfluous for God to enter into a covenant with men and bind them with an oath. We must admit unreservedly that divine law began from the time when men promised to obey God in all things by an explicit agreement" (16.205). In the state of nature, then, men are absolutely free; they are bound to obey the law—positive or divine— only when they willingly transfer their natural right to all things to the sovereign. In the Hebrew Bible, this transfer originally took the form of the Hebrew covenant with God; but such a transfer of right is later the precondition for the rational establishment of the secular state and for religion having any force in society at all. In chapter 17, Spinoza then illustrates this point by explaining that when the Hebrews departed from Egypt, "they were not bound by compact to anyone; rather they regained the natural right to all they could get." It was in this renewed state of nature that they "resolved to transfer their right" to God alone. In other words, the covenant with God comes into existence at a particular historical moment, just as the secular social contract does. As Spinoza comments, "this undertaking or transfer of right to God was made in the same way that . . . it is made in an ordinary society" (17.213). The implication of this analysis is to call attention to the secular mechanism of all state formation and political legitimacy.[50]

In chapter 19 of the *Treatise*, Spinoza elaborates the implications of the previous chapters for the conception of divine law. Here we learn that reason itself brings the divine teachings into existence in society through the secular operation of a transfer of right: "if the teachings of true reason, which are the divine teachings themselves (as we showed in ch. 4 on the divine law), are to have the full force of law, it is necessary that each person should give up his own natural right . . . and it was then and only then that we first learned what justice and injustice, equity and inequity [and all the doctrines of true reason] are." In short, human beings in society produce divine law, we might say, as law, and the historical development of society and the state are thus the precondition of religion.[51] Conversely, one might say that the structure of democratic society is homologous with the structure of the covenant. As Spinoza argues in chapter 19, "Therefore, in order that even prophetically revealed religion should have the force of law among Hebrews, each of them first had to give up his natural right, and all had to decide by common consent to obey solely what was prophetically revealed to them by God. This is exactly the same thing as we have shown occurs in a democratic state" (19.240).

Starting from scriptural hermeneutics, Spinoza has—quite remarkably—arrived at a defense of democracy. (We can appreciate Spinoza's accomplishment if we remember that Hobbes used scriptural hermeneutics to shore up his defense of absolutism.) The linchpin between these two is the critical activity of reading immanently, an activity that Spinoza represents as presuppositionless but that clearly presupposes a standard of reason (*TTP*, 7.111). Democracy is the political manifestation of Spinoza's immanent account of human nature as both determined and free, by which he means capable of critical reflection and judgment. As such, democracy is both the most natural form of government and the most rational or critical. As he writes in chapter 4 of the *Treatise*,

> But the fact that men give up their right which they receive from nature, or are compelled to give it up, and commit themselves to a particular rule of life depends on human decision. And while I entirely agree that all things are determined by the universal laws of nature to exist and act in a fixed and determined manner, I insist that these decrees depend on willed human decision, and I do so for two reasons. Firstly, in so far as man is a part of nature, he is also a part of nature's power. Hence whatever follows from the necessity of human nature (that is, from nature itself in so far as we understand it to be expressly determined by human nature) results also, albeit necessarily, from the capacity of men. Hence the decreeing of these laws may quite correctly be said to follow from human will. (4.57)

Humans beings in the state of nature make a decision to be rational: "a firm decision . . . to decide everything by the sole dictate of reason" (16.198); and this decision for reason in turn produces democracy: "Human society can thus be formed without any alienation of [*repugnantia*, "opposition to"] natural right, and the contract can be preserved in its entirety with complete fidelity, only if every person transfers all the power they possess to society, and society alone retains the supreme natural right over all things. . . . The right of such a society is called democracy" (16.200). Democracy is the most natural and most rational form of government because it presupposes the individual's natural capacity to rationally consent to government.

Democracy is also the most natural and rational form of government because thinking flourishes in democracy and is a condition for democracy's success. First, democratic states recognize the natural fact that "it is impossible for one person's mind to be absolutely under another's control," and "no one can transfer to another person his natural right, or ability, to think freely and make his own judgments" (20.250). As a result, democracies are tolerant of diverse opinions, diverse ways of thinking. But Spinoza then makes the even stronger claim that democracies can't survive without freedom of thought because "a government which denies each person freedom to speak and to communicate what they think, will be a very violent government" and will not last long (20.251). Not fearful obedience but freedom is thus "the true purpose of the state" (20.252), though Spinoza clarifies that by freedom he means freedom of thought and public expression rather than of any action contrary to the decisions of sovereign powers, which would undermine the state (20.253). He concludes, "In order, then, for loyalty to be valued rather than flattery, and for sovereigns to retain their full authority and not be forced to surrender to sedition, freedom of judgment *must necessarily* be permitted and people *must* be governed in such a way that they can live in harmony, even though they openly hold different and contradictory opinions" (20.257, my emphasis).

We could say, then, that beginning with something like Machiavelli's view of the passions and Hobbes's account of our interest in rationally agreeing to a social contract, Spinoza produces a defense of democracy and the critical use of reason that anticipates Kant's distinction between the public and private use of reason in "What Is Enlightenment?": "In a democratic state (which is the one closest to the state of nature), all men agree, as we showed above, to act—but not to judge or think—according to the common decision" (20.257). What this means is that "no one can act against the sovereign's decisions without prejudicing his authority, but they can think and judge and consequently also speak without restriction, provided they merely speak or teach by way of reason alone, not by trickery or in anger or from hatred or with the intention of introducing some alteration in the state on their own initiative" (20.252).

Spinoza takes his thinking about democracy one step further in his unfinished *Political Treatise*. Although the part that was left unfinished was the discussion of democracy, the treatise is shaped throughout by Spinoza's democratic thinking, as Louis Althusser, Antonio Negri, and others have noted. In the *Theological-Political Treatise*, Spinoza struggled to describe the origins of the state in a social contract while also denying that one could really alienate one's power—as the language of contract suggests (see chaps. 16–17). In the *Political Treatise*, Spinoza abandons the theory of the contractual origins of government, which provided a juridical legitimation of absolutism in Spinoza's time (2.17). He defines dominion as the right "which is determined by the power of the multitude." And he elaborates: "He holds dominion, to whom are entrusted by common consent the affairs of state—such as the laying down, interpretation, and abrogation of the laws, the fortification of cities, deciding of war and peace, etc. But if this charge belong to a council, composed of the general multitude, then the dominion is called a democracy" (2.17.297; see also chap. 3). As Alexandre Matheron has noted, Spinoza now defines the right of sovereignty "not by the power of the sovereign but by the power *of the multitude.* . . . Political society is not created by a contract; it is engendered and reengendered at each moment by a consensus that must be permanently renewed."⁵² This idea of a politics founded on the multitude functions in practice like a regulative idea, or like what Antonio Negri has called "a Machiavellian hypothesis of freedom," which coexists with a realism or pessimism about its realization in actuality.⁵³ But even as he admits the practical difficulties involved in realizing a perfect democracy, Spinoza also rejects the view of those who simply condescend to the common people. For everyone, in Spinoza's view, is ultimately "common" in this way. In the *Political Treatise* (7.27), Spinoza cites the same passage from Livy that Machiavelli cites in the *Discourses* about how the common people are either a humble slave or domineering master, commenting: "But all have one common nature" (7.26.340). And he adds, as Machiavelli did elsewhere in the *Discourses,* "Haughtiness is a property of rulers. Men are haughty, but by reason of an appointment for a year; how much more then nobles, that have their honours eternal[ly]" (7.27.341). Spinoza then draws the obvious conclusion that "to entrust affairs of state absolutely to any man is quite incompatible with the maintenance of liberty" (7.29.342).

Spinoza's Machiavelli

It is not surprising, then, that in the *Political Treatise* Spinoza conscripts Machiavelli for his own defense of democracy. Machiavelli's praise of civic liberty is an important precedent for Spinoza, but as the following passage makes clear, Machiavelli's rhetorical strategy is equally exemplary:

> [By] what means a prince, whose sole motive is lust of mastery, should . . . establish and maintain his dominion, the most ingenious Machiavelli has set forth at large, but with what design one can hardly be sure. If, however, he had some good design, it seems to have been to show, with how little foresight many attempt to remove a tyrant. . . . Moreover, he perhaps wished to show how cautious a free multitude should be of entrusting its welfare absolutely to one man. . . . And I am the more led to this opinion concerning that most far-seeing man, because it is known that he was favourable to liberty, for the maintenance of which he has besides given the most wholesome advice. (5.7.315)

Spinoza here alludes to the interpretive crux faced by all readers of *The Prince*: how could Machiavelli write a manual for tyrants if he was really a lover of the Florentine republic? He conjectures, as did many early defenders of Machiavelli, that Machiavelli's goal in describing the *arcana imperii* was to demystify the tyrant's ruses and thus indirectly instruct the people how to rebel against him. Spinoza clearly appreciated this rhetorical strategy, since he practiced a similar indirection in the *Theological-Political Treatise*. This strategy did not go unnoticed by Spinoza's contemporaries and later readers. The *Theological-Political Treatise* was banned in Holland in 1674. In the eighteenth century, Frederick II famously commented that Machiavelli's *Prince* is to tyrants what the work of Spinoza is to faith. As Frederick clearly understood, Spinoza's Enlightenment was in crucial respects Machiavellian.

This Machiavellianism is particularly apparent if we turn to the prefatory letter to the *Theological-Political Treatise*. Spinoza signals his debt to Machiavelli at the very beginning of the preface, where he advances an Epicurean critique of superstition with the same irony, the same rhetorical flourishes, that characterize Machiavelli's treatment of superstition and popular opinion in *The Prince*: "If men were always able to regulate their affairs with sure judgment," Spinoza writes, "or if fortune always smiled upon them, they would not get caught up in any superstition. But since people are often reduced to such desperate straits that they cannot arrive at any solid judgment and as the good things of fortune for which they have a boundless desire are quite uncertain, they fluctuate wretchedly between hope and fear. This is why most people are quite ready to believe anything" (3). And a little later on: "I think that everyone is aware of this, even though I also believe most people have no self-knowledge." In these opening lines, one cannot fail to hear an echo of Machiavelli's view of human nature, as well as his typical concession to and critique of popular opinion. For example, in chapter 18 of *The Prince*, Machiavelli wrote: "How praiseworthy it is for a prince to keep his word and live with integrity rather than craftiness, everyone understands; yet we see from recent experience that those princes have accomplished most who paid little heed to keeping their promises, but who knew how craftily to manipulate the minds of men" (*P*, 18.49; cf. 15.44–45). Or, a little later, "To anyone who sees or hears him, [the prince] should appear all honor, all humanity, all integrity, all religion. Nothing is more necessary than to seem to have this last virtue. Men in general judge more by the sense of sight than the sense of touch, because everyone can see but only a few can test by feeling. Everyone sees what you seem to be, few know what you really are; and those few do not dare take a stand against the general opinion, supported by the majesty of the government" (*P*, 18.51). In the first case, Machiavelli makes a concession to popular opinion about virtue only immediately to withdraw it; in the second case, he anticipates Spinoza's observation about the limited capacities of the people, even as he advises the prince how to use popular opinion to quell dissent.

Like Machiavelli in these passages, Spinoza accommodates his message to his audience by catering to popular opinion.[54] Even as he explicitly criticizes superstition, he adopts a pose of piety that conforms to the expectations of the multitude, not to mention the Estates General. But, just as Machiavelli hopes to educate his reader to the virtues of republicanism in the long run, so Spinoza has designed the *Theological-Political Treatise* to effect a similar transformation in the philosophically inclined reader. Although he begins with a rhetorical and practical appeal to his readers, which recognizes the necessity of persuading by words rather than equations, his goal is to lead them patiently by irony and by a series of dialectical redefinitions to accept his argument for the compatibility of reason and faith in the Dutch republic, as well as in democracies to come. This literary or narrative dimension of the *Treatise* is the rhetorical equivalent of history in Spinoza's argument. Just as Spinoza uncovers the logic of democracy by narrating the history of the Jewish people, so he gradually reveals the logic of critical thinking in the rhetoric of his own text.

We can test this argument about the narrative dimension of the *Theological-Political Treatise* by returning to the question of what Spinoza means by political theology. Initially, as we've seen, he means the theocracy of the Hebrew state. But, as so often in the *Treatise*, Spinoza's goal is to revise—or render untenable—this original definition. And he does so by showing that this revision tracks historical reality. First, Jewish history shows that theocracy, defined as the combining of sovereign and priestly power in one office, was detrimental to the state. The history of the Hebrews also shows that the independent power of priests, who refused subordination to secular power, was equally harmful. Second, theocracy of the sort instituted by Moses is no longer possible because it is no longer possible to make a political covenant with God: God has instead inscribed his divine law on the hearts of individuals (18.230). Ultimately, as we've seen, Spinoza argues that democracy, rather than theocracy, is the "most natural" form of government because the consent required to exit the state of nature is the same consent that is required to set up a democracy, or, in Spinoza's words, democracy "approaches most closely to the freedom nature bestows on every person." In a democracy, "all remain equal as they had been previously, in the state of nature" (16.202; see 20.257). But Spinoza's version of democracy presupposes its own version of political theology: it assumes the Erastian subordination of the church to the state, and the necessary mediation of divine truths by the sovereign. In Spinoza's words, "divine law depends solely upon the decree of the sovereign authorities" (19.242). Because "the entire practice of religion and the sacred ministry ensued from the commandment of kings. . . . sovereigns today . . . have and always will retain this authority [over sacred matters] absolutely" (19.249). In this way, the narrative of the *Treatise* translates Mosaic political theology into Machiavellian civil religion. At the same time, Spinoza makes it clear that it would not only be folly to try to determine people's religious beliefs by law but would actually undermine the authority of the state: "Such decrees as these, laying down what everyone must believe . . . were often introduced to appease, or rather surrender to, the fury of those who cannot tolerate free minds." But "what is more dangerous . . . than for people to be treated as enemies and led off to death, not for misdeeds or wrongdoing, but because they make a free use of their intelligence, and for the scaffold which should be the terror only of wrongdoers to become a magnificent stage on which to exhibit to all a supreme exemplum of constancy and virtue while casting the deepest reproach on the sovereign?" (20.256). So, while it is true that the sovereign has the right to determine what counts as piety, a wise sovereign will see that it is in his interest to define piety not as the observance of religious dogma but as "that which is practiced with respect to the peace and tranquility of the state" (20.253).[55]

Just as political theology undergoes revision in the course of the *Theological-Political Treatise*, so does the obedience to the state that civil religion requires. Spinoza makes it clear that this Erastian political theology is necessary to the stability of the state and the preservation of individual freedom, for its opposite—intolerance—creates only resistance and eventually revolution. But is this political theology also necessary to teach obedience to moral truths? As in the case of other crucial terms in the *Treatise*, the word "obedience" has a double valence that is relevant here: obedience is sometimes defined as obedience to positive divine or civil law, at other times simply as the love of God and reason. The vast majority of subjects learn obedience from Scripture and from positive law because they are incapable of learning it from reason. In contrast, the philosopher learns the truths implied by the notion of obedience from reason alone. So when Spinoza writes in chapter 16 of the *Treatise*, "no one knows from nature that he is bound by obedience towards God[;] indeed, he cannot discover this by reasoning either; he can only receive it from a revelation confirmed by miracles," we must read these clauses both literally and ironically: when obedience is construed as obedience to an *externally* imposed law, we cannot learn this obedience from nature or reason, which are equivalent instead to an *internal* understanding of the principles of morality and truth.

Most striking of all, Spinoza performs a similar dialectical operation on the concept of revelation. Initially, the Hebrew Bible supports the central claim of Judaism to be a revealed religion: God revealed his law to Moses on Mount Sinai. But in order for God's law to be law, "each of [the Hebrews] had first to give up his natural right, and all had to decide by common consent to obey solely what was prophetically revealed to them by God." "On the same grounds," Spinoza goes on to argue, "revealed religion no longer possessed the force of law after the destruction of the Hebrew state" (19.240). He then draws the shocking conclusion that revelation was thereafter simply a matter of reason: "It most evidently follows from all of this that . . . religion could no longer be regarded as the prescription of a particular state but as a *universal religion of reason*. I say 'of reason' because the universal religion was not yet known by revelation" (19.241, my emphasis). In this last clause, Spinoza concedes that Christianity is a religion of revelation, but this concession appears ironic in light of the fact that Spinoza has just deconstructed the very idea that revelation is necessary for the religion of reason. Here Spinoza both uses reason to dismantle the truth claim of Scripture and argues that reason is itself religious. Both points are supported by Spinoza's earlier argument that what makes Scripture *or any other text* sacred is not its content but its right *use*: "Something intended to promote the practice of piety and religion is called sacred and divine and is sacred only as long as people use it religiously. If they cease to be pious, the thing in question likewise, at the same time, ceases to be sacred. . . . From this it follows that nothing is sacred, profane, or impure, absolutely and independently of the mind but only in relation to the mind" (12.165; see 10.148, 14.178, 183–84). Here it seems that the mind's natural operations, including both reasoning and reading, are themselves a source of revelation. This redefinition of revelation in terms of the mind's natural functions, including the practice of reading, has at least two effects: the first is to emphasize that revelation can become law only through the exercise of civil power; the second is to emphasize (despite Spinoza's repeated assertions that "there is no interaction and no affinity between faith and theology, on the one side, and philosophy on the other") that "faith . . . allows every person the greatest liberty to think," not simply because faith doesn't require thinking but because thinking itself, rightly understood, is Spinoza's version of faith (14.184). Or, as Spinoza writes in chapter 12, in another passage that collapses reason and faith, "both reason and the beliefs of the prophets and Apostle evidently proclaim that God's eternal word and covenant and true religion are divinely inscribed upon the hearts of men, that is, upon the human mind. *This is God's true original text* [*eamque veram esse Dei syngraphum*]" (12.163; Lat., 230, my emphasis).[56] I'll return to this point below when I take up Spinoza's legacy to literary-critical conceptions of reading and textuality.

Spinoza's rhetorical achievement is, like Machiavelli's, the simultaneous critique of superstition and defense of civil religion. The philosophically inclined reader is educated to the truths of reason, while the people and the state are given the myths and stories they need. As we've seen, Spinoza's rhetoric—his gradual unveiling of unadorned reason—mimes the historical and cultural process by which the political theology of the Jews is replaced by the Erastian political theology of the liberal democratic state. In the one case, religious myth is replaced by reason; in the other, Mosaic political theology is historically superseded by the liberal state. But the analogy is imperfect, since in the latter case myth is also recuperated in the form of a new Machiavellian political theology or civil religion.[57] Still, there's an important difference between Machiavelli and Spinoza. While Spinoza was not naïve enough to think that the state was the embodiment of reason, unlike Machiavelli he hoped to make the state safe for philosophy. For Spinoza, then, admitting the necessity of rhetoric—writing the *Theological-Political Treatise*—is only the first step along a trajectory whose ideal endpoint is philosophy freed from the constraints of persuasion. Whether, however, the practical requirements of rhetoric are also theoretical limits—limits on the very possibility of reason—is, we might say, the ongoing question of Enlightenment.[58]

Culture Revisited

I've argued in this chapter that Spinoza is both a critic of political theology and a defender of it. He is a critic of political theology construed as theocracy, as the contemporary claim of the Jews to be the chosen people (*TTP*, chap. 3), or as the priestly manipulation of theology to subvert the state (17.211). He is a defender of political theology understood as the attempt to think the relationship between philosophy and theology and their mutual dependence upon the state. As Nancy Levene has observed, Strauss ought to have appreciated this aspect of Spinoza (and we could add, on the basis of his 1962 preface, he may have), since Strauss also wanted to think the relationship between philosophy and theology and their relation to the state.[59] But, against Strauss, Spinoza's account of the eternal truths of philosophy is not opposed to his argument that these truths emerge in history, which is to say, in culture— including the cultural artifact we know as the Bible.[60]

Spinoza can then be said to have contributed to the Enlightenment idea of culture by constructing—through biblical interpretation—what Jonathan Sheehan has called the Enlightenment's "cultural bible." Sheehan traces Enlightenment arguments according to which religion is first seen as the source of culture, and then increasingly as a cultural product itself. He argues that this view of the Bible as a cultural product in turn generates a view of culture with some of the characteristics formerly attributed to the Bible. According to Herder, for example, culture names the "entire living picture of the ways of life, customs, [and] needs" of a nation. Such an idea of culture is itself initially dependent on religion: "the real living culture of a people" begins, according to Herder, "with the awakening and cultivation of their language—and this depends on religion." "Religion alone," he wrote elsewhere, "introduced the first elements of culture and science to all peoples; more precisely, culture and science were originally nothing more than a kind of religious tradition." Significantly, Herder singled out the Jews as the "primary model for a *Nationalkultur*," because, in Sheehan's words, their "national religion was the self-contained source of [their] cultural development."[61] As the Bible itself was increasingly treated as a cultural object by Herder and his contemporaries, "the concept of culture took over all those aspects of the Enlightenment Bible—its literary quality, its pedagogical virtues, its philological exemplarity, and its historical depth."[62]

Earlier I showed that Strauss criticized Schmitt's notion of political theology as a continuation of culture when viewed from the perspective of Schmitt's political anthropology. Spinoza's biblical hermeneutics helps us see that there is a more productive traffic between political theology and culture than either Strauss or Schmitt imagined. If we think of his biblical hermeneutics as the technique that turns Scripture into a cultural artifact, we can say that Spinoza's hermeneutics anticipates the Enlightenment idea of culture as a bulwark against political theology, construed as the irrational reliance on revelation in matters of politics. But if we think of his biblical hermeneutics as a method of reading immanently that allows for the mutual coexistence of philosophy and theology, we can say that Spinoza enacts political theology, understood as this mutual coexistence, in his own writing. In particular, Spinoza's *Theological-Political Treatise* dramatizes a textual space that is analogous to the cultural and political space of Spinoza's liberal state, a space that allows for the coexistence of the freedom of philosophy and the freedom of theology, now interpreted as part of a historically evolving culture. Political theology in this second case would be very close to the Straussian project of determining, politically, a space for theology that would not interfere with the activity of philosophy.[63] But for the liberal Spinoza, in contrast to Strauss, the space of politics is understood as sheltering, rather than precluding, the space of culture. The question, of course, that all readers of Spinoza must decide is whether this mutual coexistence is something like a double truth or whether (as I currently think) the very idea of coexistence turns Scripture into secular literature or something like modern textuality. A further question, well beyond the scope of this chapter, is whether it does the same to Spinoza's idea of philosophy.

At this point we seem to have come full circle. Spinoza's philological critique of Scripture helped to produce Herder's historicist idea of culture, which in turn generated a critique of historicism and of culture on the part of figures such as Strauss. So how can culture or Spinoza be an answer to Strauss? How can culture be a response to political theology when it so often seems instead to be the source of such religious enthusiasm? One answer to this question would be to reframe the idea of culture in terms of principled judgment; the other (as I've already suggested) would be to see Spinoza as an ally of critical reason and the *Theological-Political Treatise* as an instantiation of such reason rather than its historicist subverter. Hannah Arendt explores the first possibility in her essay "The Crisis in Culture." The second possibility is articulated by Louis Althusser and Pierre Macherey in their readings of Spinoza.

Arendt, a Jew who escaped from Nazi Germany to France and then the United States, came from an intellectual milieu in some respects similar to that of Strauss. Although Strauss was raised in an Orthodox household and Arendt in a secular one, both deeply identified as Jews and both had studied philosophy with Heidegger. Like Strauss, Arendt was interested in diagnosing the failure of Weimar and the rise of the Nazi state. And like both Schmitt and Strauss, she saw these political developments as symptomatic of what Ernst Vollrath has called the "particular deficits of traditional German culture," especially the traditional perception that culture (*Bildung*) was by definition apolitical.[64] But rather than simply accepting this traditional understanding of culture and turning her attention elsewhere, Arendt wanted to rescue culture as an important part of the public sphere of deliberation and political action. In "The Crisis in Culture," Arendt elaborated a defense of the Enlightenment idea of culture and argued for its relevance to contemporary politics.[65] In some ways this is surprising, since Arendt shared Strauss's and Schmitt's sense that both the modern idea of society and modern technology had usurped the realm of the genuinely political in the twentieth century. But, against Schmitt and Strauss, Arendt—no political theologian—argued that modern society and technology had also usurped the realm of culture, which she wanted to defend.[66] With the rise of "modern mass society," she wrote, "society began to monopolize 'culture' for its own purposes, such as social position and status"; and in a line of argument reminiscent of Schmitt's critique of the language of values, she argued that, with "the first appearance of modern art," "culture . . . had become what only then people began to call 'value,' i.e., a social commodity which could be circulated and cashed in in exchange for other kinds of value, social and individual."[67] In time, mass society, which was concerned with entertainment rather than culture, devoured the artifacts of high culture and spit them out again in degraded form. Against these developments, Arendt counterposed a notion of art as separate from the world of need, exchange, and consumption. In the Kantian idea of aesthetic judgment, Arendt found a model of political judgment that firmly, if indirectly, linked the realm of culture to that of political action. As a subjective judgment that nevertheless claims the agreement of others, aesthetic judgment liberates itself from the merely subjective. As Arendt put it, "In aesthetic no less than in political judgments, a decision is made, and although this decision is always determined by a certain subjectivity, . . . it also derives from the fact that the world itself is an objective datum, something common to all its inhabitants."[68] But while Arendt distanced herself from the arbitrariness of pure (aesthetic and, by extension, political) decisionism, she also defined the realm of politics as outside philosophical claims to truth: "Culture and politics, then, belong together because it is not knowledge or truth which is at stake, but rather judgment and decision, the judicious exchange of opinion about the sphere of public life and the common world, and the decision what manner of action is to be taken in it." In locating a principled exercise of judgment in the response to works of culture, Arendt turns culture from the merely contingent product of historical conditions to the occasion for the critical analysis of society. Arendt's defense of a Kantian idea of culture is thus at the same time a defense of the realm of politics, conceived of not as a pure decision, or as the conflict of friend and enemy, as Schmitt would have it, or as a threat to philosophical truth, à la Strauss, but rather as an activity of judgment that produces consensus and action. In this way, Arendt also redefines culture: it no longer signals the degraded activity of fabrication (an ancient Greek prejudice she shares with Schmitt and Strauss); instead, it is a precondition of true politics.[69]

Although Arendt was herself critical of Spinoza for valuing the philosopher's life above political engagement, her argument has something in common with Spinoza's praise of freedom of judgment in the concluding chapter of the *Theological-Political Treatise*.[70] In his defense of the superiority of democracy, Spinoza writes, "No one . . . can surrender their freedom to judge and to think as they wish and everyone, by the supreme right of nature, remains master of their own thoughts" (20.251). This in turn means that "it is not . . . the purpose of the state to turn people from rational beings into beasts or automata, but rather to allow their minds and bodies to develop in their own ways in security and enjoy the free use of reason. . . . Therefore, the true purpose of the state is in fact freedom" (20.252). And, just as Arendt reasoned from culture to politics, Spinoza reasons from politics to culture, adding that "this liberty is absolutely essential to the advancement of the arts and sciences; for they can be cultivated [*coluntur*] with success only by those with a free and unfettered judgment" (20.255; Lat., 308).

Let me now turn to those modern admirers of Spinoza who linked the *Theological-Political Treatise* to the modern notion of textuality. Though the notion of textuality has an entirely different valence from that of culture (the former linked to the critique of the subject, the latter still implicated in humanist notions of agency), I think the two converge on the possibility of an immanent critique of ideology, including political theology. In the short posthumous essay on Spinoza that Althusser intended to include in his autobiography, he wrote that "Spinoza . . . managed to disentangle the mind from the illusion of transcendent or transcendental subjectivity as a guarantee or foundation of every meaning or every experience of possible truth." In *Essays on Self-Criticism*, Althusser elaborated on this point when he linked Spinoza to the Marxist tradition of dialectical materialism: "Spinoza's 'theory' rejected every illusion about ideology. And especially about the number one ideology of that time, religion, by identifying it as imaginary. But at the same time it refused to treat ideology as a simple error, or as naked ignorance, because it based the system of this imaginary phenomenon on the relation of men to the world 'expressed' by the state of their bodies. This *materialism of the imaginary* opened the way to a surprising conception of the First Level of Knowledge: not at all, in fact as a 'piece of knowledge,' but as the material world of men *as they live it*, that of their concrete and historical existence." In *Reading Capital*, Althusser then recast this insight in terms of modern ideas of textuality when he described Spinoza as "the first man ever to have posed the problem of *reading* and, in consequence, of *writing*. . . . With him, for the first time ever, a man linked together in this way the essence of reading and the essence of history in a theory of the difference between the imaginary and the true."[71]

Althusser's student Pierre Macherey drew on this reading of Spinoza to develop his theory of literary production. While Macherey acknowledged that Spinoza was "almost silent" on the topic of aesthetic activity, he argued with Althusser that Spinoza's understanding of textuality and reading foreshadowed something like the critique of ideology. Specifically, literary texts act out their own critique of ideology through a process of internal distantiation. This means that reading is not the deciphering of an a priori truth; instead, the contradictions within the text provide the critic with the elements of an immanent critique.[72] As I have been suggesting and as Macherey knew full well, this is precisely the task that Spinoza takes up in his *Theological-Political Treatise*. The protocols of reading that Spinoza laid out in this work are not only at the basis of the modern, Enlightenment idea of culture; they also point us to the inseparability of a certain idea of textuality and the critique of ideology, including the ideology of political theology.

"Reading" is bearing a lot of weight at this point in my argument, so it's worth pausing a moment to recapitulate. Spinoza claims to offer an immanent reading of Scripture. Rather than assuming the truth of the Bible, he declares this truth can be determined only by reading the biblical text. But, in practice, Spinoza brackets the question of truth in order to focus instead on the internal relations of the different parts of the text to each other, which he calls meaning. In bracketing the question of truth, Spinoza turns the Bible—viewed by believers as divine revelation—into a purely human *interpretation* of experience, including the historical experience of the Hebrew people. Spinoza supports this view by analyzing the various contradictions in the text, such as the prophets' different and incompatible visions of God, or the logically absurd textual fact that Moses narrates his own death, both of which help the reader see the Bible as a humanly authored artifact. So far, reading would appear to be simply a matter of attending to textual inconsistencies. But Spinoza goes still further when he develops a dialectical mode of interpretation that performs a critique of some of the central concepts of Judaism: the notion that the Jews are the chosen people, the notion of obedience to the law, even the notion of revelation itself. In reading dialectically in this way, Spinoza exemplifies his own view that it is not Scripture itself that is sacred but the capacity of the mind to liberate itself from its own prior misconceptions or forms of idolatry (including the "images and pictures, i.e. paper and ink" of the scriptural text [12.164]). Needless to say, such a notion of the sacred is utterly immanent and defines itself against the superstitious (in Spinoza's time, usual) view that God is a transcendent deity who commands humans and punishes them when they disobey him.

Spinoza, of course, is traditionally seen as a defender of reason, not of textuality; in contemporary literary theory, the latter frequently implies a kind of textual autonomy that is incompatible with historical contextualization, whereas the two are clearly compatible in Spinoza. Moreover, the *Theological-Political Treatise* makes a clear distinction between philosophy and Scripture, reason and the historical realm of human culture. But it's also fair to say that in the *Treatise* textuality—or what I would call literature—is produced by the activity of reading, when it turns its critical eye on cultural artifacts, such as the Bible, that assert authority over against the claims of reason. Because of this, what Spinoza describes as a decision for reason we might also describe as a decision for literature. There is both a historical and a theoretical reason for this redescription. Historically, scriptural hermeneutics offers the prime example of the use of reason to dismantle the authority of revelation through the critique of the biblical text. In the process of doing so, it turned Scripture into literature, i.e., into a mere text, rather than the inspired word of God. So we could say that this critique produced a decision for literature, if by decision we mean principled, rational judgment, and if by literature we mean a humanly authored text. But we could also argue, with Althusser and Macherey, that the operation Spinoza performed in his immanent critique of Scripture just is what literary texts do, by definition. Here the "internal distantiation" that is constitutive of the literary text would itself provide the model for what Arendt calls judgment and what Althusser calls the critique of ideology. To parody the theologian Karl Barth, whose manifesto I quoted earlier in this chapter, we could say that this critique is the KRISIS of theology. If we pressed this argument further, we might even say, with Derrida, that logos understood as reason is always already a matter of logos as the "word" or linguistic representation, and that linguistic

representation that knows itself as such is literature. This is undoubtedly farther than Spinoza would want to go, since in preserving the
distinction between philosophy and culture, Spinoza could also be said
to distinguish between philosophy and literature. But it is clear that
at least some of Spinoza's admirers took this additional step—among
them, Friedrich Schlegel, who wrote that he could "barely comprehend
how one can be a poet without admiring Spinoza, loving him, and becoming entirely his."[73]

Spinoza's Solitude

As the previous discussion has shown, the Spinoza revival that took
place in Germany in the 1920s had a French iteration in the 1970s. But
recently the paradigm for thinking about sovereignty has reverted from
Spinoza's critique of political theology to an assertion of its virtues. This
recent, theologically inflected version of sovereignty obviously owes
much to the influence of Schmitt's *Political Theology*, with its claim that
all significant concepts of the state are secularized versions of theological concepts and that the absolute sovereign is, like God, the one who
decides the exception. Drawing on this theological paradigm, Giorgio
Agamben has proposed a new analysis of contemporary sovereignty in
his recent book *The Kingdom and the Glory*, which focuses on "power
as government [or] effective management" and "power as ceremonial or
liturgical reality," two aspects of sovereignty that he implausibly claims
"have been curiously neglected by both political philosophers and
political scientists." To the question "why does power need glory?"—
not only in the early modern period but even now in the twenty-first
century—Agamben replies that this question can be answered only by
"bringing these questions back to their theological dimension." And
this prompts Agamben to offer a history of ideas of government and
investiture as they developed in Christianity. Agamben anticipates the
objection that such an investigation into the theology of investiture will
seem antiquarian and irrelevant. In response, he insists that "the function of acclamation and glory, in the modern form of public opinion and
consensus, is still at the center of the political apparatuses of modern
democracy.[74]

For Agamben, "glory" is a "realm of indistinction" between theology
and law. By his own admission, Agamben is drawing here on Kantorowicz's study of medieval "imperial acclamations," which compared the
ruler to Christ, and which Kantorowicz ultimately traced to pagan imperial acclamations at the time of Augustus. Agamben, however, rejects

this secular, pagan genealogy of ideas of sovereignty. "More interesting than taking sides with one thesis or another," he writes, ". . . is to try to understand the functional relationship that links the two principles [of theology and politics]. Glory is the place at which this bilateral . . . character of the relation between theology and politics clearly emerges into the light." But Agamben is not so even-handed in his conclusion: "The *theology* of glory," he asserts, "constitutes the secret point of contact through which theology and politics continuously communicate and exchange parts with one another." Christian theology, it turns out, is for Agamben the discourse best suited to exploring democracy.[75]

This revival of the theological paradigm for thinking about sovereignty is not limited to literary and cultural critics. In a recent book, the legal scholar Paul W. Kahn has argued that Schmitt prompts us to rethink what he calls the "sacral character" of popular sovereignty in the United States. Kahn is one of a group of scholars who argue that Schmitt is not just a defender of absolutism. While Schmitt's early definition of sovereignty is derived from Hobbes, his later work on constitutionalism lends itself to understanding the modern popular conception of sovereignty as the locus of power to decide in modern democratic states. Drawing on Schmitt, Kahn argues that "the popular sovereign is understood [in the United States] as a collective, transtemporal subject in which all participate." Asserting that "our political life remains deeply embedded in a web of conceptions that are theological in their origin and structure," he describes popular sovereignty as "the mystical corpus of the state, the source of ultimate meaning for citizens."[76] And he goes on to assert that "the popular sovereign can always demand a life; it can demand of citizens that they kill and be killed for the state." This, apparently, is a good thing for Kahn; he writes: "The fundamental character of the relationship of citizen to sovereign is not contract—as in the social contract [tradition]—but sacrifice. To be a citizen is to imagine the possibility of a sacrificial act." And he draws a further comparison: "Arguably, we live at a moment when this set of beliefs is becoming more, not less, prevalent. The symbolic message of the terrorist is that political identity in and of itself is a matter of life and death." The problematic implication here is that at least terrorists have a genuine conception of the political, unlike liberals, who obscure the political by virtue of their emphasis on rational discourse and human interests.[77] It's arguments like this that make one long for yet another revival of interest in Spinoza, another redemption of Spinoza from his condition of solitude.

I'm thinking here of Althusser's essay "Machiavelli's Solitude." Althusser used the phrase to conjure up Machiavelli's break with the classical and Christian traditions of thinking about politics. Solitude also captures the situation of the new prince, who must found the new principality alone, on the basis of his own *virtù* (rather than being dependent on others). But Machiavelli is also solitary, according to Althusser, because no one has followed his steps. To use Althusser's metaphor, no one has "thought in his thought." This is because the natural rights tradition of the seventeenth century blocked the insights of Machiavelli, displacing his concern with solitude and, eventually, national unity with a focus on the "rights of the individual as a subject." According to Althusser, this new bourgeois political philosophy "attempted to deduce theoretically the existence of positive law and the political state from the attributes that legal ideology confers on the human subject (liberty, equality, property)." This is a very different world of thought from Machiavelli's, Althusser argues, not least of all because "the number-one object and stake of the philosophy of natural law is absolute monarchy: whether the theoreticians want to give it a rightful basis (like Hobbes) or to refute it by right (like Locke and Rousseau), absolute monarchy is their starting point and their subject of discussion."[78] It is surprising that Althusser doesn't mention Spinoza as someone who thought Machiavelli's thought, especially given that he suggests as much in another essay, where he describes Machiavelli as "the greatest materialist philosopher in history—the equal of Spinoza, who declared him '*acutissimus*,' most acute."[79]

It's been an implicit argument of this chapter that we need to recover the tradition of Spinoza and Machiavelli rather than tracing the sources of popular sovereignty to religion or some quasi-secular idea of political theology. Writing before divine right absolutism, Machiavelli cannot even imagine a theological model of sovereignty, if by this we mean that absolutism is modeled on the omnipotence of God. Writing in the heyday of divine right absolutism in Europe, Spinoza narrates the historical supersession of the Hebrew theocracy in order to disable this theological model and to put democracy in its place. To be sure, Machiavelli and Spinoza both discuss religion, but they do so in a very different way from Schmitt or his modern acolytes. For Machiavelli, religion is important only as a political tool; this means the best form of religion is a purely civil religion. While offering lip service to Christianity, Spinoza basically makes the same point about the civil and political usefulness of religion. For both, power was a relation of forces, a shifting calculus, through which individuals and the multitude could exert their wills.

Neither was naive about the virtues of the people or their intelligence. Each conceded the vulnerability of the people to manipulation. At the same time, each tried to construct his texts so as to dramatize the process of critical thinking that would promote not only a more secular but also a more democratic polity, and enable the people to reclaim their own agency.

5   Freud's Spinoza/Freud's Illusions

If by political theology we mean the critique of religion in the tradition of Spinoza, Freud is one of the great political theologians of the early twentieth century. Of all the figures discussed in this book, he was the most resolutely atheist and the most skeptical of theological modes of explanation. Almost a century later, it is still quite a bracing experience to read Freud's attack on religion in *The Future of an Illusion*. Who now dares to describe religion as a mass delusion or obsessional neurosis? Yet this was precisely Freud's position in 1927. Religious illusion, he argued, is dangerous because it is not susceptible to rational refutation. By contrast, artistic illusion declares itself as such. In sustaining a balance between illusion and its own demystification, art for Freud comes to stand for the highest achievements of civilization. But this easy contrast between religious and artistic illusion is upset, as Freud realizes in *Moses and Monotheism* (1938)—his own theological-political treatise—when art is put in the service of political theology.[1]

In this chapter I argue that Freud's thoughts about the differences between religious illusion and artistic illusion, and between religion and psychoanalysis, were developed through a dialogue with Renaissance culture. It's well known that Freud read *Hamlet*, the most famous English Renaissance work of art, as a confirmation of the

Oedipus complex. But in this chapter I will be focusing not on Shakespeare but on the figures who, I believe, were even more important for Freud: Leonardo da Vinci, Michelangelo, and—above all—Spinoza.[2] I trace Freud's engagement with and analysis of illusion, from his early reflections on Renaissance art to what we might call his "discovery of the early modern" in the 1920s and '30s. As we'll see, in these last decades of Freud's life, which coincided with the end of World War I and the beginning of World War II, Freud turns away from his celebration of the secular culture of the Renaissance to draw out the more troubling implications of Spinoza's account of political theology for his own modern moment. But he does not abandon his distinction between artistic and religious illusion, nor does he renounce his fierce atheism.

Although Freud's interest in the Renaissance has often been noted, it's important to see this is not simply a contingent fact, as though Freud could have used writers and artists from other periods to the same effect. Like Jacob Burckhardt, whose work he knew well, Freud saw the Italian Renaissance as the period that asserted—for the first time since antiquity—the value of the individual personality (what Burckhardt called "das Individuum" or "die Persönlichkeit") and the shaping power of the individual will in society, art, and politics.[3] Unlike Burckhardt, however, Freud seems not to have been ambivalent about this achievement; instead, he saw himself as furthering it by means of psychoanalysis. In Freud's essays on Leonardo and Michelangelo, psychoanalysis appears as the logical development of Renaissance individualism: in the genealogy Freud constructs, his own heroic achievements are prefigured by Leonardo da Vinci, Michelangelo, and Spinoza.

Freud saw the Renaissance as the great period of confrontation between Christianity and secular reason. In this respect, too, Freud was following in the steps of Burckhardt. In *The Civilization of the Renaissance in Italy*, Burckhardt had famously portrayed the liberating encounter with classical philosophy in fifteenth-century Italy.[4] In ancient philosophy, Renaissance Italians encountered what from a Christian perspective appeared to be a "godless universe" or a world of "cosmotheism," in which god was identified with nature. They encountered as well un-Christian accounts of the will and necessity, including that of Epicurus.[5] These encounters fostered a degree of skepticism about their own beliefs, the ability to imagine the tolerance of other faiths, or the loss of faith altogether. Freud, too, understood that the Renaissance by definition raised the question of the relationship of religion and secular reason, and he clearly took the side of the latter. But he went beyond Burckhardt in explicitly associating ancient cosmotheism and secular reason with Spinoza, whose great influence he acknowledged in his correspondence. In a letter to an acquaintance who inquired about his indebtedness to Spinoza, Freud replied: "I readily admit my dependence on Spinoza's doctrine." Elsewhere he wrote, "Throughout my long life I have sustained an extraordinarily high respect for the person as well as for the intellectual achievements [*Denkleistung*] of the great philosopher Spinoza."[6]

Spinoza is in fact a leitmotiv in Freud's shifting attitudes toward religious illusion and aesthetic illusion, secular reason and political theology. For Freud in the nineteen teens, Renaissance artists advanced a Spinozist critique of superstition, one that supplanted religion by nature and allied science with art. The essays on Leonardo (1910) and Michelangelo (1914) dramatize Freud's conviction that there is a difference between religious illusion and aesthetic illusion, a distinction he would reiterate much later in *The Future of an Illusion* (1927). They also enact the reoccupation, in Hans Blumenberg's terms, of religion by art. By contrast, in *Moses and Monotheism* (1938), Freud offered a Spinozist reading of Moses that drew out the theological-political dimension of illusion that he had neglected earlier. In returning to and revising his earlier essays on Leonardo and Michelangelo, *Moses and Monotheism* dramatizes Freud's own hermeneutic repetition compulsion, his attempt to master the question of the relation of religion to secular reason, and of religious illusion to artistic illusion. It also dramatizes Freud's increasing pessimism about the victory of reason over religion.

What was missing from the earlier work of the nineteen teens was a deeper reflection on culture in relationship to politics and the human propensity to violence. By Freud's own account, it took World War I and the beginning of the Second World War for him to turn his attention to these larger questions of culture and barbarism in works such as *Beyond the Pleasure Principle* (1920), *The Future of an Illusion*, *Civilization and Its Discontents* (1930), and *Moses and Monotheism*. In fact, it's fair to say that Freud was drawn into the orbit of political theology by these historical events. In *Beyond the Pleasure Principle*, Freud hypothesized the existence of a death drive to explain the traumatic "war neuroses" of returning veterans. In *The Future of an Illusion* and *Civilization and Its Discontents*, Freud turned his attention to the cultural violence wrought by religion. And in *Moses and Monotheism*, Freud engaged the Spinoza of the *Theological-Political Treatise*, who is concerned with politics and history, in particular the history of Moses's construction of the Jewish people. This is also the Spinoza who enacts in his own text the narrative dimension and rhetorical appeal that cannot be reduced to, are always in excess of, the strict law of reason. In *Moses and Monotheism*, Freud too focuses on the fictional and historical dimension of Jewish monotheism, and in doing so—as we'll see—complicates his earlier understanding of the opposition between religion and art. As Freud himself wrote to Lou Andreas-Salomé in 1935, "In *The Future of an Illusion* I expressed an essentially negative valuation of religion; later I found a formula that does better justice to it: its power is to be sure based on its truth content, but this truth is not a material but a historical one."[7] It will be one of the tasks of this chapter to unpack this gnomic assertion.

Leonardo's Unbelief

Freud's essay on Leonardo da Vinci (1910) was clearly influenced by Burckhardt's picture of the Renaissance as an age of heroic and secular individualism. We see this not least of all in the fact that Freud focuses primarily on Leonardo the genius and only secondarily on his art. But Burckhardt is not the only ghost haunting the essay on Leonardo. Equally important, as we'll see, is Spinoza. In Freud's reading, Leonardo is a Spinoza avant la lettre, one who helps Freud articulate the difference not only between reason and religion but also between religion, on the one hand, and science and art on the other.

Spinoza initially emerges in the essay as a figure of scientific curiosity. In Freud's account, Leonardo was a towering genius whose intellectual orientation was similar to "Spinoza's mode of thinking." From Freud's assertion that Leonardo's "affects were controlled and subjected to the instinct for research; he did not love and hate, but asked himself about the origin of what he was to love or hate," we can guess that Leonardo's scientific inquiries were driven by an intellectual rigor not unlike Spinoza's in the *Ethics*.[8] But the mention of Spinoza also points in the direction of a critique of religion, for Freud then argues that the young Leonardo's intellectual curiosity would inevitably have produced religious skepticism. Moreover, he notes that Vasari confirms this hypothesis in the first edition of his *Lives*, where he describes Leonardo as an unbeliever.[9]

What is important, for our purposes, is that Freud then links Leonardo's religious unbelief to the quality of Leonardo's art. He notes contemporary comments that Leonardo "took from the sacred figures the last remnant of their connection with the Church and made them human, so as to represent by their means great and beautiful human emotions." And he adds that, while Leonardo "expresses his admiration for the Creator . . . there is nothing which indicates that he wishes to maintain any personal relation with this divine power." Such lack of interest in a personal relation with God amounts, in Freud's book, to disbelief:

> There is scarcely any doubt that Leonardo had prevailed both over dogmatic and personal religion, and had by his work of research removed himself far from the position from which the Christian believer surveys the world.[10]

In Freud's account, Leonardo's art is not only a daring form of sublimation that, like science, refuses subordination to dogmatic authority. It also reoccupies the terrain of religion, reappropriating its forms for purely human, secular purposes. If we recall that Freud used the term *Besetzung* or "occupation" to describe the relationship of the drive to its object, we might say that an analogous *Besetzung* or reoccupation is dramatized in the art of the Renaissance, which "took from the sacred figures the last remnant of their connection to the Church and made them human."[11] We might even say that the Renaissance is one grand *Besetzung* in relation not only to antiquity but also to Christianity. In emphasizing the secular interpretation of Christian subjects, Freud's interpretation of Leonardo's art validates Burckhardt's view of the Renaissance.

So far, I have left aside the oddest part of Freud's essay, but I now want to suggest that here too we may find an allusion to Spinoza. Freud notoriously supports his claim regarding Leonardo's scientific orientation with the analysis of the bizarre childhood dream that Leonardo recorded as an adult. In this dream, the baby Leonardo is visited in the cradle by a bird ("un nibio" or kite) that opens his mouth with its tail and strikes its tail against his lips. Freud famously misinterpreted the lowly *nibio* as a vulture and proceeded to build an elaborate scaffolding on this misinterpretation, linking the vulture to the ancient Egyptian god Mut, and to Leonardo's mother (Mutter), to whom he in turn traced Leonardo's homosexuality.[12] In Freud's fantastic interpretation, which scholars have understandably been quick to dismiss, the adult Leonardo's voracious learning brought him in contact with fables about the Egyptian vulture in the *Hieroglyphics* of Horapollo, and he in turn used these to construct a memory of himself as a "vulture-child," with a mother but no father.[13] The fantasy thus points to the truth that the young Leonardo spent an inordinate amount of time alone with his mother, and this in turn, according to Freud, explains his intense scientific curiosity.[14]

Of course, there needs no Horapollo come from the grave to tell us that, especially since Freud's interpretation of the dream yields the picture of Leonardo's childhood he already held. Yet, while Freud's recourse to Horapollo may appear far-fetched, on closer inspection it is compatible with Freud's Spinozist reading of Leonardo. As Freud—who was fascinated with all things Egyptian—may have known, Horapollo's treatise on Egyptian hieroglyphics was discovered in 1419 on the island of Andros and brought to Florence, where it set off a period of intense fascination with Egyptian wisdom, which scholars have described as Egyptomania.[15] For some, Egyptian hieroglyphics were gestures toward the secret of one god, a monotheism compatible with Judaism and Christianity. More often, however, the Egyptians were perceived as advancing what the Egyptologist Jan Assmann has called "cosmotheism," an equation of God and nature, which by the seventeenth century was regularly identified with Spinoza. Egyptian wisdom even became a kind of code for Spinozism, and the New Testament notion that Moses had Egyptian knowledge (Acts 7:22) or that Moses was an Egyptian (available in Strabo and later Toland) was equivalent to saying Moses was a Spinozist. According to this argument, Moses accommodated his Spinozist knowledge of the sublime mysteries of nature by presenting them in the form of a theistic, personal God. But the philosophical few would know that "the world *is* God."[16] Given Freud's great admiration for Spinoza, and his undoubted familiarity with some of the works arguing for the connection between Moses's Egyptian knowledge and Spinoza's cosmotheism,[17] it is possible that the reference to Horapollo is intended to attribute a Spinozist curiosity to the young Leonardo and a Spinozist view of god and nature to the mature Leonardo. This Spinozist view of nature is borne out by the end of the essay, which stresses the role of chance and necessity in our lives. In response to the objection that he has made too much of the chance circumstances of Leonardo's parentage, Freud remarks, "If one considers chance to be unworthy of determining our fate, it is simply a relapse into the pious view of the Universe. . . . we are all too ready to forget that in fact everything in our life is chance, from our origin out of the meeting of spermatozoon and ovum onwards—chance which nevertheless has a share in the law and necessity of nature, and which merely lacks any connection with our wishes and illusions."[18] Or as Spinoza wrote in the *Theological Political Treatise*, "Nature is not bound by the laws of human reason . . . but rather by numberless other things that concern the eternal order of the whole of nature (of which human beings are but a small part), and all individual things are determined to live and behave in a certain way only by the necessity of this order" (16.197). In his heroic recognition of the role of necessity in our lives, a recognition explicitly contrasted to a conventionally "pious" view of the universe, Freud could also be said to reveal his allegiance to Spinoza.[19]

By the end of the essay, then, Leonardo seems to stand for the supersession of religion by art, and of art by science—an Enlightenment narrative of the sort Cassirer advanced in *The Philosophy of Symbolic Forms*. Religious illusions are purged, art is entertained and put aside, as though it could not really satisfy Leonardo's Spinoza-like hunger for knowledge. This narrative would change, however, some four years later, when Freud wrote "The Moses of Michelangelo." In this essay, Freud grapples more seriously with the mysterious power of art, and both the statue of Moses and Michelangelo himself become alter egos for the founder of psychoanalysis.

Freud's Jewish Question

There were lots of reasons for Freud, the Jewish founder of psychoanalysis, to identify with Moses, the leader of the Jewish people. But what is striking about Freud's engagement with Moses in the nineteen teens is that it is an engagement mediated by Michelangelo. Freud's Moses is first and foremost a Renaissance Moses, a statue of Moses that—Freud will imply—has more in common with the powerful Pope Julius II and with Michelangelo himself than with the religious figure of the Hebrew Bible. As we'll see, Michelangelo's art comes to stand for some of the critical potential of psychoanalysis, the science that aspires to demystify our illusions, even as it reveals the inevitability of illusion and its centrality to civilization as we know it.

Critics have been quick to note the relevance of Freud's essay to the "religion" of psychoanalysis. In one prominent interpretation, the essay is an allegory of Freud's relationship to the Jewish Question, construed as the question of the acceptance of "the Jewish science" of psychoanalysis by mainstream Austrian society. In the early years of the twentieth century the members of the Viennese Psychoanalytic Society were primarily Jewish, but if psychoanalysis could attract Christian followers such as Carl Jung, Freud wrote in a 1907 letter to Karl Abraham, it could more plausibly claim to be a science of universal principles rather than a matter of Jewish particularism.[20] Hence Freud's severe disappointment at the defection of Jung in 1913, precisely the time Freud was composing his essay on Michelangelo's *Moses*. In 1909, Freud had written of his hopes to Jung, "you will as Joshua, if I am Moses, take possession of the promised land of psychiatry, which I am only permitted to glimpse from afar." Later, he wrote to Sandor Ferenczi, "At the moment the situation in Vienna makes me feel more like the historical Moses than the Michelangelo one."[21] But—this interpretation argues— Freud ultimately identified with Michelangelo's Moses: just as Moses (in Freud's interpretation of the statue) mastered his anger at the defection of the Jews from monotheism, so Freud saw himself as the Moses of psychoanalysis, needing to restrain his anger against Jung in order to save the Law.

I don't want to contest this interpretation so much as suggest that there is another Jewish Question—or another dimension of the Jewish Question—at the heart of Freud's essay, and that is Spinoza's question of the relationship between religion, reason, and culture. As we've seen, this question was replayed in the nineteenth and early twentieth century, in debates about Jewish assimilation to the German tradition of *Bildung*. At the center of this debate was the question of the relationship of Jewish belief to Christian culture, including the question of whether one needed to assimilate to the other. But, as Bruno Bauer recognized, the further question was whether religion needed to cede altogether to secular culture.

Even more than the essay on Leonardo, the essay on Michelangelo's *Moses* shows that Renaissance art is the prism through which Freud takes up the question of religious illusion in relation to art and psychoanalysis. In this context, it's striking that the unbelief that Freud attributed to Leonardo shadows Freud's own response to Michelangelo's work. We see this powerfully at the very beginning of the essay in Freud's gripping description of his encounter with the statue in the Church of San Pietro in Vincoli in Rome:

> How often have I mounted the steep steps of the unlovely Corso Cavour to the lonely place where the deserted church stands, and have essayed to support the angry scorn of the hero's glance! Sometimes I have crept cautiously out of the half-gloom of the interior as though I myself belonged to the mob upon whom his eye is turned—the mob which can hold fast no conviction, which has neither trust nor patience and which rejoices when it has regained its illusory idols [*das keine Überzeugung festhalten kann, das nicht warten und nicht vertrauen will und jubelt, wenn es die Illusion des Götzenbildes wieder bekommen hat*].[22]

Freud is particularly impressed by the conviction expressed in Moses's gaze, which he contrasts with the weak faith of the mob worshiping the golden calf. Thematically, or in terms of its content, then, the passage aligns Moses's austere monotheism with true faith, in contrast to the weak conviction of the idolaters. Significantly, Freud includes himself among those who are rebuked for their lack of conviction ("as though I myself belonged to the mob"). This is perhaps not surprising, given that Freud treats the church as though it were simply a museum housing a great Renaissance work of art. Freud may then be suggesting that his own powerful aesthetic response to the statue is itself a form of idolatry, one that needs to be checked by something like Moses's iconoclasm, i.e., by translating the meaning of the statue into verbal form.[23] In this case, Freud the art connoisseur would be like the worshipers of the golden calf, while Freud the founder of "the talking cure" would be occupying the place of Moses.

But Freud's description of his response also recuperates aesthetic response over against a religious interpretation of the statue. In his description of his response to the statue, Freud alludes ironically to Vasari's description of how the Jews of sixteenth-century Rome admired Michelangelo's statue when it was first completed:

> every part of the statue is finished so expertly, that today more than ever Moses can truly be called a friend of God. For through the skill of Michelangelo, God has wanted to restore and prepare the body of Moses for the Resurrection before that of anyone else. And well may the Jews continue to go there (as they do every Sabbath, both men and women, like flocks of starlings) to visit and adore the statue, since they will be adoring something that is divine rather than human.[24]

As Julia Lupton has commented on this passage from Vasari, "the appearance of contemporary Jews on the site of Christian typology signals the limits of Pauline exegesis. After all, these are not the Chosen People of the Old Testament who happily prefigure the order that will have superseded them, but rather Jews of modern Rome, who . . . prefer not to convert."[25] In this narrative, the Christian allegorization of the statue is resisted by the Jews of Renaissance Rome, and the refusal to convert is linked to the purely aesthetic appreciation of the work of art.

There is still another way to read the passage that sees Freud's powerful aesthetic response in even more positive terms. If we read the passage in terms of Freud's comment on the statue's form and aesthetic effect, then Moses's gaze appears as the result of Michelangelo's artistic conviction, and the artistic illusion of "the hero's glance" is contrasted to illusory religious idols worshiped by "the mob." Artistic conviction, that is, produces an illusion of a different sort, one that does not deceive or lead astray. Freud would then be thinking of Michelangelo's powerful art as a model for himself, in particular, for the scientific discipline of psychoanalysis. In this second case, Freud would be occupying the place of Michelangelo as well as Moses, of the artist as well as the iconoclast.

But Freud goes one step further in his identification with Michelangelo, whom he portrays as an almost blasphemous interpreter of Scripture. As Freud notes, the chief interpretive crux for viewers of the statue is the significance of Moses's posture: is he about to rise and dash the tablets to the ground when he sees the Jews idolizing the golden calf, or does he represent instead, as the art historian Henry Thode argued, "a character-type, embodying an inexhaustible inner force which tames the recalcitrant world"?[26] Freud eventually synthesizes these two interpretations. He proposes that Moses's sudden movement in response to the worship of the golden calf actually precedes the moment represented by the statue. Michelangelo's Moses is tempted to leap up and dash the tablets but restrains himself: "it was to preserve them that he kept his passion in check. . . . He remembered his mission and renounced for its sake an indulgence of his feelings."[27] As Freud goes on to note, this amounts to a bold revision of the scriptural text, in which Moses did dash the tablets to the ground in a fit of rage. Moreover, it amounts to a better representation of Moses. In this account, art displaces religion and sculpture replaces sacred text:

> Michelangelo has placed a different Moses on the tomb of the Pope, one superior to the historical or traditional Moses. He has modified the theme of the broken Tables; he does not let Moses break them in wrath, but makes him be influenced by the danger that they will be broken and calm that wrath, or at any rate prevent it from becoming an act. In this way he has added something new and more than human to the figure of Moses; so that the giant frame with its tremendous physical power becomes only a concrete expression of the highest mental achievement that is possible in a man, that of struggling successfully against an inward passion for the sake of a cause to which he has devoted himself.[28]

Michelangelo—according to Freud—has "reoccupied" or reinterpreted Scripture for human purposes, presenting in Moses an allegory of "the highest mental achievement that is possible in a man," the successful sublimation of a powerful passion in the service of his civilizing mission or "cause." But Freud nowhere remarks that this mission is a religious one. Unusually, he is less interested in the content of the imagined scene than in the formal relationship between suppressed passion and civilization.[29] Freud's Michelangelo is a Renaissance artist who uses religious themes to glorify the human form and celebrate the human power of art. He is like Freud's Leonardo, who "took from the sacred figures the last remnant of their connection with [institutional religion] and made them human." Moses the divine lawgiver becomes a supremely secular figure of willpower and restraint. At the same time, Freud's interpretation ironically suggests that in containing his anger at idolatry, in refusing the iconoclastic moment, Michelangelo's Moses accepts the failure of monotheism to purge the world of idols. It is impossible not to think of Freud himself here, aware of his own cherished illusion that the world might be purged of religious illusions. In this, as Freud was undoubtedly aware, he was following in Spinoza's footsteps.

Unlike the Leonardo essay, then, the Michelangelo essay puts art and the artist front and center. Art is not something to be transcended in the direction of science. Instead, the work of art is itself an act of interpretation, which the viewer must try to reconstruct. In Freud's gloss on Michelangelo, the shaping power of the artist is an emblem for the heroic project of civilization, construed as the sublimation and redirection of our instincts, and the even more heroic secular project of psychoanalysis, construed as the demystification of our illusions. It's almost as if Freud were suggesting that, just as Renaissance artists turned the Bible into an occasion for art, so psychoanalysis turns illusion into an occasion for analysis, even as it concedes the inevitability of idolatry, whether religious or aesthetic.

The Claims of Reason

In the story I've told so far, Freud turned to the Renaissance in order to discover, as Burckhardt did, the gradual supplanting of religion by art and science.[30] This was a secularizing narrative that was utterly congenial to Freud's own view of religion, and it allowed him to analogize the heroic achievements of Renaissance art to his own adventures in psychoanalysis. Judging from Freud's correspondence and his comments on

Leonardo's Egyptian wisdom, Spinoza was an important influence on this narrative, not least of all because Spinoza had advanced the equation of God and nature and an account of human passions and desires that left no room for a transcendent divinity. But in the last two decades of Freud's life, Freud turned away from this heroic picture of the Renaissance. With the political crisis of the 1930s and the onset of World War II, Freud began to confront the contemporary reality of political theology and to reflect more generally on the political uses of religion. The Spinoza who is most relevant to this late work is the Spinoza of the *Theological-Political Treatise*. In fact, we could say that Freud becomes in his late work a Spinoza-like political theologian of the psyche, one who distinguishes increasingly between the enlightened few and the many "who have no self-knowledge" and for whom religion is both a necessary and a potentially dangerous illusion (*TTP*, preface, 3). To the extent Freud engages this Spinoza, he does so, like the other figures in this book, in order to discover the roots of the political crisis of the 1930s. In this section, I explore the events and works that intervened between Freud's heroic view of the Renaissance and his discovery of the early modern.

In contrast to his essays on Leonardo and Michelangelo, Freud's late thoughts on art and culture were shaped by his experience of two world wars and his "discovery" of the death drive. In his first major postwar publication, *Beyond the Pleasure Principle*, Freud reflected on the "war neuroses" produced by the traumatic violence of World War I. He noted that the compulsion to repeat unpleasant experiences could not be described as a function of the pleasure principle and conjectured that veterans were trying to master trauma by repeating it. Freud famously compared the repetition compulsion to the *fort/da* game of the child who plays with making an object disappear and then retrieving it in an effort to master the disappearance of its mother from sight. In a move that anticipated *Civilization and Its Discontents*, Freud analogized this play to the "cultural achievement" of renouncing instinctual satisfaction more generally, including through the artistic play with or imitation of painful experiences. Art, he suggested, could make an unpleasant subject pleasurable by imitating it and by allowing it to be "worked over" in the mind. But art could not fully master the death drive, an instinct of aggression against the self and a desire to return to an inanimate state.[31] These thoughts about death and art, or what Freud sometimes called thanatos and eros, would inflect Freud's analysis of religion in *The Future of an Illusion* (1927) and of the psychic costs of culture in *Civilization and Its Discontents* (1930).

Freud returned to the question of the relationship between art and religion in *The Future of an Illusion*, transforming the simple oppositions of the earlier essays on Leonardo and Michelangelo into a powerful, if negative, dialectic. Freud's most virulent attack on religion as an illusion, even a delusion, also reveals that illusion itself is an antithetical primal word—perhaps *the* antithetical primal word—in the world of psychoanalysis. Freud wanted to defend psychoanalysis's claim to be a science—one that can give us purchase on our own susceptibility to illusions, including artistic and religious illusions—at the same time that he conceded that illusion, with its genesis in wish fulfillment, is a fundamental process of the human psyche, including the psyche of the scientist.[32]

Freud was deeply attuned to the powerful effects of religious illusion in the lives of individuals and of nations. All illusions, he argued, are disguised fantasies of wish fulfillment; in the case of religion, the motive force is the powerful wish to be protected against the violence of nature, of others, and even arguably of one's own harsh superego. Religion also channels the enduring power of phantasmatic identification in the form of a communal bonding that transcends the individual, even as it separates friend from enemy. Such phantasmatic identification might be thought of as a residue of political theology, if by political theology we understand Freud's account in *Totem and Taboo* (1913). There, Freud described the primal scene in which a band of brothers kills their father and establishes fraternal society, at the same time that they reinscribe the father in the form of religious totem. But Freud would never have equated all fantasy or illusion with political theology, precisely because he was intent on distinguishing between illusions that are harmless and religious illusions that are, by definition, closer to delusions.

What is at stake in this distinction, as Freud declares in *The Future of an Illusion*, is reason itself: not a reason that ignores the power of religion but precisely one that is capable of criticizing it because all illusions are not the same: "Illusions need not necessarily be false—that is to say, unrealizable or in contradiction to reality. For instance, a middle class girl may have the illusion that a prince will come and marry her. This is possible, and a few such cases have occurred. That the Messiah will come and found a golden age is much less likely." As Freud comments on his own witty understatement: "Whether one classifies this belief as an illusion or something analogous to a delusion will depend on one's personal attitude." By the end of *The Future of an Illusion*, however, it's clear that this classification is not at all a subjective judgment but the objective conclusion of reason.[33]

In *The Future of an Illusion*, Freud takes up the general problem of culture or civilization (he "scorns to distinguish between [them]").[34] Civilization, which involves the repression of instinct and mastery of nature, also produces what Freud calls "mental wealth," in the form of cultural ideals, including religion and art.[35] Of the latter he writes, "art offers substitutive satisfactions for the oldest and still most deeply felt cultural renunciations, and for that reason it serves as nothing else does to reconcile a man to the sacrifices he has made on behalf of civilization." But Freud's chief concern in this essay is religion—"perhaps the most important item in the psychical inventory of a civilization"—which he equates with illusion, defined not as error but as the fulfillment of "the oldest, strongest, and most urgent wishes of mankind."[36] These include the wish, above all, to be protected from feelings of helplessness.

Freud's initial arguments about religion are a combination of Lucretius and Spinoza. On the one hand, he agrees with Lucretius that religion was invented to allay our fears of the natural world: The gods have a "threefold task: they must exorcize the terrors of nature, they must reconcile men to the cruelty of Fate, particularly as it is shown in death, and they must compensate them for the sufferings and privations which a civilized life in common has imposed on them. . . . And thus a store of ideas is created, born from man's need to make his helplessness tolerable and built up from the material of memories of the helplessness of his own childhood and the childhood of the human race."[37] On the other hand, Freud agrees with Spinoza that the scriptures are unreliable and cannot themselves be accepted as proof that they are revealed truth: "They are full of contradictions, revisions, and falsifications. . . . It does not help much to have it asserted that their wording, or even their content only, originates from divine revelation, for this assertion is itself one of the doctrines whose authenticity is under examination, and no proposition can be a proof of itself."[38] Freud also rejects two defenses of religion, one ancient and one contemporary: Tertullian's "I believe because it is absurd," and Hans Vaihinger's theory of the "as if," which turns religion into a fiction that people believe because it is necessary for the health of society. Freud argues that Tertullian's maxim offers no justification for believing one absurdity over another, and Vaihinger's notion that religion is a fiction deprives religion of the "guarantee"— Freud appears to mean the ontological or epistemological bedrock— that most people expect even in their "ordinary activities," let alone ones that give meaning to their lives. Here Freud sharply distinguishes between the truth claims of religion and the workings of fiction, which, however much it may enrich our lives, does not pretend to console as religion does.

Freud then proceeds to reject the consolations of religion as an insult to reason. He first notes that, although religious illusions (like all illusions) are not necessarily errors, religious illusions are uniquely "insusceptible of proof" or refutation.[39] But Freud is not content with this position, which implies, like Pascal's wager, that it might be a good idea to believe precisely in the absence of decisive refutation. Instead, he insists (drawing on his earlier argument about the need for a "guarantee") that no respectable intellectual would base such important matters on mere ignorance. He also rebuts the charge that his critique of religion deprives ordinary believers of their one consolation. Instead, he asserts, "civilization runs a greater risk if we maintain our present attitude to religion than if we give it up." Ultimately, Freud sees religion as a grand, communal obsessional neurosis and guesses that "the time has probably come . . . for replacing the effects of repression by the results of the rational operation of the intellect." And he adds, "We need not deplore the renunciation of historical truth [e.g., of a religious dogma that was once held to be true at a particular historical time] when we put forward rational grounds for the precepts of civilization." From the perspective of reason, illusory symbols should give way to reality, that is, to truth.[40]

It is all the more striking then that, almost from the beginning, the essay is characterized by a recurrent, striking detour into artistic illusion or fiction. As though he were writing a Platonic dialogue, Freud invents an urbane but critical interlocutor, who is unpersuaded by Freud's arguments and who chastises him for his vehemence. When, late in the essay, Freud admits he might himself be chasing an "illusion" in hoping that civilization will be improved by the elimination of religious education, his imaginary interlocutor charges Freud with being "an enthusiast . . . carried away by illusions"—in the precise Freudian sense of a wish (that there be no more religious illusions).[41] Freud's interlocutor pleads for the pragmatic use of religion, not its truth value. Like Spinoza, he sees religion as "a proved and emotionally valuable illusion" for the masses. Freud responds by distinguishing once again between illusions that are and are not capable of correction. "Observe the difference between your attitude to illusions and mine," Freud urges.

> You have to defend the religious illusion with all your might. If it becomes discredited . . . then your world collapses. There is nothing left for you but to despair of everything, of civilization

and the future of mankind. . . . Our god, *Logos*, is perhaps not a very almighty one, and he may only be able to fulfill a small part of what his predecessors have promised. If we have to acknowledge this we shall accept it with resignation. We shall not on that account lose our interest in the world and in life, for we have one sure support which you lack. We believe [*wir glauben daran*] that it is possible for scientific work to gain some knowledge about the reality of the world, by means of which we can increase our power and in accordance with which we can arrange our life. If this belief is an illusion, then we are in the same position as you. But science has given us evidence by its numerous and important successes that it is no illusion.[42]

As though conceding, if only in jest, the charge that his work is motivated by prophetic monotheism, Freud refers to Logos as a "god," though "perhaps not a very almighty one." This god is weak in comparison with its predecessor gods in the sense that it cannot console and does not promise salvation, as they did. Reason is also weak, perhaps, because it cannot persuade those who are determined to worship the false idols of religion. But reason is strong in that it can survive the disenchantment of religion as a false consolation. For this reason, Freud insists, belief in reason is not the same thing as belief in religion. Freud goes on to address the charge of relativism, the charge that science, "being bound to the conditions of our own [perceptual] organization, . . . can yield nothing else than subjective results, while the real nature of things outside ourselves remains inaccessible." To this he replies, "the task of science is fully covered if we limit it to showing how the world must appear to us in consequence of the particular character of our organization." And, as though he were Hegel criticizing Kant's distinction between the noumenal and phenomenal worlds, he adds, "the problem of the nature of the world without regard to our percipient mental apparatus is an empty abstraction, devoid of practical interest."[43]

Although Freud begins the essay by differentiating between illusion and error, by the end it is clear he thinks religious illusion is indeed an error: "In the long run nothing can withstand reason and experience, and the contradiction which religion offers to both is too palpable." This at least is true insofar as we think of God as providing consolation for earthly existence, for such a figure is an obvious projection of our desires. But, Freud argues, if we do not think of God as providing consolation or if we think of him as remote from our concerns, we will lose interest in him.[44] (Lucretius had also suggested as much in *De rerum natura*.) Like Spinoza and Cassirer, Freud sees religion as a myth that must in time give way to rational and ethical universalism, even as he preserves a place for the sense-making activity of art.[45] This means that Freud in effect distinguishes between good and bad illusion, though his economic theory of the instincts cannot justify such value judgments.[46] What he can do is argue for the difference between rational argument, which invites refutation of individual claims, and religious illusion, which does not. In this contrast, art is on the side of reason. After comparing "religious consolations" to the effect of a "narcotic," as Marx famously did years earlier, Freud links art to the "education to reality":

> As honest small-holders on this earth [men] will know how to cultivate their plot in such a way that it supports them. By withdrawing their expectations from the other world and concentrating all their liberated energies into their life on earth, they will probably succeed in achieving a state of things in which life will become tolerable for everyone and civilization no longer oppressive to anyone. Then, with one of our fellow unbelievers [*Unglaubensgenossen*], they will be able to say without regret: *Den Himmel überlassen wir/Den Engeln und den Spatzen* (Heaven we leave to the angels and the sparrows).[47]

Heine, the author of these lines, famously referred to Spinoza as an *Unglaubensgenossen*. Here Freud adduces Heine, the poet, unbeliever, and follower of Spinoza, as evidence of the reality principle, of an interpretation of life that withdraws its expectations from the other world and concentrates instead on creating symbols that enhance rather than diminish our understanding. In contrast to his distinction between religious illusion and reality, or even between illusion and reality tout court, Freud suggests here that art escapes, or transfigures, the antithesis between the real and the illusory; it cannot be demystified by asserting that what it represents does not exist. Rather, it offers us a symbolic world, an interpretation of experience.

Paul Ricoeur has argued that, to the extent Freud focuses on art as an activity of interpretation, he may also unwittingly provide a different way to think about religion. In particular, Ricoeur claims that Freud's conception of hermeneutics is more compatible with the phenomenology of religion than with Freud's own "economic" model of psychoanalysis:

For Freud an illusion is a representation to which no reality corresponds. His definition is positivist. Is there not, however, a function of the imagination which escapes the positivist alternative of the real and the illusory? A lesson that we have learned, which is parallel to Freudianism but independent of it, is that myths and symbols are carriers of a meaning which escapes this alternative. A different hermeneutics, distinct from psychoanalysis and closer to the phenomenology of religion, teaches us that myths are not fables, i.e., 'false' and 'unreal' stories. As opposed to all positivism, this hermeneutics presupposes that the 'true' and the 'real' cannot be reduced to what can be verified by mathematical and experimental methods but has to do with our relation to the world, to other beings, and to being as well. It is this relationship which in an imaginative mode . . . myth has begun to explore. Freud is both very close and very far from recognizing this function of the imagination, with which, in a different vein, Spinoza, Schelling, and Hegel were all acquainted. What brings him close to it is his *practice* of "interpretation," but what separates him from it is his "metapsychological" *theorizing*, i.e., the implicit philosophy of the economic model [of the instincts] itself.[48]

Ricoeur rightly takes Freud to task for his sometimes simplistic opposition between the real and the illusory, or the true and the illusory. In place of this opposition, Ricoeur insists that religion is itself an activity of sense-making. As we've seen, in *The Future of an Illusion* Freud himself complicated the distinction between the real and the illusory, and he would later further dismantle this opposition in *Moses and Monotheism*. But he would not have accepted Ricoeur's recuperation of religion. Instead, he would have responded not only that Ricoeur's idea of "myth" is encompassed by art and culture more generally, but that the history of Christianity in particular shows how harmful such myths can be.[49] As Philip Rieff has remarked of Freud's analysis of religion in *The Future of an Illusion*, "Freud refers not to Christianity but to 'Christian culture'" in order to highlight "his view of Christianity as the chief instrument of coercion in the larger system of coercions defined as culture."[50] Three years later, in *Civilization and Its Discontents*, Freud made it clear that he thought religion had failed miserably in its civilizing mission: "its technique consists in depressing the value of life and distorting the picture of the real world in a delusional manner—which presupposes an intimidation of the intelligence." And, like Nietzsche, he singled out Christianity for special criticism: "How has it happened that so many people have come to take up this strange attitude of hostility to civilization? . . . A factor of this kind hostile to civilization must already have been at work in the victory of Christendom over the heathen religions. For it was very closely related to the low estimation put upon earthly life by the Christian doctrine." In contrast to this depreciation of life, Freud affirmed the aesthetic attitude, the "useless" appreciation of this-worldly beauty: "we require civilized man to reverence beauty wherever he sees it in nature and to create it in the objects of his handiwork as far as he is able." Such aesthetic experience "offers little protection against the threat of suffering, but it can compensate for a great deal. . . . Beauty has no obvious use; nor is there any clear cultural necessity for it. Yet civilization could not do without it."[51]

Freud's late work is clearly infused with a tragic sense of culture, the sense that civilization exacts too high a price in the form of the repression of individual desires and that civilization must ultimately fail in its civilizing mission because "man is a wolf to man."[52] Like Carl Schmitt and Leo Strauss, Freud was not optimistic about the power of education to transform human nature. (In *Civilization and Its Discontents* he refers to "the undeniable existence of evil.")[53] Even as he asserted his belief in science and its eventual triumph over illusion, he conceded that few individuals were capable of scientific reason just as few were capable of appreciating the great works of civilization. Science has indeed increased man's "control over nature," but this control has not increased human happiness.[54] Freud here adumbrates something like Adorno and Horkheimer's dialectic of enlightenment, but with a special emphasis on its affective dimension. For Adorno and Horkheimer, the dialectic of enlightenment involves the process by which mastery of external nature also produces the alienation and oppression of human nature, just as the Enlightenment emphasis on reason produces its own barbaric underside. In a similar way for Freud, civilization consoles man for the sublimation of his instincts, at the same time that civilization and man are locked in a tragic conflict.[55] But this tragedy—as Freud asserted much earlier in *Beyond the Pleasure Principle* and reiterates here—is not simply externally imposed but also internal to the human psyche.

It's therefore appropriate that, in describing the process of sublimation, Freud conjures up the notions of contingency and fate that together figure so prominently in Renaissance ideas of tragedy, including, of course, *Hamlet*.[56] When Freud writes that "sublimation is a vicissitude which has been forced upon the instincts entirely by civilization," the German for "vicissitude forced upon the instincts" is *Triebschicksal*, more literally translated as instinctual fate. Chief among these fateful instincts is eros, in the form of self-love or self-preservation. Freud's elaboration of the tragic conflict between self-love and the commandment to love one's neighbor as oneself leads to a critique of Pauline universalism or cosmopolitanism.[57] Such universalism, he argues, produces intolerance of the excluded, of those who refuse universal notions of community. This critique is fueled by the hypothesis of an instinct to aggression, which makes one see that the command to love's one's neighbor "is really justified by the fact that nothing else runs so strongly counter to the original nature of man."[58] In Freud's anthropology, the high ideals of civilization may themselves harbor "illusions" about human nature, and Freud's definition of "Kulturkampf" is not a struggle over competing notions of civilization but rather the struggle that constitutes civilization—the struggle between eros and death.[59] In contrast to a naive celebration of *Bildungsideologie*, Freud is ever sensitive to what cannot be simply sublated by culture: the human propensity to violence and the irreducible fact of human mortality.

In the conclusion to *Civilization and Its Discontents*, Freud refuses the stance of a "prophet" who offers his readers "consolation" for the depredations of civilization and hope for the future.[60] Yet, precisely because of his pessimism, Freud does indeed prove to be a prophet in the concluding words of the essay:

> Men have gained control over the forces of nature to such an extent that with their help they would have no difficulty in exterminating one another to the last man. They know this, and hence comes a large part of their current unrest, their unhappiness and their mood of anxiety. And now it is to be expected that the other of the two 'Heavenly Powers,' eternal Eros, will make an effort to assert himself in the struggle with his equally immortal adversary. But who can foresee with what success and with what result?[61]

As the editor notes, "this final sentence was added in 1931—when the menace of Hitler was already beginning to be apparent." Subsequent events made Freud only more acutely aware of his contemporaries' susceptibility to myth. In the 1935 postscript to his *Autobiographical Study*, Freud tells us that *The Future of an Illusion* and *Civilization and Its Discontents* marked a return to "the cultural problems" that had fascinated him in his youth, and that the essays elicited considerable public interest. "They may have played a part in creating the short-lived illusion that I was among the writers to whom a great nation like Germany was ready to listen." In 1930, Freud tells us in the postscript, this illusion was strengthened when he was awarded the Goethe Prize. He then comments on his own subsequent tragic moment of reversal and recognition, a recognition, we can guess, of the political theology that informed the Nazi state: "This was the climax of my life as a citizen. Soon afterwards the boundaries of our country narrowed and the nation would know no more of us [*wollte nichts von uns wissen*; literally, 'wanted to know nothing of us'].''[62] The English translation, while not quite accurate in its temporal ambiguity, captures something of the prophetic force of this statement in hindsight. Although Freud escaped to London in 1938 and died there in 1939, wartime Germany under Hitler *would* eventually know nothing more of the Jews, having exterminated them.

The Persistence of Illusion

While World War I was a catalyst for Freud's hypothesis of the death drive, it seems to have taken the political crisis of the 1930s and the onset of World War II for Freud to confront the contemporary reality of political theology. In his last major work, *Moses and Monotheism*, Freud returns to the constellation of issues that he broached in his essays on Leonardo's Egyptian wisdom and Michelangelo's civilizing Moses by arguing, notoriously, that Moses *was* an Egyptian, who learned his monotheism as a follower of Akhenaton and then imposed it on the Jews. But this later work also breaks with the earlier essays by developing a far more pessimistic Spinozist account of political theology and religious illusion, one that arrives at a more complicated view of the relationship between religion and art, reason and illusion. In elaborating a "historical" account of the development of monotheism, Freud also comes to understand better the universal, psychological reasons for the persistence of religious illusion. In doing so, he revises the optimistic, implicitly secularizing narratives of the essays on Leonardo and Michelangelo.

As numerous critics have noted, the publication history of *Moses and Monotheism* was determined by Freud's own theological-political calculations. He began the work in 1934 and published sections of it in 1937, but delayed publication of the final part for fear that it would arouse the Church's hostility against psychoanalysis in a time of great political uncertainty: "We are living here in a Catholic country under the protection of that Church, uncertain how long that protection will hold out."[63] In particular, Freud seems to have hoped that the Church would "protect Austria from Nazi domination." After the Anschluss and Freud's emigration in 1938, he decided to publish the work as a whole. But the dire political situation and the ever-increasing anti-Semitism were not simply an occasion of prudence; they also seem to have inspired, at least in part, Freud's analysis of Jewish monotheism. In a letter to Stefan Zweig, Freud wrote, "In the face of new persecutions, one once again has to ask how the Jew has become what he is and why he attracts such eternal hatred. I have found the following formula: Moses created the Jew and my work will have as its title, *Moses: A Historical Novel.*"[64]

Despite the fantastic elements of this text (which Freud himself acknowledges in his fanciful subtitle), it's hard to imagine a more demystified reading of Moses, one more clearly designed to outdo Spinoza's own revolutionary interpretation, not least of all by calling even greater attention to the role of fiction, poetry, and legend in the constitution of history, including the history of political theology. Freud presents the Bible as a tendentious work, "embellished by poetic invention"; he describes it as a text with its own rhetorical "vicissitudes," including "noticeable gaps, disturbing repetitions and obvious contradictions."[65] Early in the text, Freud examines the role of fantasy (in particular the family romance) in shaping not only the psychic reality of the child but also "the poetic fiction" of the hero's birth. He also stresses the role of poetry and legend in creating the figures of Moses, Cyrus, and Romulus (shades of Machiavelli) and compares the Bible's construction of a tradition to the poetry of national epics.[66] Not least of all, Freud suggests that texts have a kind of rhetorical unconscious in the sense that all texts enact what they are repressing: "In its implications the distortion of a text resembles a murder: the difficulty is not in perpetrating the deed, but in getting rid of its traces." In this famous and telling metaphor, the comparison not merely is illustrative but in fact disguises—one might even say, allegorizes—Freud's central hypothesis that the Jews literally murdered the Egyptian Moses and the murder was occluded in the scriptural text (more on this below).[67]

Such doubling of fantasy and reality, fiction and disguise, is a characteristic feature of Freud's text. As Michel de Certeau has described *Moses and Monotheism*:

> The text initiates a play between religious legend (*Sage*) and Freudian construction (*Konstruction*), between the object under study and the discourse performing analysis. Their play takes

place in the fuzzy area of an ambivalence, in what gives 'fiction' the meaning both of a production (*fingere*, to fashion, to fabricate) and of a disguise or a deceit. Everything is unraveled in the field of relations between the labor that constructs and the ruse that would 'make us believe' in the fiction—a mixed terrain of production and lure. What history creates and what narrative dissimulates will meet in that very place. *Moses and Monotheism* is situated at this intersection of history and fiction. But its elucidation does not escape what it is elucidating. In the fashion of a fantasy, it *tells* a story of what is *produced* in a tradition. This theory of fiction is indeed a 'theoretical fiction.'[68]

De Certeau captures brilliantly the doubling or layered effect of Freud's text—the way Freud's theory is exercised both on and from within fictions (in this case, myths and legends), and the way Freud uses the literary techniques of close reading (the analysis of gaps, repetitions, and contradictions) to construct the repressed "truth" of Moses in Jewish "history." This history in Freud's analysis is arguably a product of fantasy more than reality; or perhaps it would be more accurate to say that human reality for Freud is always inextricable from human fantasies and desires. Moreover, any reconstruction of this fantastic history is itself bound to reenact or repeat the displacements and distortions of desire that it aims to uncover and bring to the surface.[69]

What de Certeau does not observe is how Freud imitates in narrative form, in the form of a historical novel, Moses's putatively historical use of fiction to fabricate the Jewish people. Nor does he observe the link to Spinoza. If he had, he would have seen a whole other layer of doubling in the text. For just as the Jewish people, in Freud's account, forget their murder of the original Moses, only to have that murder leave traces in the text, so Freud "forgets" his indebtedness to Spinoza in order to produce his own Spinozist account of Moses as a political theologian. Freud could also be said to forget his indebtedness to Spinozism in advancing the Egyptian origin of Moses, an argument that—as we've seen—was historically associated with the reception of Spinoza. In both cases, Freud elaborates a psychoanalytic account of political theology, that is, of the role of fiction and fantasy in the constitution of religion. In doing so, Freud revises the optimistic, implicitly secularizing narratives of the essays on Leonardo and Michelangelo's *Moses*.

Jan Assmann, who has done the most to link *Moses and Monotheism* to debates about the relationship between Jewish monotheism and Egyptian cosmotheism, and thus to the tradition of Spinozism, also does not note the link to Spinoza's own political theology. He argues that "Freud's construction of Moses as the creator of his nation goes against all historical probability." And yet, he continues, it is precisely this insistence on Moses the politician and lawgiver that proves Freud's indebtedness to ancient texts about Moses's Egyptian origin:

> it is precisely this construction of Moses as the creator of a nation that forms the strongest link between Freud's text and the Moses/Egypt discourse. The orthodox Jewish tradition tends to play down Moses' role in the Exodus. In the Passover Haggadah, the annual reenactment of the Exodus from Egypt in the form of a family liturgy, Moses is not even mentioned. Rather, it is one of the presuppositions of the discourse on Moses and Egypt that is shared by all participants, including the ancient sources. It is not 'Moses the prophet' but 'Moses the lawgiver' who forms the thematic focus of the discourse. . . . It is Moses the lawgiver and political creator who needs his Egyptian education.[70]

But there was a source nearer at hand, which was not the Spinozism of Egyptian cosmotheism, but Spinoza himself, specifically the Spinoza of the *Theological-Political Treatise*, for whom Moses was first and foremost not a prophet but a legislator in the period after the exodus from Egypt.[71]

In the *Theological-Political Treatise*, Moses is a political theologian who imposes religion on the Hebrews after the Exodus from Egypt: in a passage that echoes Machiavelli's account in chapter 6 of *The Prince*, Spinoza writes that the Hebrews "were all of rude intelligence and down-trodden by the miseries of slavery. Government therefore had to remain in the hands of one man alone who would rule the others, compel them by force, and make laws for them, and interpret those laws subsequently." This role was assumed by Moses (*TTP*, 5.74). "Hence, Moses remained the sole maker and interpreter [*lator et interpres* (Lat., 275)] of the divine laws. He was also the supreme judge whom no one else could judge and who alone among the Hebrews acted for God, i.e. he held sovereign majesty" (17.214). In this capacity, Moses promulgated the notion that the Jews were the chosen people because the Jews were obstinate and needed special persuasion to obey God's commandments (3.52). Spinoza then gives an account of the Hebrews' feeling of chosenness that anticipates Freud's analysis of how Jewish monotheism produced both heightened self-esteem and extreme intolerance: "For having transferred their right to God, they believed their kingdom was the kingdom of God, that they alone were the children of God and that other nations were enemies of God, whom for that reason they regarded with extreme hostility" (17.222; cf. *MM*, 105–6).

Spinoza then recounts the fragmentation and decline of the Hebrew theocracy, especially after the worship of the golden calf. Particularly striking in light of Freud's own preoccupations is Spinoza's account of the Jews' resentment against Moses for setting up his own tribe, the Levites, as the priesthood after every other tribe proved guilty of idolatry (17.227). Spinoza quotes the passage from Deut. 31:27 where Moses says to the people, "I know your rebellion and your disobedience. If while I have lived among you, you have been unruly against God, how much more will you be so after my death?"—a passage that Freud could have cited as a warrant for his hypothesis about the Jews' murder of Moses, but that Spinoza cites as prefiguring the dissolution of the Hebrew commonwealth. Spinoza's account of Moses, then, like his account of the Hebrew Bible as a whole, is simultaneously respectful and demystifying: it turns Moses into a figure of political force, cunning, and "craft" (*arte* [Lat., 286]) by craftily attributing this interpretation to the resentful Jews themselves (17.227). But Spinoza's account also turns the Hebrew commonwealth into a specific historical institution, one whose "historical truth"—including the laws and narratives of the Hebrew bible—means that it has been superseded.

Moses and Monotheism is a theological-political treatise in the tradition of Spinoza, which uses the insights of psychoanalysis to explain the persistence of religious illusion. Like Spinoza, Freud presents Moses as a political theologian, one whose political ambitions coincided with his desire to preserve the monotheistic religion he had embraced as an Egyptian follower of Akhenaton.[72] Like the Moses of the *Theological-Political Treatise*, Freud's Moses imposed monotheism on the Hebrews by force and in so doing "made" the Jews ("Es war der Mann Moses, der die Juden geschaffen hat" [47]). Freud's Moses, then, is an Old Testament Michelangelo, a biblical *homo faber*, whose chief work of art was the creation of the Jewish people. And Freud follows in his steps in creating his own artistic interpretation of Moses, his own "statue," as he described *Moses and Monotheism* in his correspondence—thereby perhaps suggesting he himself thought of this late text as a return to and rethinking of Michelangelo's work.[73]

Yet, even as Freud presents Moses as a *homo faber*, he also stresses the differences between religious and artistic illusion. In particular, religion differs from art in involving what Freud calls "the characteristic of compulsion," whether this is owing to guilt at original sin or to the force of belief or ethical obligation. This kind of compulsion, he argues, means that neurosis rather than art is the appropriate analogy for religion. And this in turn means that, ultimately, religion, like neurosis, has a traumatic force that art may not be able to counteract.[74]

Trauma is, in fact, spectacularly encoded in Freud's hypothetical history of the "making" of the Jews. While Freud's Moses is, like Spinoza's, a willful creator, against whom the Hebrews revolt (*TTP*, 17.227), Freud goes one step further than Spinoza when he argues that the "savage Semites" eventually murdered Moses, a fact that is only indirectly revealed in Scripture.

> The people's defection from the new religion is also described in the text—only as an episode, it is true: namely in the story of the golden calf. In this, by an ingenious turn, the breaking of the tables of the law (which is to be understood symbolically: "he has broken the law") is transposed on to Moses himself, and his furious indignation is assigned as its motive.[75]

According to this ingenious explanation, guilt for the murder of Moses is displaced onto Moses himself: in the biblical narrative composed after his death, the people justify his murder proleptically by reading Moses's breaking of the tablets as a figure for his having broken the law.

In this account of the murder of Moses, Freud drew on his analysis of the origins of society and religion in *Totem and Taboo*. There, as we've seen, Freud hypothesized that the first form of society was a primal horde of brothers, with a single father at its head. In time, the father was slain by his sons, who rebelled against his authority and sexual monopoly. To expiate their guilt, they then erected a totem in his place, whom they worshiped and propitiated with sacrifices. This, according to Freud, was the beginning of religion. Later, the totem was replaced by the figure of God, whose patriarchal qualities were a displaced version of the original father.[76]

Freud draws the conclusion that all religion derives its psychic power from the oedipal complex, whose social and political resolution produces both gods and godlike kings. This is the "historical truth" of religion, but it is a historical truth grounded on a material, psychological truth: "Psychoanalytic investigation of the individual teaches with especial emphasis that god is in every case modeled after the father . . . and that god at bottom is nothing but an exalted father" (*TT*, 190). Guilt at the murder of the primal father in turn produces the internalization of the father in the form of the psychological compulsion, that is, conscience and the strict, ethical observance of the law that is central to Judaism. Moses the Egyptian may have "made" the Jews, but far more powerful, for Freud, was the primal traumatic violence that his murder both activated and reenacted.

Jan Assmann has argued that, in identifying Moses as an Egyptian, Freud is deliberately breaking down the "Mosaic distinction"—the distinction between Hebrew monotheism and the cosmotheism of Egypt.[77] By cosmotheism, as we've seen, Assmann means the equation of God and nature, an equation that was recovered in the Renaissance through Horapollo's *Hieroglyphics* and that was quickly identified with Spinoza. Freud then would be trying to make Judaism more like Christianity, or vice versa, by equating all monotheism with the esoteric truth of cosmotheism, that is, with a monotheism like Akhenaton's—and Spinoza's—that was genuinely universal, open to all, and not just to the chosen people.[78] In support of Assmann, we could also say that Freud is trying to break down the Mosaic distinction by proposing a secular explanation of religion on the basis of universal, psychological attributes. In Freud's account, the psychological truth of the oedipal complex and the dynamic of the primal horde are not exclusive to Judaism. They are also at work in Christianity. Freud gives the example of the ritual of the Eucharist, which he claims reenacts "the content of the old totem meal." Similarly, the theology of Christianity effectively dethrones God the Father, in much the same way as the primal horde dethroned the primal father.[79] And yet Christianity, like Judaism, "has not escaped the fate of having to get rid of the father," which is to say the paternal, authoritarian structure of religion that, as Freud suggests in *The Future of an Illusion*, persists even in the Enlightenment and after, and continues to produce neurosis.

And yet, against Assmann, we could also say that in *Moses and Monotheism* Freud preserves the Mosaic distinction, that is, he insists on the difference between Judaism and Christianity.[80] He does so not only through his literal reading of figures, but also more generally through his Old Testament insistence on the law over against New Testament grace. Although Freud first presents Saint Paul as a political theologian, a "politico-religious agitator," whose doctrine of original sin made psychological sense, given the murder of the primal father, he then tells us that Paul's most brilliant creation was the "fantasy of atonement," the idea that "a son of God allowed himself to be killed without guilt and had thus taken on the guilt of all men." Whereas "Judaism had been a religion of the father; Christianity became a religion of the son." In doing so, it both universalized and destroyed Jewish monotheism. Unlike Judaism, which was a monotheism of the chosen people alone, Paul's religion restored the universality of the original monotheism of Akhenaton, which embraced all men. But in elevating Christ to the position of the godhead along with God the Father, and reinventing the "great mother-goddess" in the cult of Mary, Paul's religion "was no longer strictly monotheist." In a brilliant move that reverses the supersessionist claims of Christianity, Freud asserts that the new religion of Christianity involved a "cultural regression" to pagan polytheism. In contrast, the Jewish insistence on the law amounts to a higher form of reason and spirituality. "It was," Freud writes, "as though Egypt was taking vengeance once more on the heirs of Ikhnaton."[81] And this, according to Freud, in turn explains anti-Semitism: Judaism provokes hatred because of its exclusivity, its rigid upholding of the Mosaic distinction.[82]

In Freud's text, then, the Mosaic distinction itself is overdetermined. On the one hand, it seems to stand for Jewish iconoclasm against the Christian cult of images and the doctrine of the incarnation. On the other hand, it seems to stand for a sense of compulsion and psychic violence—the trace of the original trauma—that Christianity tries to sublate in its ethos of love. In both cases, Freud would be implicitly identifying his Egyptian Moses with Spinoza the fierce rationalist. But in the first case, it would be the rationalist who hopes to transcend the necessity of myth and narrative, the necessity of the appeal to fantasy, whereas in the second case, it would be the rationalist who recognizes the psychic force of the imagination, of fantasies and desires, that can't simply be sublated by reason. Far from being an iconoclast, this Spinoza acknowledges the necessity of myths and stories, narratives and rhetoric to appeal to and channel these forces.

We can now return to Freud's remarks to Lou Andreas-Salomé in 1935: "In *The Future of an Illusion* I expressed an essentially negative valuation of religion; later I found a formula that does better justice to it: its power is to be sure based on its truth content, but this truth is not a material but a historical one." In *Moses and Monotheism*, such historical truth is inseparable from the insight that "the man Moses" "made" the Jewish people, in much the same way that Michelangelo sculpted his *Moses* for the tomb of Pope Julius II. Freud thus presents the historical truth of Judaism as a contingent product of human history and human art, including the art of political theology. But he also presents all religion as an illusion whose historical power is predicated on the real or material truth—the powerful compulsion—of psychic needs and desires.[83] Religion is not simply a fiction in the sense of an artful illusion imposed by a single, heroic individual. It is also a powerfully compelling illusion whose "ground" is a communally shared fantasy of violence, a communally shared ambivalence about paternal authority.

This argument (which is, of course, an argument about the unconscious) has implications for Freud's activity as a writer and his authority as a theorist. While Freud clearly saw himself as a kind of Michelangelo figure, sculpting his Egyptian Moses, the text also bears signs of compulsion that Freud does not control. Given that the *Moses and Monotheism* we have is really three separately published essays, three separate efforts to come to terms with the figure of Moses the Egyptian and the history of monotheism, we could say that this last major work of Freud's dramatizes in quite spectacular fashion Freud's own repetition compulsion, his effort to master the historical trauma of monotheism, the trauma of being a Jew in the 1930s in Austria, and, not least of all, it's been argued, his oedipal relation to his observant Jewish father.[84] And, if we recall Freud's own powerful response to Michelangelo's *Moses* or his account of the uncanny power of Shakespeare's *Hamlet*, a power Freud famously attributed to its dramatization of the Oedipus complex, the founding compulsion of religion becomes even more difficult to distinguish from the compulsion of art.

In response, I think Freud would say that it is not the nature of the underlying desires that distinguishes religion from art or psychoanalysis, but the form that they take.[85] Religion takes the form of a communal neurosis that claims to offer a historical truth that cannot be refuted by reason. It is a neurosis in particular because it hands over to religious authority the autonomy that Freud thinks individuals should assume for themselves. (Hence, perhaps, Freud's representation of himself as a solitary individual in the deserted Church of San Pietro in Vincoli: a representation that conforms to the Renaissance individualism sketched by Burckhardt and even more to the individual's successful resolution of the oedipal complex, in contrast to its neurotic formation in the fantasy of religion.) Psychoanalysis—which, Freud argues, is a science and thus open to refutation—takes the form of exposing the material truth behind this fantasy, the material truth of fantasy, at the same time that it counsels liberation from the bonds of religion. Art for Freud makes no assertions and so does not need to be refuted, but it too, according to Freud, interprets our fantasies in a form that liberates rather than constrains. But both art and psychoanalysis may prove to be weak against the powerful illusions of religion.

In contrast to the earlier essays on Leonardo and Michelangelo, then, Freud's *Moses and Monotheism* offers a more pessimistic assessment of the future of religious illusion. Freud now suggests that something like political theology is—at least for many people—not just a political strategy but a principle of psychic life. As we've seen, Spinoza thought that political theology was necessary because most people are incapable of reason. In Freud's case, political theology is a principle of psychic life because religion reenacts in communal and, in Freud's view, neurotic form the oedipal conflict of the individual. This is true whether we consider political theology to involve the use of religion to mediate psychic and political conflict or to refer to the way theological notions of sacrifice provide an affective bond for communities, both assuaging guilt (for rebelling against authority) and creating new notions of authority (*TT*, 201, 193). In this way, Freudian psychoanalysis claims to provide a universal explanation for religion, but one that rejects the presumption of Pauline universalism to eradicate difference and transcend violence.

The question that inevitably follows is whether it is possible to live without such theologically charged symbols of authority. Freud clearly thought it was, if only for the few. Yirmiyahu Yovel has argued that Freud may not have been entitled even to this degree of optimism, given his own pessimistic account of human nature: "Freud saw the need to indicate (in his theory of transference) a source of libidinal energy by which resistance and repression can be removed. Where, then, in parallel manner, do we find the auxiliary eros by which the intellect (*logos*) is to win its long-fought battle against religion and for the demystified acceptance of *ananke* [necessity]?"[86] Freud himself anticipated this objection by putting it in the mouth of his critical interlocutor in *The Future of an Illusion*, who announces triumphantly: "I think I have now shown that your endeavours come down to an attempt to replace a proved and emotionally valuable illusion by another one, which is unproved and without emotional value."[87] As we've seen, in response Freud distinguished between illusions that are capable of correction (his own) and ones that are not (religious illusions), but he did not provide an answer to Yovel's question.

Freud clearly found one positive source of eros in "the artist's joy in creating" and another in the "scientist's in solving problems or discovering truths." At the same time, he confessed his own inability to explain such pleasures: "At present we can only say figuratively that such satisfactions seem 'finer' and 'higher.'"[88] As we've seen, however, this does not mean Freud was naive about or blind to the continuing power of religion. To the contrary, he consistently acknowledged it. And, in *The Future of an Illusion*, he even went so far as to predict that defenders of religion would use psychoanalysis to explain the affective charge of religion as something positive, thereby enlisting psychoanalysis itself in the service of political theology—construed here as the view that theology is politically necessary to bind citizens to the state.[89] As I argued in the introduction, this prediction has been borne out in modern criticism.

How much can Freud's view of Renaissance art help us as we think about the dangers of political theology? It's tempting to say that Freud's first illusion in his essays on Michelangelo and Leonardo was that art was merely the product of sublimated libido, except for the fact that Freud himself was so conscious of the limitations of psychoanalysis's genetic or economic explanation of art. Like Marx, he marveled that great works of art from the past continue to move us, and he did not think that tracing the subject matter of art to its "origins" in childhood could adequately account for art's continuing appeal. Nor did he think his "ars poetica"—the notion that the pleasure we derive from formal complexity is merely a lure and that the deeper pleasures of art come from the way aesthetic pleasure lifts our inhibitions—could offer a complete explanation of the power of Michelangelo, Leonardo, or Shakespeare.[90]

Paradoxically, Freud's own model of psychoanalysis may provide us with some help here. For Freud, psychoanalysis was both part of culture and an analysis of the tensions, contradictions, and conflicts that are constitutive of culture. Psychoanalysis so conceived performs the work of immanent critique in much the same way that scriptural hermeneutics did for Spinoza or allegory did for Benjamin. To the extent that psychoanalysis provides us not just with an economic model of drives but also a hermeneutic of culture, as Ricoeur has argued, it is compatible with these other, more capacious understandings of the work of culture, according to which cultural artifacts are not just symptoms of social and political contradictions but also an interpretation of them—and, at times, a critique. Art, which, in Freud's view, is cut loose from the reality principle, has a particular role to play here. As Herbert Marcuse claimed long ago, in a spirit admittedly more utopian than Freud's, "art challenges the prevailing principle of reason," and its sidekick, the ideologically laden reality principle.[91] Or as Adorno remarked, "culture, in the true sense, [does] not simply accommodate itself to human beings; but it always simultaneously [raises] a protest against petrified relations" under which individuals live.[92] By this definition, "culture in the true sense"—like psychoanalysis—is iconoclastic, a breaking of "petrified relations."

In the end, however, Freud does not promise us rationalism without remainder. If Freud's critique of religion has some affinity to Spinoza's political theology and to Feuerbach's critique of religion as man's first indirect form of self-consciousness, Freud does not believe that the disenchantment of religion—imagining for a second that such a thing were completely possible—could ever mean the full return of the subject to itself, in absolute self-consciousness.[93] In fact, by definition, there is no such thing in Freudian psychoanalysis, for this would mean discounting Freud's main discovery of the unconscious and its corollary: an enduring future for illusion, whether religious or artistic.[94] In his own version of the dialectic of enlightenment, demystification cannot fully eradicate illusion. In the end, Freud provides us with the tools for dismantling his own illusion that religious illusion might be superseded altogether, even as he gives us good reasons for preferring the very different illusions and secular pleasures of Renaissance art.

Coda

In *Spinoza and Other Heretics*, Yirmiyahu Yovel argued that Spinoza and Freud belong to a group of thinkers one might call "philosophers of the dark enlightenment," a group beginning in the early modern period with Machiavelli and Hobbes.

This process of dark enlightenment provoked a sharp awakening from religious and metaphysical illusions, incurring pain and conflict in its wake. For it challenged accepted self-images and enshrined cultural identities, and thereby endangered a whole range of vested psychological interests. But for these very reasons, it was also a movement of emancipation, serving to inspire a richer and more lucid self-knowledge in man, even at the price of unflattering consequences which often shock and dismay. This is the true 'Oedipal drive'—not of Freud's Oedipus but of the original protagonist of Sophocles' tragedy, of whom Freud himself is an avid follower. The Freudian Oedipus theory (regardless of how accurate it may be) is a modern way of fulfilling the wish for the mythological king who did not rest until he discovered the hidden truth about himself and his real situation in the world, even

at the price of tragedy and the loss of his two eyes. Freud, like
the other 'dark enlighteners,' brought to light the hidden layers
in human existence buried in unconscious depths and whose
budding consciousness has long been repressed.[1]

Yovel helps us to see that the early modern/late modern debate I have
been tracing is, ultimately, a debate about the Enlightenment and its
values of lucidity, heightened self-consciousness, and demystified self-
knowledge. But what is interesting about the moderns whom I have
engaged in this book is that they looked not to the eighteenth century
but to the Renaissance, which they read as the true break with earlier
theological modes of explanation, the true "origin" of a new conception
of reason not grounded in any transcendent or supernatural element,
the true prefiguration of modernity.

Freud, of course, was not naive about the values of lucidity and demystified self-knowledge. Although he wrote that the goal of psychoanalysis was "to strengthen the ego, to make it more independent of the
super-ego, to widen its field of perception and enlarge its organization,
so that it can appropriate fresh portions of the id," he was also aware
of the forces and energies militating against this goal. In Yovel's words,
"From this point of view Freud stands midway between Nietzsche
and Spinoza. Like Spinoza, he accepts the principle of intellectual self-
knowledge and the value of truth as a nonrelative ideal; like Nietzsche,
he acknowledges the limitations and the fragility of this ideal and the
volcanic depths seething beneath it."[2]

Yovel goes on to make the point that a critical philosophy of immanence of the sort adumbrated by Freud must ultimately be a philosophy
of finitude:

> As finite beings we can neither affirm the transcendent domain
> nor rid ourselves completely of its empty yet meaningful hori-
> zon. By 'empty' I mean that it cannot be filled with any positive
> contents or even be asserted to exist. Yet this empty horizon is
> meaningful as a memento of our own finitude.[3]

In Blumenberg's terms, we could say that transcendence has been reoccupied by finitude, and that this reoccupation generates an account of
value as neither transcendent nor merely relative: "A critical philosophy of immanence rejects the timelessness of man-made norms as well
as their dismissal as meaningless. Humans exist by placing value on
things beyond their naturally given state. This is the way we transcend

ourselves and give our lives structure, meaning, direction and identity for which it is worthwhile struggling and making sacrifices even in the absence of timeless absolutes."[4] Placing values on things might be described as the activity of fiction-making, but we should not construe such values as "mere fictions," since this would involve passing judgment on them from the position of absolute transcendence, which is not a position we can occupy.

For this reason, among others, I remain unpersuaded by the arguments of Strauss and Schmitt, both trying in their different ways to resist what they described as the historicism and relativism of modern life, Strauss by recovering a classical notion of reason and natural right, Schmitt by advocating a Catholic paradigm of political representation and concrete order against a liberal idea of the law and formal equality. It has been one of the wagers of this book that Strauss and Schmitt are worth engaging nevertheless for their often brilliant and always provocative analyses of early modern texts: worth engaging because they saw the turn to poiesis in the early modern period, even though they were wrong to see this as the source of the ills of modern life. Against their reactionary stance, the early modernisms of Machiavelli, Hobbes, Shakespeare, and Spinoza, and the later modernism of Kantorowicz, Cassirer, and Benjamin, seem more attuned to the capacity of human beings to create the values that bind them and give their lives meaning. In their different ways, each understood the profound insight that Hannah Arendt articulated in her essay "On Authority" and that has inspired the project of this book: "To live in a political realm with neither authority nor the concomitant awareness that the source of authority transcends power and those who are in power, means to be confronted anew, without the religious trust in a sacred beginning and without the protection of traditional and therefore self-evident standards of behavior, by the elementary problems of human living-together."

Notes

PREFACE

1. Strauss and Arendt are also deeply engaged with Nietzsche and Heidegger, not least of all with Heidegger's ideas
about "poetry" or *Dichtung*, but that engagement is well
beyond the scope of this book.

INTRODUCTION

1. See Charles Taylor, *A Secular Age* (Cambridge: Harvard
University Press, 2007); Giorgio Agamben, *The Time That
Remains: A Commentary on the Letter to the Romans*, trans.
Patricia Daley (Stanford: Stanford University Press, 2005);
Slavoj Žižek, *The Fragile Absolute* (London: Verso, 2000), and
On Belief (London: Routledge, 2001); Terry Eagleton, *Reason,
Faith, and Revolution: Reflections on the God Debate* (New
Haven: Yale University Press, 2009). See also Jürgen Habermas
et al., *An Awareness of What Is Missing: Faith and Reason in a
Post-Secular Age*, trans. Ciaran Cronin (Cambridge, UK: Polity
Press, 2010); and Habermas and Joseph Ratzinger, *The Dia-
lectics of Secularization: On Reason and Religion*, trans. Brian
McNeil, C.R.V. (San Francisco: Ignatius Press, 2006). Habermas has elaborated his own turn to religion as a cognitive
resource in *Religion and Rationality: Essays on Reason, God,
and Modernity*, ed. Eduardo Mendieta (Cambridge: MIT Press,
2002), and *Between Naturalism and Religion* (Cambridge, UK:
Polity Press, 2008). The term "political theology" first appears
in the work of Marcus Varro and Saint Augustine, resur-
faces in Spinoza (as "theologico-politicus") and others in the

seventeenth century, and reappears in modern times in the work of Giuseppe Mazzini and Mikhail Bakunin. For the history of the term, see Hent de Vries's introduction to *Political Theologies*, ed. de Vries and Lawrence E. Sullivan (New York: Fordham University Press, 2006), esp. 25–26.

2. See Stephen D. Smith, *The Disenchantment of Secular Discourse* (Cambridge: Harvard University Press, 2010), criticizing John Rawls, among others.

3. A very recent exception is the collection of essays *Political Theology and Early Modernity*, ed. Graham Hammill and Julia Reinhard Lupton (Chicago: University of Chicago Press, 2012).

4. In the following pages, I refer to the early twentieth-century figures as "modern," and to the present moment (2012) as contemporary.

5. Although it's often assumed that the early modern period subscribed to the political theology of the divine right of kings, numerous writers in the period posed serious challenges to the divine legitimation of political power. The political influence of the papacy in Italy, the religious wars on the continent, and sectarian strife in England all prompted contemporaries to rethink the relationship between religion and the state. In one strain of this rethinking, a number of radical religious movements across Europe stressed the subversive political potential of the theological appeal to conscience and argued for a religiously inspired republican, protodemocratic, or anarchist critique of the state. There is a distinguished secondary literature on these radical religious movements in the Reformation, one that modern historians and theorists of political theology would do well to remember. The moderns I focus on in this book, however, were concerned with a very different understanding of politics and theology in the sixteenth and seventeenth centuries. For them, what was central was the critique of theological modes of understanding and the emergence of a new, secular understanding of the sphere of politics and the state.

6. See Jacques Derrida, "Force of Law: The 'Mystical Foundation of Authority,'" in *Deconstruction and the Possibility of Justice, Cardozo Law Review* 11 (1990): 919–1046 ; "Faith and Knowledge: The Two Sources of 'Religion' at the Limits of Reason Alone," trans. Samuel Weber, in *Religion*, ed. Derrida and Gianni Vattimo (Stanford: Stanford University Press, 1998), 163: "the fundamental concepts that often permit us to isolate or to *pretend* to isolate the *political* . . . remain religious or in any case theologico-political." Derrida's attitude toward religion is contested. On this point, see Neil Saccamano, "Inheriting Enlightenment, or Keeping Faith with Reason in Derrida," *Eighteenth-Century Studies* 40 (2007): 405–24. See also Stanley Fish, "Are There Secular Reasons?," February 22, 2010, http://opinionator.blogs.nytimes.com/2010/02/22/are-there-secular-reasons/, and "Does Reason Know What It Is Missing?," April 12, 2010, http://opinionator.blogs.nytimes.com/2010/04/12/does-reason-know-what-it-is-missing/; Agamben, *The Time That Remains*; and Hent de Vries, *Religion and Violence: Philosophical Perspectives from Kant to Derrida* (Baltimore: Johns Hopkins University Press, 2002), 235–36. William E. Connolly, *Why I Am Not a Secularist* (Minneapolis: University of Minnesota Press, 2000), also forms part of this conversation, insofar as Connolly argues that secularists have been intolerant of the religious perspective in the public sphere.

7. Michael Allen Gillespie, *The Theological Origins of Modernity* (Chicago: University of Chicago Press, 2008), 270, 280. See also 271–73, 286.

8. Claude Lefort, "The Permanence of the Theologico-Political?," in *Democracy and Political Theory*, trans. David Macey (Minneapolis: University of Minnesota Press, 1988), 222–23.

9. Eric L. Santner, *The Royal Remains: The People's Two Bodies and the Endgames of Sovereignty* (Chicago: University of Chicago Press, 2011), 5.

10. Quoted in Santner, *Royal Remains*, 21; cf. 30. See also Santner, *On the Psychotheology of Everyday Life* (Chicago: University of Chicago Press, 2001), 116: for Rosenzweig, "revelation opens up the possibility of converting what had functioned as a support of ideological captivation into a locus of suspension and interruption. Revelation converts the 'surplus cause' of our relational surrender, our passionate attachments to ideological formations—or various forms of *idolatry*—into a 'remnant' of them." In *Political Theology: Four New Chapters on the Concept of Sovereignty* (New York: Columbia University Press, 2011), Paul W. Kahn argues for a specifically modern American version of political theology: not the notion that the state is subordinated to the church but the idea that popular sovereignty (like Schmitt's sovereign) has the power to decide the exception and that it is impossible to understand citizens' willingness to sacrifice themselves for the state without recourse to theological ideas (18–19). Later, he asserts that modern political theology is a secular inquiry into the analogies between "the political and the religious in the social imaginary . . . entirely independent of any beliefs about God and Church" (124). I discuss this argument at greater length in chapter 4.

11. See Debora Kuller Shuger, *Political Theologies in Shakespeare's England: The Sacred and the State in "Measure for Measure"* (Houndsmills, UK: Palgrave Macmillan, 2001), on political theology as divine right. See also Regina Schwartz, *Sacramental Poetics at the Dawn of Secularism* (Stanford: Stanford University Press, 2008); and Ken Jackson and Arthur Marotti, "The Turn to Religion in Early Modern English Studies," *Criticism* 46 (2004): 167–90. In *Citizen-Saints* (Chicago: University of Chicago Press, 2005), Julia Reinhard Lupton traces the emergence of a protoliberal idea of citizenship from within Pauline universalism. She pursues her interest in the liberal potential of political theology in *Thinking with Shakespeare* (Chicago: University of Chicago Press, 2011) and subsequent essays. Lupton seeks to "develop an approach to political theology for early modern studies that remains faithful to the potentialities and achievements of liberalism" ("Invitation to a Totem Meal: Hans Kelsen, Carl Schmitt, and Political Theology," in *The Return to Theory in Early Modern English Studies*, ed. Paul Cefalu and Bryan Reynolds [Houndsmills, UK: Palgrave Macmillan, 2011], 123). See also Graham L. Hammill, *The Mosaic Constitution: Political Theology and Imagination from Machiavelli to Milton* (Chicago: University of Chicago Press, 2012). In Hammill's view, political theology is an effect of secularization, but "the problem with constituting power is that it endlessly falls into theological modes of thinking and representation." He goes on to clarify that he does "not mean to suggest that political communities are determined by God or Platonic ideals but rather that political making assumes supplemental discourses—myths and founding fictions—that

play the role of the transcendent for particular political communities" (5).
Elsewhere, however, Hammill seems to equate the capacity for metaphor with
the theological imaginary and the capacity for transcendence with the divine.
See 10–11 on Blumenberg and 75 on Spinoza.

12. See *PT*. In *Meaning in History* (Chicago: University of Chicago Press,
1949), Karl Löwith argued that modern teleological versions of history,
including the historicist kind elaborated by Hegel, were secularized versions
of the Christian providential notion of history, but he criticized both models
as unconvincing attempts to impose meaning on the flux of history. See Jeffrey
Andrew Barash, "The Sense of History: On the Political Implications of Karl
Löwith's Concept of Secularization," *History and Theory* 37 (1998): 69–82.
I discuss the concept of secularization in the introduction to a special journal
issue, "Early Modern Secularism," *Representations* 105 (2009): 1–11.

13. Hannah Arendt, "On Authority," *Between Past and Future: Six Exercises in Political Thought* (Cleveland: Meridian Books, 1968), 102.

14. See Hans Blumenberg, *The Legitimacy of the Modern Age*, trans.
Robert M. Wallace (1966; Cambridge: MIT Press, 1995), 3–124. A full legitimation of curiosity required the *deus absconditus* (absent God) of nominalist
theology, who vacates the world and thus makes room for human activity,
including aesthetic activity. With the legitimation of curiosity, the question of
salvation did not disappear but was instead reoccupied by an interest in what
one could expect from the secular world. See the discussion of Petrarch and
aesthetic curiosity, 341–46.

15. Ibid., 65 and 80 (on reoccupation), and 446–47, 453 (citing Vico). We
could call this modern project the project of autofoundation and the critique
of transcendence. See Carole Widmaier, "Leo Strauss et le problème de la sécularisation," in *Modernité et sécularisation: Hans Blumenberg, Karl Löwith,
Carl Schmitt, Leo Strauss*, ed. Michael Foessel, Jean-François Kervégan, and
Myriam Revault d'Allones (Paris: CNRS, 2007), 81–91. Strikingly, Blumenberg presents his defense of early modernity and critique of the secularization
thesis as a critique of Carl Schmitt: see *Legitimacy of the Modern Age*, 94–101.
On Blumenberg's critique of Schmitt in his later work, see Graham Hammill,
"Blumenberg and Schmitt on the Rhetoric of Political Theology," in Hammill
and Lupton, *Political Theology and Early Modernity*, 84–101.

16. Hannah Arendt, "Religion and Politics," in *Essays in Understanding,
1930–1954*, ed. Jerome Kohn (New York, 1994), 372; cited by Samuel Moyn,
"Hannah Arendt on the Secular," *New German Critique* 105 (2008): 76.

17. In "The Political," in *The Power of Religion in the Public Sphere*, ed.
Eduardo Mendieta and Jonathan Vanantwerpen (New York: Columbia University Press, 2011), Jürgen Habermas implicitly criticizes this equation of the
political with the symbolic resources of religion. He first defines "the political"
in early societies in terms of the essentially religious symbolic legitimation of
political authority: "It is this symbolic dimension of the fusion of politics and
religion for the description of which the concept of 'the political' can properly
be used" (18). But Habermas goes on to argue that, under "the completely
changed conditions of the modern period," "the political" finds "an impersonal
embodiment in the normative dimension of a democratic constitution" (21).

18. Moyn, "Hannah Arendt on the Secular," 95. According to Moyn, "the religious idea of miracles as a model of political revolution is precisely the case that Schmitt himself cited as the best evidence for political theology" (96). Moyn's main argument is that Arendt is defending a secular notion of politics, but he thinks her use of theological metaphors shows that "far from contradicting her argument about the difficulty of overcoming political theology, Arendt *performs* it, unwittingly" (96).

19. This seems to be the point of Blumenberg's critique of Schmitt in *The Legitimacy of the Modern Age*, 89–102, esp. 93–94.

20. Erich Auerbach, *Mimesis: The Representation of Reality in Western Literature*, trans. Willard R. Trask (Princeton: Princeton University Press, 1953). I discuss Auerbach's reading of Dante in chapter 2.

21. Erich Auerbach, *Literary Language and Its Public in Late Latin Antiquity and the Middle Ages*, trans. Ralph Mannheim (Princeton: Princeton University Press, 1993), 7. On Vico, see also Auerbach, "Vico and Aesthetic Historicism," in *Scenes from the Drama of European Literature* (1959; Minneapolis: University of Minnesota Press, 1984), 183–200; and Auerbach, "Philology and *Weltliteratur*," trans. Maire Said and Edward Said, *Centennial Review* 13 (Winter 1969): 1–17.

22. Auerbach, "Vico and Aesthetic Historicism," 189.

23. Auerbach, *Literary Language and Its Public*, 12, 13.

24. Edward W. Said, *The World, the Text, and the Critic* (Cambridge: Harvard University Press, 1983), 291, 26, 27.

25. Ibid., 292.

26. On Auerbach's engagement with theological-political questions, see Jane O. Newman, "Force and Justice: Auerbach's Pascal," in Hammill and Lupton, *Political Theology and Early Modernity*, 159–80; and Earl Jeffrey Richards, "Erich Auerbach's *Mimesis* as a Meditation on the Shoah," *German Politics and Society* 59 (2001): 62–91, cited in Newman.

27. Carl Schmitt's argument in *The Concept of the Political* that anything can become political once it becomes the vehicle of "the most intense and extreme antagonism" is relevant here (*CP*, 29).

28. Hannah Arendt, *The Human Condition* (Chicago: University of Chicago Press, 1958), 272. See also 299 and 264.

29. Ibid., 295; see also 301 and 308 on poiesis. Elsewhere, Arendt argued explicitly that "the modern suspicion towards man's truth-receiving capacities" led Vico to "turn his attention from natural science to history, which he thought to be the only sphere where man could obtain certain knowledge, precisely because he dealt here only with the products of human activity" (298).

30. Ibid., 306.

31. Ibid., 296. See Martin Heidegger, "The Age of the World Picture," in *The Question concerning Technology and Other Essays*, trans. William Lovitt (New York: Harper and Row, 1977), 134. All of this was a baleful development for Arendt, especially the shift to understanding fabrication in terms of process rather than the finished product. For this idea of process undermined the notion of "fixed and permanent standards" of judgment and an "inherent *telos*" of human nature. This disaster was compounded by the Christian

reversal of classical values, which gave rise to the notion that life itself, and ultimately mere biological life, was the highest good. Once "the [pagan] aspiration towards immortality" was "equated with vainglory," individual life "came to occupy the position once held by the 'life' of the body politic" (*Human Condition*, 314).

32. Arendt, *Human Condition*, 304, 307, 314, 313 (*homo laborans*).

33. Hannah Arendt, "The Crisis in Culture," *Between Past and Future: Six Exercises in Political Thought* (Cleveland: World, 1968), 220.

34. Ibid., 223.

35. At issue was the interpretation of article 48 of the German Constitution, which, Schmitt argued, permitted Hindenburg to establish temporary dictatorial powers against extremist parties, including the National Socialists. See *PT*, 11–12; George Schwab's introduction to *PT*, xix–xx; and Joseph Bendersky, *Carl Schmitt, Theorist for the Reich* (Princeton: Princeton University Press, 1983). Lutz P. Koepnik contests this interpretation in "The Spectacle, the *Trauerspiel*, and the Politics of Resolution: Benjamin Reading the Baroque Reading Weimar," *Critical Inquiry* 22 (1996): 283.

36. Carl Schmitt, "Der Führer schütz das Recht: Zur Reichstagsrede Adolf Hitlers vom 13. Juli 1934," *Deutsche-Juristen Zeitung* 39 (1934): cols. 945–50, reprinted in Schmitt, *Positionen und Begriffe im Kampf mit Weimar-Genf-Versailles, 1923–1939* (Berlin: Duncker und Humblot, 1994). For a discussion of this article and the argument that Schmitt was forced to write it, see David Bates, "Political Theology and the Nazi State: Carl Schmitt's Concept of the Institution," *Modern Intellectual History* 3 (2006): 415–42

37. Leo Strauss, *Natural Right and History* (Chicago: University of Chicago Press, 1953), 42.

38. Ibid., 52 and 61.

39. I owe this information and the following reference to Jane O. Newman. See Hew Strachan, *The First World War: To Arms* (Oxford: Oxford University Press, 2003), 1116–17. Newman also argues that the German bombing of Belgium and France during World War I was justified by a "Lutheran 'war theology'": see her "Enchantment in Times of War: Aby Warburg, Walter Benjamin, and the Secularization Thesis," *Representations* 105 (2009): 133–67.

40. Eric Voegelin, *Political Religions*, trans. T. J. DiNapoli and E. S. Easterly (Lewiston, NY: E. Mellen Press, 1986), and Raymond Aron, "The Future of Secular Religions," *The Dawn of Universal History: Selected Essays from a Witness to the Twentieth Century*, trans. Barbara Bray (New York: Basic Books, 2002), 177–202. Voegelin traces the political and spiritual crisis signaled by the rise of Nazi Germany to "the secularization of the spirit" which is a consequence of "the concept of humanism" (3). But he also saw Nazism as a degenerate pseudoreligion: "Even where the secular *Ekklesia* finds itself in a sharp debate with the Christian Church on religious matters, as in German National Socialism, even there, the basic form of mystical *corpus*, bound by the *Pneuma* into an entity, lives in the furtherance of spiritual conformity" (37). See also 66: "The engendering of the myth and its propagation through the newspaper and radio, through speeches and communal festivals, gatherings and parades, the planning for and the dying in war, are the intramundane

forms of the *unio mystica*." Voegelin sees the Führer as a latter-day Hobbesian sovereign (68). See also Franz Neumann, *Behemoth: The Structure and Practice of National Socialism, 1933–1944* (London: Oxford University Press, 1942), 83–98 on the charismatic leader in the Nazi state, whose origins Neumann traced to the early modern period, specifically to the theology of Calvin, as well as to the tradition of thaumaturgic kingship. For more on the specifically Nazi connotations of political theology, see Karl Loewenstein, *Hitler's Germany: The Nazi Background to War*, 2nd ed. (New York, 1940), and David Bates, who discusses Neumann's "secularized theology of the Nazi state" in his "Political Theology and the Nazi State," 418. On the use of the term "political theology" in twentieth-century Germany, see also John Stroup, "Political Theology and Secularization Theory in Germany, 1918–1939: Emanuel Hirsch as a Phenomenon of His Time," *Harvard Theological Review* 80 (1987): 321–68, and Uriel Tal, "On Structures of Political Theology and Myth prior to the Holocaust," in *The Holocaust as Historical Experience*, ed. Yehuda Bauer and Nathan Rotenstreich (New York: Holmes and Meier, 1981), 43–74.

41. Barash, "Sense of History," 74, summarizing Löwith. Not all of the early moderns thought political theology or its religious sources were pernicious. Benjamin had a complicated relation to messianism, whose utopian potential he tried to salvage. According to Barash, the same was true of Ernst Bloch, who thought "the major mistake of orthodox Marxism arose from its inability to integrate and demystify the religious aspirations that, over the past centuries, have constantly nourished social demands." Thus Bloch declared, "There will be no successful attack on the irrational front without dialectical intervention, no rationalization and conquest of these areas without its own 'theology,' adjusted to the always still irrational revolutionary content." See Barash, 80 n. 20.

42. See Anson Rabinbach, *In the Shadow of Catastrophe: German Intellectuals between Apocalypse and the Enlightenment* (Berkeley: University of California Press, 1997), 39.

43. Walter Benjamin, "Theologico-Political Fragment," in *Reflections*, ed. Peter Demetz, trans. Edmund Jephcott (New York: Harcourt Brace Jovanovich, 1978), 312.

44. Strauss traced the origins of liberalism to the early modern period, while Schmitt located full-blown liberalism in the nineteenth century. Still, as we'll see, even Schmitt saw Spinoza, and eventually Hobbes, as the beginning of modern liberalism.

45. Strauss, *Natural Right and History*, 35–80.

46. *PT*, 36. See *PT*, 46, where Schmitt describes his method in exploring the concept of sovereignty as "a sociology of juristic concepts": "The presupposition of this kind of sociology of juristic concepts is thus a radical conceptualization, a consistent thinking that is pushed into metaphysics and theology. The metaphysical image that a definite epoch forges of the world has the same structure as what the world immediately understands to be appropriate as a form of its political organization. The determination of such an identity is the sociology of the concept of sovereignty." See also David William Bates, *States of War: Enlightenment Origins of the Political* (New York: Columbia

University Press, 2012), 19–24 on Schmitt's concept of "the political." Bates writes: "For Schmitt, the concept of the political was first revealed in the early-modern period, because the [early modern and especially Hobbesian] state emancipated itself from the completing logics of theology and morality" (23).

47. Carl Schmitt, *Political Romanticism*, trans. Guy Oakes (Cambridge: MIT Press, 1986), 17–18: "To a great extent, it holds true that different and, indeed, mundane factors have taken the place of God: humanity, the nation, the individual, historical development, or even life as life for its own sake, in its complete spiritual emptiness and mere dynamic. This does not mean that the attitude is no longer metaphysical. . . . What human beings regard as the ultimate, absolute authority, however, certainly can change, and God can be replaced by mundane and worldly factors. I call this secularization."

48. *TM*, 297.

49. In the words of Peter E. Gordon, Cassirer "wished to show how an essentially Kantian theory regarding the formative powers of transcendental consciousness might guide his own inquiry into the nature of scientific symbolism as well as the 'deeper' and historically prior modes of symbolic expression such as language and myth." See *Continental Divide: Heidegger, Cassirer, Davos* (Cambridge: Harvard University Press, 2010), 13.

50. See Ernst Cassirer, *Individual and Cosmos in Renaissance Philosophy*, trans. Mario Domandi (New York: Barnes and Noble, 1963). For Cassirer the new primacy of form was not at all equivalent to mere subjectivism but rather to a proto-Kantian dialectic of subject and object. In the Renaissance, he writes, "[t]he antinomy freedom-necessity is transformed into a correlation. For the common characteristic joining the world of pure knowledge to that of artistic creation is that both are dominated, in different ways, by a moment of genuine intellectual generation. In Kantian language, they both go beyond any 'copy' view of the given; they must become an 'architectonic' construction of the cosmos. As science and art become more *conscious* that their primary function is to give form, they conceive of the law to which they are subject more and more as an expression of their essential freedom" (143; see also 51 and 159–61). This view of the new centrality of form-giving in the Renaissance, in contrast to the Middle Ages, is shared by Erwin Panofsky in *Renaissance and Renascences in Western Art* (New York: Harper and Row, 1972).

51. Leo Strauss, review of *The Myth of the State*, in *Social Research* 14 (1947): 128; this review is republished in Strauss, *What Is Political Philosophy? and Other Studies* (Chicago: University of Chicago Press, 1988), 292–96.

52. *CP*, 72. For an argument that Schmitt does have an idea of culture that is based on his idea of *nomos* as the "structure-determining convergence of order and orientation," see David Pan, "Historical Event and Mythic Meaning in Carl Schmitt's *Hamlet or Hecuba*," afterword to *Carl Schmitt's "Hamlet or Hecuba*," ed. Jennifer R. Rust and Julia Reinhard Lupton, trans. Pan and Rust (New York: Telos Press, 2009), 78. See also 82: "the sovereign's decision is always bounded by a cultural understanding of that which constitutes the group's way of life and consequently what would threaten this constitution." Such a notion of culture, I note, utterly precludes its critical or antagonistic relation to the status quo.

53. See Julia Reinhard Lupton, *Afterlives of the Saints: Hagiography, Typology, and Renaissance Literature* (Stanford: Stanford University Press, 1996), chap. 1, for a compelling discussion of the differences between Burckhardt's *Kulturgeschichte* and Benjamin's method in the *Trauerspiel* book. Lupton reads Benjamin's emphasis on the ruin as analogous to the Jewish remnant or that which is excluded from "the dominant historiography," which is modeled on Christian typology (30). Lupton also calls attention to Benjamin's "Theologico-Political Fragment" of the early 1920s, where "Benjamin distinguishes the messiah from the ends of history in order to reassert the sublime gap between the sacred and profane articulated by allegory" (32).

54. See now the magisterial account of Benjamin's exploration of the relevance of the baroque to interwar political and cultural debate by Jane O. Newman, *Benjamin's Library: Modernity, Nation, and the Baroque* (Ithaca: Cornell University Press, 2011). For Benjamin's attempt to distance himself in the *Trauerspiel* book from his earlier engagement with conservative cultural politics of Gustav Wyneken, see John McCole, *Walter Benjamin and the Antinomies of Tradition* (Ithaca: Cornell University Press, 1993). In his later essays, as is well known, Benjamin explicitly criticized the fascist aestheticizing of politics. See Walter Benjamin, "The Author as Producer," in *The Essential Frankfurt School Reader*, ed. Andrew Arato and Eike Gebhardt (New York: Continuum, 1982), 254–69.

55. Although Cassirer was critical of the influence of Machiavelli and Hobbes on the myth of the state, his lifelong work was a celebration of the human capacity for culture. It took the experience of World War II and exile in the United States for Cassirer to finally turn his attention to "the myth of the state," including the modern "political theology" of Nazism. On Cassirer's Kantianism, see Edward Sidelsky, *Ernst Cassirer: The Last Philosopher of Culture* (Princeton: Princeton University Press, 2008).

56. As Steven B. Smith has argued in *Spinoza, Liberalism, and the Question of Jewish Identity* (New Haven: Yale University Press, 1997), "The Jewish Question was not an incidental or peripheral aspect of the Enlightenment but an integral part of it. The Jews were, even for the most advanced thinkers of the *Aufklärung*, the quintessential 'Other,' the exotic or 'Oriental,' a vestige of the East within the West. The capacity to assimilate this Other would be the true test of the program of emancipation through *Bildung*" (167). On *Bildung*, see "Bildung," in *Geschichtliche Grundbegriffe*, ed. Otto Brunner, Werner Conze, and Reinhardt Koselleck (Stuttgart: Klett-Cotta, 1972); Josef Chytry, *The Aesthetic State: A Quest in Modern German Thought* (Berkeley: University of California Press, 1989); George L. Mosse, *German Jews beyond Judaism* (Bloomington: Indiana University Press, 1985), and Mosse, "Jewish Emancipation: Between Bildung and Respectability," in *The Jewish Response to German Culture: From the Enlightenment to the Second World War*, ed. Jehuda Reinharz and Walter Schatzbert (Hanover: University Press of New England, 1985), 1–16; Robert A. Pois, *Friedrich Meinecke and German Politics in the Twentieth Century* (Berkeley: University of California Press, 1972), chap. 5; Geoffrey Hartman, appendix, "Culture and Civilization," in *The Fate of Reading* (Chicago: University of Chicago Press, 1984).

57. Marx, paraphrasing Bauer, in "On the Jewish Question," in *The Marx-Engels Reader*, ed. Robert C. Tucker (New York: Norton, 1972), 25. For the similarities between Bauer and Carl Schmitt, see Raphael Gross, *Carl Schmitt and the Jews*, trans. Joel Golb (Madison: University of Wisconsin Press, 2007), 111–12, 117. Gross argues that Schmitt's debate with Hans Kelsen about constitutional law "can . . . be read as a continuation of the debates about Jewish emancipation between Bauer and Marx. . . . In polemicizing against the idea of 'pure' legal theory advocated by Kelsen, Schmitt made particular use of Bauer's attack on what he saw as the abstract, positive nature of Jewish law" (131).

58. Marx, "On the Jewish Question," 28.

59. Ibid., 43.

60. Ibid., 36, 50.

61. Ibid., 46: "What is the profane basis of Judaism? *Practical* need, *self-interest*. What is the worldly cult of the Jew? *Huckstering*. What is his worldly god? *Money*."

62. Ibid., 47. In the *Grundrisse*, Marx attributed these characteristics not to Jews but to Lutherans. See Enzo Traverso, *The Marxists and the Jewish Question*, trans. Bernard Gibbons (Atlantic Highlands, NJ: Humanities Press, 1990). Traverso argues that this "demonstrates that for Marx—at least in his maturity—the 'cult of money' was not a Jewish specificity and that his argument was not inspired by an anti-Semitic prejudice" (21). For a subtle appreciation both of Marx's anti-Judaism and the centrality of Judaism as a social power in Marx's theory, see Dennis Fischman, "The Jewish Question about Marx," *Polity* 21 (1989): 755–75, esp. 767: "As a religion, [Marx] holds Judaism in greatest contempt. As a social power, on the other hand, Marx regards Judaism as supremely important. What Marx chooses to call 'Jewish' is nothing less than the driving force of his social and political theory: the reality of human need, as expressed in the contradictions of capitalist society."

63. Marx, "On the Jewish Question," 46, 51.

64. As Theodor Adorno wrote in "Freudian Theory and Fascist Propaganda," in Arato and Gebhardt, *Essential Frankfurt School Reader*, 134: "the objective aims of fascism are largely irrational in so far as they contract the material interests of great numbers of those whom they try to embrace, notwithstanding the prewar boom of the first years of the Hitler regime."

65. Initially associated with Hegel's *Geistesgeschichte*, the progress of reason or spirit in history, by the early twentieth century historicism had come to embrace a variety of historiographical approaches from Dilthey's *Geisteswissenschaften* and Ranke's attempt to capture "wie es eigentlich gewesen [ist]" (how it really was) to the Hegelian political history of Friedrich Meinecke, the cultural history of Jacob Burckhardt, and Ernst Troeltsch's sociology of religion. Wilhelm Dilthey distinguished between natural sciences (*Naturwissenschaften*), which seek causal explanations, and the historical and textual sciences or *Geisteswissenschaften*, which require hermeneutical "understanding." Of particular concern was the way historicism produced a crisis of religious faith. Allan Megill argues in particular for the theological origins of the crisis of historicism in "Why Was There a Crisis of Historicism?," *History and Theory* 36 (1997): 416–29. Efforts to investigate the historical life of

Jesus prompted skepticism about his existence, just as scriptural hermeneutics exposed contradictions in the biblical text that were corrosive to faith. On the theological dimension of the crisis of historicism, see also Jeffrey Andrew Barash, *Martin Heidegger and the Problem of Historical Meaning*, rev. ed. (New York: Fordham University Press, 2003); and Thomas Albert Howard, *Religion and the Rise of Historicism: W. M. L. de Wette, Jacob Burckhardt, and the Theological Origins of Nineteenth-Century Historical Consciousness* (Cambridge: Cambridge University Press, 2000). The primary and secondary literature on historicism is enormous. In addition to the works already cited, see Ernst Troeltsch, "Die Krisis des Historismus," in *Die Neue Rundschau* 33 (1922): 572–90; Troeltsch, *Der Historismus und seine Probleme* (Tübingen: J. C. B. Mohr, 1922); Friedrich Meinecke, *Historism*, trans. J. E. Anderson (1936; n.p.: Herder and Herder, 1972). More recently, see Georg Iggers, *The German Concept of History*, rev. ed. (1966; Wesleyan, CT: Wesleyan University Press, 1988); Charles R. Bambach, *Heidegger, Dilthey, and the Crisis of Historicism* (Ithaca: Cornell University Press, 1995); Paul Hamilton, *Historicism* (London: Routledge, 1996); David N. Myers, *Resisting History: Historicism and Its Discontents in German-Jewish Thought* (Princeton: Princeton University Press, 2003); and Jeffrey Andrew Barash, *Politiques de l'histoire: L'historicisme comme promesse et comme mythe* (Paris: Presses Universitaires de France, 2004). For a discussion of historicism that doesn't identify it with nineteenth-century Hegelianism, see Donald R. Kelley, *Foundations of Modern Historical Scholarship* (New York: Columbia University Press, 1970), introduction.

66. To give just one example, for Benjamin, in the early decades of the twentieth century, culture emerged as an issue in debates about Zionism as a possible solution to the Jewish Question. The young Benjamin expressed his enthusiasm for a new journal founded by the Zionist Ludwig Strauss with the following comment: "Precisely for the Jewish Question we need an area where the Jewish spirit can be isolated and reveal its nature." But, as we've seen, Benjamin rejected Strauss's Zionism. As Anson Rabinbach summarizes Benjamin's break with Strauss, "from the standpoint of 'liberal culture,' Zionism had to be rejected." Benjamin's concern with culture would intensify after the First World War, which he and many of his contemporaries interpreted "in terms of the collapse of Western culture and the triumph of technology and civilization." See Rabinbach, *In the Shadow of Catastrophe: German Intellectuals between Apocalypse and the Enlightenment* (Berkeley: University of California Press, 1997), 43 and 47.

67. The questions raised here about the relationship between culture and politics, and between modernity and the early modern period, resonate beyond the circle I have described—in both time and space. In *The Protestant Ethic and the Spirit of Capitalism*, Max Weber traced the defining features of modern culture and politics—the capitalist work ethic and instrumental reason—to the Protestant Reformation. Other early twentieth-century scholars of the Renaissance saw their work as intervening in late nineteenth- and early twentieth-century debates about the relationship between culture and the state. Hans Baron's *Crisis of the Early Italian Renaissance* was influenced by Werner Jaeger's work on Greek ideals of culture or *paideia*, which was in

turn indebted to Wilhelm von Humboldt's defense of humanistic learning. But Baron also explicitly conceived of his exploration of Renaissance Italian civic humanism as a response to Nazi Germany and "the fragility of European cultural traditions." See Riccardo Fubini, "Renaissance Historian: The Career of Hans Baron," *Journal of Modern History* 64 (1992): 541–74, here 567, 569. Ernst Robert Curtius shared Baron's sense of the fragility of these traditions. Both emphasized the useful work the historicist interpretation of literary texts could do to stem the tide of "barbarism."

Moreover, as Allan Megill, F. R. Ankersmit, and Charles Bambach have argued, at least some of these issues concerning culture and historicism are at the heart of postmodernism. If historicism is construed as the positivist notion that we can recover the past as it really was, then postmodernism, with its epistemological skepticism, is certainly critical of historicism. For the same reason, postmodernism would be equally critical of culture construed as an ideal of *Bildung*, according to which the individual reenacts the progress of civilization, for such an ideal presupposes "a homogenous, prescriptive pattern of ethical and aesthetic standards and set erudition." But if historicism is construed as a form of nominalism and anti-essentialism, then postmodernism and historicism have much in common. See F. R. Ankersmit, "Historiography and Postmodernism," *History and Theory* 28 (1989): 137–53, here 151, quoting E. H. Kossmann, and 149. See also Allan Megill, *Prophets of Extremity: Nietzsche, Heidegger, Foucault, Derrida* (Berkeley: University of California Press, 1987), and Bambach, *Heidegger*. And just as the late nineteenth-century crisis of historicism provoked new, existentially charged forms of faith in the twentieth century, so postmodern historicism seems to be generating new forms of theism in the twenty-first.

68. See, among others, Aamir R. Mufti, *Enlightenment in the Colony* (Princeton: Princeton University Press, 2007). I encountered this book when the present study was almost complete, but I am in complete agreement with Mufti's argument for the centrality of the Jewish Question for modern discussions of secularism, and in complete sympathy with Mufti's appreciation and analysis of figures like Adorno, Horkheimer, Arendt, Auerbach, et al. for what they can tell us about "culture and critique" (9). There is, of course, one obvious difference between the Muslim Question and the Jewish Question, since the former raises the specter of religiously motivated violence in a way that the latter did not in the nineteenth century.

CHAPTER ONE

1. On Schmitt and early modernity, see now the essays in *Political Theology and Early Modernity*, ed. Graham Hammill and Julia Reinhard Lupton (Chicago: University of Chicago Press, 2012); and *Carl Schmitt's "Hamlet or Hecuba,"* a special issue of the journal *Telos* 153 (2010), ed. David Pan and Julia Reinhard Lupton. Older works include John McCormick, "Fear, Technology, and the State: Carl Schmitt, Leo Strauss, and the Revival of Hobbes in Weimar and National Socialist Germany," *Political Theory* 22 (1994): 619–52;

and McCormick, *Carl Schmitt's Critique of Liberalism* (Cambridge: Cambridge University Press, 1997).

2. On Schmitt's anti-Semitism and the way it permeates his critique of legal positivism (especially the work of the Jewish jurist Hans Kelsen), see now the excellent book by Raphael Gross, *Carl Schmitt and the Jews*, trans. Joel Golb (Madison: University of Wisconsin Press, 2007).

3. Carl Schmitt, "The Age of Neutralizations and Depoliticizations," trans. Matthias Konzett and John P. McCormick, *Telos* 96 (1993): 130–42; here 131. Schmitt emphasizes that this is not a unidirectional, unidimensional process: "there is always a plurality of diverse, already spent stages coexisting" (131).

4. Ibid., 133.

5. *CP*, 65–66, 72 ; McCormick, *Carl Schmitt's Critique of Liberalism*, 66.

6. Carl Schmitt, *Political Romanticism*, trans. Guy Oakes (Cambridge: MIT Press, 1986), 18–19.

7. Karl Löwith, "The Occasional Decisionism of Carl Schmitt," in *Martin Heidegger and European Nihilism*, ed. Richard Wolin, trans. Gary Steiner (New York: Columbia University Press, 1995), 141, 146. This essay was originally published in 1935.

8. Peter Bürger, "Carl Schmitt oder die Fundierung der Politik auf Ästhetik," in *Zerstörung, Rettung des Mythos durch Licht*, ed. Christa Bürger (Frankfurt: Suhrkamp, 1986), 173. See *PT*, 15: "The exception is more interesting than the rule." In Schmitt's later work, he moved away from defining politics in terms of the exception and toward a conception of the "concrete order" of politics. See Schmitt, *On the Three Types of Juristic Thought*, trans. Joseph W. Bendersky (New York: Praeger, 2004).

9. Richard Wolin, "Carl Schmitt: The Conservative Revolutionary Habitus and the Aesthetics of Horror," *Political Theory* 20 (1992): 433, 443, 445. On Schmitt's aestheticization of politics, see also Jürgen Habermas, "The Horrors of Autonomy: Carl Schmitt in English," in *The New Conservatism*, ed. and trans. Shierry Weber Nicholsen (Cambridge: MIT Press, 1992), 137; and the essays in *Telos* 153 (2010).

10. On Schmitt's attack on the liberal notion of culture, see the excellent article by Miguel E. Vatter, "Taking Exception to Liberalism: Heinrich Meier's *Carl Schmitt and Leo Strauss: The Hidden Dialogue*," *Graduate Faculty Philosophy Journal* 19 (1997): 323–44, esp. 331–32, referring to Kant's *Critique of Judgment*, section 84.

11. *PT*, 5, 33, citing Hobbes, *Leviathan*, chap. 26.

12. From the perspective of a seventeenth-century scholar, Schmitt is right when he describes Hobbes as preoccupied with the question "Who decides?" and right to isolate this question as the central question regarding sovereignty in the tumultuous years leading up to and including the English civil war. From James I's early political treatises through the parliamentary pamphleteers of the 1640s, reasoning about the exceptional case (or, in the rhetoric of the period, reason of state) was a burning political issue. In fact, as contemporaries on both sides of the struggle perceived, the English civil war was fought to decide the question of who decides.

But a scholar of seventeenth-century England might also have some questions for Schmitt. Reading seventeenth-century parliamentary debates, one is repeatedly struck by the worry that the exception can be feigned. In the years leading up to the civil war, one of Parliament's complaints was that Charles I had pretended there was a military emergency—pirates near the British coastline—simply in order to raise taxes without the consent of Parliament (this was the famous Shipmoney case of 1637–38). Schmitt doesn't consider this possibility of the faked (or fictional) emergency because his exception is incapable of reproduction; it is by definition opposed to what he calls in *Political Theology* "a mechanism that has become torpid by repetition" (15). It is thus opposed to the reiteration or convention that is a necessary part of any system of representation, or misrepresentation. To put this another way, if Schmitt's sovereign is faking it, it doesn't matter because there is no standard of the real exception apart from the sovereign—i.e., there is no way (and no need) to tell the real apart from the fictional.

13. *PT*, 13.

14. See *PT*, 47–48, on Hobbes's personalistic conception of sovereignty.

15. Ibid., 32–33, 34.

16. Ibid., 42.

17. Ibid., 63.

18. See Joseph Bendersky, *Carl Schmitt: Theorist for the Reich* (Princeton: Princeton University Press, 1983), 207, on how later editions of *The Concept of the Political* reflect Schmitt's accommodation to the Nazi regime: among other changes, Schmitt deleted references to Marx and Lukács that had appeared in the first edition.

19. Carl Schmitt, *The Crisis of Parliamentary Democracy*, trans. Ellen Kennedy (Cambridge: MIT Press, 1992), 66.

20. Ibid., 67, 68.

21. Ibid., 76.

22. *RC*, 25.

23. Ibid., 28–29.

24. Ibid., 21.

25. Ibid., 13–24. See 21 on materialism, and 19 on the incarnation.

26. On mere fictions, see Leo Strauss's comments in NCP, 93, 94.

27. *CP*, 38, 28

28. Ibid., 27, 33, 36.

29. Ibid., 53, 61, 67.

30. Ibid., 72.

31. To a literary critic, Schmitt's distinction between myth and representation seems remarkably close to Goethe's *aesthetic* preference for symbol over allegory, which Walter Benjamin famously criticized in his book on German tragic drama.

32. On the mutually reinforcing relationship between myth and technology, see McCormick, "Fear, Technology, and the State," 642, citing Walter Benjamin, "The Artwork in the Age of Its Mechanical Reproducibility" (1936). McCormick also points out that the mutual relationship between myth and

technology is more familiar to us as the relationship between myth and enlightenment in Adorno and Horkheimer's *Dialectic of Enlightenment*.

33. Helpful discussions of Strauss's commentary on Schmitt can be found
in John McCormick, "Fear, Technology, and the State"; McCormick, *Carl
Schmitt's Critique of Liberalism*, 250–66; Vatter, "Taking Exception to Liberalism"; and Robert Howse, "From Legitimacy to Dictatorship—and Back Again:
Leo Strauss's Critique of the Anti-Liberalism of Carl Schmitt," in *Law as
Politics: Carl Schmitt's Critique of Liberalism*, ed. David Dyzenhouse (Durham: Duke University Press, 1998), 56–91. Vatter and Howse, who completely
disagree about Strauss's views, are a good introduction to the conflicting interpretations of Strauss's work in general.

34. NCP, 86.

35. Ibid., 91.

36. Ibid., 92–93.

37. Ibid., 97.

38. Ibid., 100, 105. Strauss's critique of Schmitt's indecision anticipates all
those modern readers who have argued that Schmitt falls into the errors of romanticism or aesthetics that he criticized both in *The Concept of the Political*
and in *Political Romanticism*. Strauss cites the passage from *CP* where Schmitt
asserts that a world without the political is a world "of culture, civilization"
and above all "entertainment." According to Schmitt, this world might be very
"interesting" (here one is reminded that the interesting was the mark of the
aesthetic for Kierkegaard), but it could never be serious (NCP, 101, 103, 116).
This is Schmitt's aporia, according to Strauss: Schmitt cannot critique the aesthetic and affirm the seriousness of the political without making a moral claim,
a moral distinction between the political and the ostensibly apolitical world of
modernity. To do so, he must either affirm the moral seriousness of the political by subjecting the political to the liberal concept of morality from which
he earlier distinguished it, or elaborate a different notion of morality, a new
"transprivate" basis of "obligation" (104). But Schmitt has not done so. He
has not described the new "order of the human things" (106). He has merely
substituted the notion of "necessity" for that of obligation, thereby concealing
his moral judgment (105). In doing so, he has acted in accordance with the
individualism of liberal society.

39. Of course, Strauss was also vulnerable to the charge of existentialist
historicism. See McCormick, "Fear, Technology, and the State," 648 n. 31.

40. See Leo Strauss's pejorative remarks about how *Leviathan* anticipates
the eighteenth-century notion of the aesthetic in *The Political Philosophy of
Hobbes*, trans. Elsa M. Sinclair (Chicago: University of Chicago Press, 1952),
161 n. 2. The book was originally published in 1936. McCormick argues that
Strauss's book on Hobbes pointed Schmitt to the importance of myth in instill-
ing fear of violent death, but gives no specific references to Strauss's discussion
of myth ("Fear, Technology, and the State," 636). In contrast, I believe Strauss
saw the myth of Leviathan as complicit with the rise of the aesthetic. I discuss
Strauss's work on Hobbes in the 1930s in more detail in chapter 4.

41. Carl Schmitt, *The Leviathan in the State Theory of Thomas Hobbes*,

trans. George Schwab and Erna Hilfstein (Westport, CT: Greenwood Press, 1996), 34, 44.

42. Ibid., 57, 75.

43. See Thomas Hobbes, *Leviathan*, ed. Richard Tuck (Cambridge: Cambridge University Press, 1994), "Review and Conclusion." All subsequent references are to chapter first, then page.

44. According to Schmitt, this is the dilemma of liberal democracy; cf. *Crisis of Parliamentary Democracy*, 28.

45. Ibid., 73.

46. McCormick, *Carl Schmitt's Critique of Liberalism*, 275–76. McCormick makes the point that Schmitt could have argued that the Nazi state overcomes the dilemmas of liberalism, but conspicuously he does not. For another reading of *Leviathan in the State Theory of Thomas Hobbes* as an indirect criticism of the Nazi state, see George Schwab, *The Challenge of the Exception: An Introduction to the Political Ideas of Carl Schmitt between 1921 and 1936* (New York: Praeger, 1989), and Schwab's introduction to *CP*, 13.

47. On this point, see also McCormick, *Carl Schmitt's Critique of Liberalism*, 278.

48. Schmitt, *Leviathan in the State Theory of Thomas Hobbes*, 82, 85.

49. Hobbes, *Leviathan*, 17.120.

50. Ibid., 16.111 and 112.

51. *RC*, 21.

52. Of course, the emergency power of the Weimar Reichspräsident also means that he did not represent the people in any mimetic way. But whereas Hobbes stresses convention, Schmitt stresses personalism.

53. Schmitt, *Leviathan in the State Theory of Thomas Hobbes*, 98.

54. Carl Schmitt, *Hamlet oder Hekuba: Der Einbruch der Zeit in das Spiel* (Düsseldorf: Klett-Cotta, 1956). I quote from the English translation, *HH*.

55. Goethe, *Wilhelm Meister's Apprenticeship*, trans. R. Dillon Boylan (London: Bell and Daldy, 1873), 270. Though he doesn't refer to Schmitt's book on *Hamlet*, Jürgen Habermas discusses *Wilhelm Meister* as an illustration of the demise of Schmitt's concept of "representative publicness" in *The Structural Transformation of the Public Sphere*, trans. Thomas Burger with Frederick Lawrence (Cambridge: MIT Press, 1991), 12–14.

56. Friedrich Schlegel, *On the Study of Greek Poetry*, trans. Stuart Barnett (New York: State University of New York Press, 2001), 34–41, esp. 37; Hegel, *Aesthetics*, trans. T. M. Knox (Oxford: Oxford University Press, 1979), 231, 583–84, 1225–32; the quote is from 1228.

57. Friedrich Schlegel, "Über nordische Dichtkunst," in *Characteristiken und Kritiken II (1802–1829)*, ed. Hans Eichner (Munich: F. Schöningh, 1975), 257 and 244. This equation of *Hamlet* with Germany helps to explain why *Hamlet* figured so prominently in Walter Benjamin's veiled critique of twentieth-century German politics in his book on German tragic drama.

58. See Jane O. Newman, *Benjamin's Library* (Ithaca: Cornell University Press, 2011), 125–27.

59. There is an extensive secondary literature on the cultural appropriation of Shakespeare by the Third Reich. See, among others, Werner Habicht,

"Shakespeare and Theater Politics in the Third Reich," in *The Play Out of Context: Transferring Plays from Culture to Culture*, ed. Hannah Scolnicov and Peter Holland (Cambridge: Cambridge University Press, 1989), 110–20; and Wilhelm Hortmann, *Shakespeare on the German Stage: The Twentieth Century* (Cambridge: Cambridge University Press, 1998). I am grateful to Richard Burt for these references.

60. On the last page of *Hamlet oder Hekuba*, Schmitt also refers to the poem by Ferdinand Freilingrath, whose first line is "Deutschland ist Hamlet!" Schmitt may also have been responding to Karl Jaspers's 1947 book *Von der Wahrheit*, which included a discussion of Greek and Shakespearean tragedy that clearly allegorized the events of the Second World War and the Nazi perversion of tragic rhetoric, the pseudotragic evocation of "the racial past." Jaspers's discussion of tragedy has been translated as *Tragedy Is Not Enough*, trans. Harald A. T. Reiche, Harry T. Moore, and Karl W. Deutsch (Boston: Beacon Press, 1952), here 101. According to Jaspers, "tragically, the individual represents the genuine exception which, though opposing the law, yet has truth on his side" (48). Jaspers also criticized the merely aesthetic understanding of tragedy, in which "the play becomes devoid of moral obligation" (87). Jaspers includes a brief analysis of *Hamlet*, in which he argues that Hamlet can be condemned for inaction only by someone who equates action with unthinking reflex (65).

61. Gopal Balakrishnan, *The Enemy: An Intellectual Portrait of Carl Schmitt* (New York: Verso, 2000), 255. For the transcript of this exchange and commentary, see Joseph W. Bendersky, "Schmitt at Nuremberg," *Telos* 72 (1987): 91–106. The quotations from Schmitt's subsequent reflection on his exchange with Kempner appear on 122 and 123. Bendersky states that Schmitt's ideas were ignored by the Nazi regime and that he was interrogated mostly because of his notorious reputation outside of Germany.

62. Balakrishnan, *Enemy*, 7–8.

63. On Benjamin's reading of Shakespeare in the tradition of the German *Trauerspiel*, see Newman, *Benjamin's Library*, 115–37. As Newman shows, Benjamin read Shakespeare in the second edition of the Schlegel-Tieck German translation.

64. "In tragedy the common public sphere (which in every performance encompasses the author, the actors, and the audience) is not based on the accepted rules of language and play but upon a shared historical reality" (*HH*, 143).

65. *HH*, 63, citing Hegel, *Rechtsphilosophie*, paras. 93 (misprinted as 98) and 218.

66. Benjamin sent Schmitt a copy of his *Trauerspiel* book in 1930, along with a letter in which he declared his indebtedness to Schmitt's representation of the doctrine of sovereignty in the seventeenth century. On the history of this letter, see Samuel Weber, "Taking Exception to Decision: Walter Benjamin and Carl Schmitt," *Diacritics* 22 (1992): 5–18. For good discussions of Schmitt's reading of Benjamin on *Hamlet*, see David Pan, "Political Aesthetics: Carl Schmitt on Hamlet," *Telos* 72 (1987): 153–59; and Carlo Galli, "*Hamlet*: Representation and the Concrete," in Hammill and Lupton, *Political Theology and*

Early Modernity, 60–83. For a discussion of Schmitt's relationship to Benjamin that briefly touches on Schmitt's *Hamlet oder Hekuba*, see Horst Bredekamp, "From Walter Benjamin to Carl Schmitt, via Thomas Hobbes," *Critical Inquiry* 25 (1999): 247–66.

67. See *T*, 70–71.

68. On the "discontinuous temporality of decision" in *Trauerspiel*, see Weber, "Taking Exception to Decision," 16–17. In Weber's words, "the plotter begins where the sovereign hopes to end: with the ex-clusion of the state of exception" (17).

69. *T*, 66, 81.

70. *T*, 138.

71. *T*, 82, 83.

72. *T*, 160.

73. *T*, 176, 180, 182.

74. John McCole, *Walter Benjamin and the Antinomies of Tradition* (Ithaca: Cornell University Press, 1993), 152.

75. In this context, Benjamin also seems to be criticizing Schmitt's decisionist definition of sovereignty in *Political Theology*. As Lutz Koepnik has argued, "What is essential about the Trauerspiel is that it exhibits critical self-contradictions inherent in the secularized paradigm of power and, in turn, also exposes the flaws of Schmitt's alternative to the precarious legitimacy of twentieth-century parliamentarism. Understood as a shrewd commentary on both the seventeenth and the early twentieth century, Benjamin's mapping of power in baroque drama reveals nothing other than the hidden aestheticism on which Schmitt bases the differentiation of an autonomous logic of political action in the modern age. For to counterbalance its decisionist impoverishment of practical reason, the new model of pure politics activates aesthetic resources; as it seeks to increase loyalty through omnipotent visibility, baroque monarchy implements spectacular modes of self-representation and consequently functionalizes art for its political end. Even though it may seem counterintuitive, in order to stabilize the tendency of politics in modernity to become autonomous, absolute sovereignty seeks to recast the public scenes of political action as highly theatrical spectacles." See Lutz P. Koepnik, "The Spectacle, the *Trauerspiel*, and the Politics of Resolution: Benjamin Reading the Baroque Reading Weimar," *Critical Inquiry* 22 (1996), 287–88.

76. *HH*, 40, 41.

77. *HH*, 44.

78. *HH*, 45. My emphasis. Cf. *The Crisis of Parliamentary Democracy* and *The Concept of the Political* on liberalism's relativizing of different points of view. *Spiel* is associated not only with fiction but also with liberal relativism. On *Spiel* and the "Unverspielbarkeit" (unplayability) of the tragic, see *HH*, 40 n. 96.

79. *HH*, 16–18, 21.

80. *HH*, 25; see also 27–30.

81. *HH*, 45, my emphasis.

82. *HH*, 45, 47. I am grateful to David Bates for discussion of this point.

83. There may also be an autobiographical element here. As Jennifer R.

Rust and Julia Reinhard Lupton note, "Schmitt was born in Westphalia, into a Catholic family that resided in a Protestant town." And they remind us that the Peace of Westphalia of 1648–68 "determined the borders of many modern European states and affirmed the principle that each prince would determine the religion of his state: cuius region, eius religio." See the introduction to *HH*, xxxviii.

84. Schmitt, *Crisis of Parliamentary Democracy*, 67.

85. *HH*, 43.

86. *HH*, 47, 48.

87. *HH*, 47, 63. This opposition between civilization and barbarism owes something to Nietzsche's critique of civilization in *The Genealogy of Morals*, or perhaps to Spengler's defense of "blood and tradition" against civilization in *The Decline of the West*. Students of Benjamin will also recall his maxim that every achievement of civilization is simultaneously a record of barbarism.

One is also reminded here of Schmitt's celebration in *Roman Catholicism and Political Form* of "the antithesis of [the] empire of technology . . . nature untouched by civilization, wild and barbarian." In that earlier work, however, Schmitt rejected this idealization of the barbaric: "Such a dichotomy between a rationalistic-mechanistic world of human labor and a romantic-virginal state of nature is totally foreign to the Roman Catholic view of nature," which Schmitt was defending (10). Cf. *Crisis of Parliamentary Democracy* on the revolutionary use of force by the masses as an expression of immediate life and barbarity (68–72). Benjamin himself, according to Schmitt, neglected the differences between Elizabethan England and absolutist France and so missed the distinction between the barbaric and the political. He thus misapplied Schmitt's conception of the sovereign to Shakespeare's *Trauerspiel*: "In Shakespeare's Elizabethan England the baroque theatrification of life was still unfounded and elementary—not yet incorporated into the strict framework of the sovereign state and its establishment of public peace, security and order, as was the theater of Corneille and Racine in the France of Louis XIV. In comparison with this classic theater, Shakespeare's play in its comic as well as melancholic aspects was coarse and elementary, barbaric and not yet 'political' in the sense of the state at that time" (140).

88. Franco Moretti reads Shakespearean tragedy in terms of the shift from a theological to a secular worldview in *Signs Taken for Wonders* (London: Verso, 1983), 42–82. (Moretti briefly discusses the relevance of Schmitt's notion of sovereignty for Tudor-Stuart drama early in this essay.) Stephen Greenblatt reads *Hamlet* as dramatizing contemporary anxiety about the shift from a Catholic notion of purgatory and fullness of ritual to a vitiated Protestant theatricality in *Hamlet in Purgatory* (Princeton: Princeton University Press, 2001). Schmitt draws on Lilian Winstanley, *Hamlet and the Scottish Succession* (Cambridge: Cambridge University Press, 1921), and J. Dover Wilson, *What Happens in "Hamlet"* (Cambridge: Cambridge University Press, 1951).

89. The first quarto was a pirated edition, half as long as the second quarto of 1604, and is not considered a reliable text. It may have been edited or pirated for performance in the provinces. For an excellent modern account of the differences between the first quarto, the second quarto, and the first folio

editions of *Hamlet*, see Leah S. Marcus, "Bad Taste and Bad *Hamlet*," in her *Unediting the Renaissance* (New York: Routledge, 1996), 132–76. Marcus makes it clear that the Hamlet of the first quarto is far less self-reflective and melancholic, and far more capable of action, than the later Hamlets: "While Q2 frequently doubles back upon itself and slows down the action with long meditative speeches, Q1 *Hamlet* has no time for prolonged meditation and very little time for soliloquies"; "But what is lost in terms of Hamlet's relentless, nearly manic probing of the dark borders of human existence is partly gained back by his increased capacity for action" (145).

90. Shakespeare, *Hamlet*, 2.2.527–43, in *The Norton Shakespeare*, gen. ed. Stephen Greenblatt (New York: Norton, 1997).

91. It's as though Hamlet were anticipating Benjamin's analysis of the indecision and theatricality characteristic of German baroque drama in contrast to genuine tragedy. In *T*, Benjamin writes: "In the European *Trauerspiel* as a whole . . . the stage is also not strictly fixable, not an actual place, but it too is dialectically split. Bound to the court, it yet remains a travelling theatre; metaphorically its boards represent the earth as the setting created for the enactment of history; it follows the court from town to town" (119).

92. *HH*, 141.

93. In this light, Hamlet's decision to act would be analogous to what Löwith, "Occasional Decisionism of Carl Schmitt," describes as Schmitt's "decision in favor of decisiveness" (158), or as the "radical *indifference* of purely formal decision to any kind of political *content*" (150).

94. Schmitt himself writes that Elizabethan society "largely perceived its own action as theater," but his remarks on Hamlet and Hecuba seem designed precisely to eradicate the difference between theater and historical fact (*HH*, 41).

95. For a different reading of Schmitt's analysis of Hamlet's speech, see Johannes Türk, "The Intrusion: Carl Schmitt's Non-Mimetic Logic of Art," *Telos* 142 (2008): 87: "The political message would be that politics is different from art and it is art alone that can reflect this difference. This is Schmitt's version of aesthetic education: tragedy is a sphere in which other spheres can be reflected in their difference. The result is a privilege of art over other spheres. But it is an *exorbitant* art that no longer abides by the Romantic and idealist notions that tried to contain it." This is a sophisticated argument but one that fails to note that, pace Schmitt, Hamlet does not move directly to action after the speech but instead to the staging of a play.

In "Hecuba against Hamlet: Carl Schmitt, Political Theology, and the Stake of Modern Tragedy," *Telos* 153 (2010): 94–112, Katrin Trüstedt argues, in a way entirely compatible with the argument of this book, that Schmitt's Hamlet book is "a proxy of his debate with [Hans] Blumenberg." Whereas Blumenberg insists on a break between the medieval period and modernity, Schmitt wants modern politics to be continuous with or legitimated by medieval theology. As a result, Schmitt privileges the political and tragic over the mere play of modern politics. But Schmitt's own reading of *Hamlet* shows the impossibility of separating play and seriousness, the necessity of their confrontation for the tragic to emerge. She concludes, "Moreover, the element of struggle, detour, and play may be what constitutes modernity's legitimacy against its historical burdens. Read in this way, Schmitt's essay on *Hamlet* shows that there is no need for a political theology in his (literal) sense. Rather, there is a need for a politics *against* theology, for a play *working through* tragic material—or, in Schmitt's code, Hecuba *against* Hamlet" (112).

96. Samuel Weber, "Taking Exception to Decision," 17. See *T*, 119, on spectatorship.

97. For a variety of arguments regarding Shakespeare's theatrical critique of absolutism, see Moretti, *Signs Taken for Wonders*; Annabel Patterson, *Shakespeare and the Popular Voice* (Cambridge, MA: Wiley-Blackwell, 1989); Constance Jordan, *Shakespeare's Monarchies* (Ithaca: Cornell University Press, 1997); Lorna Hutson, "Not the King's Two Bodies," in *Rhetoric and Law in Early Modern Europe*, ed. Victoria Kahn and Lorna Hutson (New Haven: Yale University Press, 2001), 266–98; Julia Reinhard Lupton, *Thinking with Shakespeare* (Chicago: University of Chicago Press, 2011). Lupton and others have argued that the play dramatizes the possibility of a constitutional monarchy, even a protoliberal state, and they have bolstered such readings with references to Schmitt's own identification of the sovereign with the popular will in his *Constitutional Theory*. In "Steward of the Dying Voice: The Intrusion of Horatio into Sovereignty and Representation," *Telos* 153 (2010): 113–31, Timothy Wong argues that *Hamlet* dramatizes two Schmittian notions of sovereignty: absolute decisionist sovereignty and constituent sovereignty or the sovereign power of the popular will to establish a legal order (125). "*Hamlet*," he writes, "is emblematic of the political schisms of the time, in which the English parliament and the people slowly began to gain strength, culminating in the execution of King Charles less than fifty years after *Hamlet* was written. . . . Although this situation does not create the modern sovereign executive who represents the people to themselves, it does create the conditions for the possibility of such an executive" (127). We could then say that Schmitt's suppression of the issue of election in *Hamlet* goes hand in hand with his one-sided interpretation of mediation, including artistic mediation. Whereas Schmitt sees Catholic representation as the best form of political representation, *Hamlet*, for Wong, Lupton, and others, explores the constitutionalist and liberal notions of representation avant la lettre.

98. To the extent Schmitt discusses the Elizabethan public sphere, he equates it with the public's shared knowledge of the religious conflicts of the Reformation and the Elizabethan succession crisis. But the public sphere is more vexed, more conflict-ridden, than Schmitt will allow.

99. *T*, 79, 89, 92, 86.

100. *T*, 73, 157. As though to illustrate his point about the "neo-antique" or pagan elements of the play, Benjamin then goes out of his way to link the immanence and contingency of the baroque world of *Trauerspiel* with Machiavelli: "The sovereign intriguer is all intellect and will-power. And as such he corresponds to an ideal which was first outlined by Machiavelli." In support of this view, Benjamin quotes Dilthey: "Machiavelli saw the roots of political thought in anthropological principles. The uniformity of human instinct and the emotions, especially the emotions of love and fear, and their limitlessness—

these are the insights on which every consistent political thought or action, indeed the very science of politics must be based. The positive imagination of the statesman, capable of calculating with facts, has its basis in this knowledge, which teaches us to understand man as a force of nature and to overcome emotions in such a way that they bring other emotions into play" (95–96). See also 98.

101. See Newman, *Benjamin's Library*, 123–25, on the possible sources of Benjamin's Christian reading of the play, and 182–84 on the precariousness of any possibility of redemption or transcendence in the *Trauerspiel* and in Benjamin's theory of allegory more generally.

102. *T*, 137.

103. *T*, 158.

104. On this point, see David Pan's concluding essay in *Hamlet or Hecuba*, "Historical Event and Mythic Meaning in Carl Schmitt's *Hamlet or Hecuba*." Pan argues, "The Christian aspect of *Hamlet* for Benjamin is not an explicit story of salvation but a spiritually grounded awareness of a melancholy imprisonment in a world of action that has been decoupled from salvation" (108).

105. *HH*, 61.

106. *HH*, 59, 65.

107. *HH*, 62.

108. See Wolin, "Carl Schmitt," 434.

109. Søren Kierkegaard, *Either/Or*, trans. David F. Swenson and Lillian Marvin Swenson with revisions by Howard A. Johnson, vol. 1 (Garden City, NY: Doubleday, 1959), 139.

110. Ibid., 141, 139–40.

111. Ibid., 141, 153.

112. Kierkegaard allows for modern tragedy but argues that the proportion of subjective and objective, pain and sorrow, differs from that of ancient tragedy.

113. Kierkegaard, *Either/Or*, 143, 145.

114. Ibid., 148, 144.

115. Heinrich Meier, *The Lesson of Carl Schmitt*, trans. Marcus Brainard (Chicago: University of Chicago Press, 1998), 11.

CHAPTER TWO

1. On George's ideal "Kulturnation" and "das Künstlerische," see Kay E. Schiller, "Dante and Kantorowicz: Medieval History as Art and Autobiography," *Annali Italianistica* 8 (1990): 396–411, here 399. On Stefan George, see also Robert E. Norton, *Secret Germany: Stefan George and His Circle* (Ithaca: Cornell University Press, 2002); and Andrew L. Yarrow, "Humanism and Deutschtum: The Origins, Development and Consequences of the Politics of Poetry in the George-Kreis," *Germanic Review* 58 (1983): 1–11. On George's anti-Semitism, see Martin A. Ruehl, "'In This Time without Emperors': The Politics of Ernst Kantorowicz's *Kaiser Friedrich der Zweite* Reconsidered," *Journal of the Warburg and Courtauld Institutes* 63 (2000): 187–242. Unless

otherwise indicated, I quote Shakespeare's *Richard II* from the edition of Kenneth Muir (New York: New American Library, 1963).

2. See Friedrich Nietzsche, *Beyond Good and Evil*, trans. Judith Norman (Cambridge: Cambridge University Press, 2002), 87 (section 5, para. 200). George seems to have thought that Dante's ideal emperor in *De Monarchia* (especially book 3) was Frederick. See Charles Davis, "Kantorowicz and Dante," in *Ernst Kantorowicz: Erträge der Doppeltagung*, ed. Robert L. Benson and Johannes Fried (Stuttgart: Franz Steiner Verlag, 1997), 240–64, esp. 249.

3. See Schiller, "Dante and Kantorowicz," 400.

4. Norman F. Cantor, *Inventing the Middle Ages* (New York: Morrow, 1991), 102–3, has suggested that the book responds in part to the late nineteenth-century *Kulturkampf* (cultural struggle) "over the relationship between church and state in imperial Germany. Projected back into the Middle Ages, this dispute inspired a study of the emotional pull of kingship in society, and of the way that medieval kingship, especially in the First German Empire, from the late tenth to the mid-thirteenth century, used religious ideas to assert its sovereignty over the clergy and the church's intellectual and cultural resources." According to Cantor, for Kantorowicz and other conservative historians, "the problem of kingship was the central problem in medieval history. It also offered a highly attractive alternative to the liberal democratic republic in which they lived from 1919 to 1933, for which they had no respect, and to the communism they detested with all their beings."

5. On Frederick's revival of classical ideals and anticipation of the Renaissance, see Yarrow, "Humanism and Deutschtum," 7.

6. See David Norbrook, "The Emperor's New Body? *Richard II*, Ernst Kantorowicz, and the Politics of Shakespeare Criticism," *Textual Practice* 10 (1996): 329–57, and Ruehl, "'In This Time without Emperors.'"

7. The letter to George is cited and discussed by Ruehl, "'In This Time without Emperors,'" 231.

8. *TKTB*, xi.

9. Although it was published in 1957, Kantorowicz's *TKTB* was particularly influential in the 1980s, with the rise of New Historicism. There are a variety of reasons for this, not least of which is that Foucault mentioned Kantorowicz with approval in *Discipline and Punish*. It didn't hurt from a Foucauldian perspective that "body" figured prominently in Kantorowicz's title, and that the body that counted was the symbolic body, the charismatic royal body constituted by discourse. And, of course, it positively helped that the book included a chapter on Shakespeare. In short, by focusing on what Clifford Geertz called "the symbolic aspects of power," *TKTB* offered a model of New Historicism avant la lettre and thus validated its approach. Like his earlier biography of Frederick II, *TKTB* advocated a historiography that deals with myth rather than fact, perceptions rather than positivist ideas of knowledge. It thus provided a methodological model in its attention to symbolic forms and in the pride of place it gave to literature. In fact, one could even argue that *TKTB* was influential not only because of the centrality of myth, literature, and representation but also because *TKTB* is essentially about the power of *metaphor*. But it may also be that Kantorowicz caught on just when

he did because his analysis of divinized kingship served as a surrogate for the lost plenitude of subjectivity after the ravages of deconstruction and the critique of the human sciences. In place of the king as representative sovereign subject, we have the construction of kingship through the fiction of the royal body; in place of full presence, we have the social energy of charisma.

10. Only a few scholars have commented on this connection between Schmitt and Kantorowicz, among whom see Richard Faber, "Walter Benjamin's *Ursprung des deutschen Trauerspiels* und Ernst H. Kantorowicz's *Die Zwei Körper des Königs*. Ein Vergleich," esp. 176–79, and Anselm Haverkamp, "Stranger Than Paradise: Dantes irdisches Paradies als Antidot politischer Theologie," 96. Both essays appear in *Geschichtskörper: Zur Actualität von Ernst H. Kantorowicz*, ed. Wolfgang Ernst and Cornelia Vismann (Munich: Wilhelm Fink Verlag, 1998). See also Haverkamp, "*Richard II*, Bracton, and the End of Political Theology," *Cardozo Studies in Literature and Law* 16 (2004): 313–26; Carl Landauer, "Ernst Kantorowicz and the Sacralization of the Past," *European History* 27 (1994): 1–25, esp. 19; Giorgio Agamben, *Homo Sacer: Sovereign Power and Bare Life*, trans. Daniel Heller-Roazen (Stanford: Stanford University Press, 1998); Alain Boureau, *Histoires d'un historien: Kantorowicz* (Paris, 1990), 162–67; Richard Halpern, "The King's Two Buckets: Kantorowicz, *Richard II*, and Fiscal Trauerspiel," *Representations* 106 (2009): 67–76. Jennifer Rust also discusses Schmitt's and Kantorowicz's alternative accounts of political theology in "Political Theologies of the *Corpus Mysticum*: Schmitt, Kantorowicz, and de Lubac," in *Political Theology and Early Modernity*, ed. Graham Hammill and Julia Reinhard Lupton (Chicago: University of Chicago Press, 2012), 102–24.

11. *TKTB*, viii.

12. Ernst Cassirer, *The Myth of the State* (New Haven: Yale University Press, 1946), 282. On *TKTB* as engaging Cassirer's naive view of myth in *The Myth of the State*, see Joseph Mali, *Mythhistory: The Making of a Modern Historiography* (Chicago: University of Chicago Press, 2003), 193–94.

13. Cassirer, *Myth of the State*, 296.

14. Ibid., 292.

15. Peter Eli Gordon, "Continental Divide: Ernst Cassirer and Martin Heidegger at Davos, 1929—An Allegory of Intellectual History," *Modern Intellectual History* 1 (2004): 219–48, here 247 and 225.

16. *TKTB*, 87.

17. Rust, "Political Theologies of the *Corpus Mysticum*," rightly cautions that Schmitt's is only one interpretation of the Catholic tradition and should not be taken to represent Catholicism as a whole. She argues further that Kantorowicz is influenced by Henri de Lubac's analysis of "the *corpus mysticum* as a mode of communal organization that implicitly counters the authoritarian tendencies of Schmittian decisionism" (102–3).

18. *RC*, 18–19; See Samuel Weber, "'The Principle of Representation': Carl Schmitt's *Roman Catholicism and Political Form*," *Targets of Opportunity: On the Militarization of Thinking* (New York: Fordham University Press, 2005), 36. Weber argues that Schmitt's model here is the crucifixion—not simply incarnation.

19. It is likely that Schmitt was influenced here by nineteenth-century "Germanist" (as opposed to Romanist) legal scholars who saw the idea of the *persona ficta* as incompatible with the organic idea of community (*Genossenschaft*). See note 26 below.

20. *RC*, 21. On Hobbes's personalism, see *PT*, 39–40. Schmitt changed his views about whether the people could be representative in the same way that the vicar of Christ could be. At times, Schmitt argued that the democratic notion of the people could constitute a genuine representation (*RC*, 21); at other times, he appeared to reject the juristic fiction whereby the people could constitute the body politic (*PT*, 49). At times, Schmitt saw Hobbes as defending a personalistic idea of sovereignty (*PT*, 47) ; at other times, as attacking it (*RC*, 21).

21. *RC*, 23, 22.

22. *TKTB*, 302ff. See also Paul Vinodograff, "Juridical Persons," *Columbia Law Review* 24 (1924): 594–604, here 602, referring to the view of F. W. Maitland and Otto von Gierke. Vinodograff distinguishes between fictional and realist interpretations of the corporation as a juridical person on 600. See also *TKTB*, 209, on *corpus verum* (an individual person's body) and *corpus fictum* (a collective of any size) and on the juridical person as a fictive person.

23. *TKTB*, 306 and n. 81. On poetic and legal fiction, see, for example, Kathy Eden, *Poetic and Legal Fiction in the Aristotelian Tradition* (Princeton: Princeton University Press, 1986), and Lorna Hutson, *The Invention of Suspicion: Law and Mimesis in Shakespeare and Renaissance Drama* (Oxford: Oxford University Press, 2007).

24. *TKTB*, 338.

25. *TKTB*, 319.

26. *TKTB*, 341, 359. Although it is beyond the scope of this chapter to explore this point, Kantorowicz is drawing on the legal scholarship of Otto von Gierke and F. W. Maitland, both of whom he cites in *The King's Two Bodies*. Gierke is most famous for his distinction between *Gesellschaft* and *Genossenschaft*, between "mechanistic" Roman legal ideas of corporations as contractual arrangements and "organic" German ideas of corporate bodies that have a real and not merely fictive group personality. Maitland made a similar distinction between the continental (Roman law) idea of the legal fiction of the corporation and the commonsense view that groups were persons in a more than fictional sense. On Gierke and Maitland, see David Runciman, *Pluralism and the Personality of the State* (Cambridge: Cambridge University Press, 1997), esp. 91–99. Like Ernest Barker, who wrote an introduction to the 1933 English translation of Gierke's work, Kantorowicz in 1957 seems eager to distance himself from what might appear to be the fascist connotations of *Genossenschaft*.

27. Whether Kantorowicz's genealogy of English constitutionalist thinking is accurate is another question altogether. For a very different account, see Alan Cromartie, "The Constitutionalist Revolution: The Transformation of Political Culture in Early Stuart England," *Past and Present* 163 (1999): 76–120. See also Norbrook, "Emperor's New Body?" According to Norbrook, in stressing instead the way arguments for royal absolutism could fuel early modern

republicanism, Kantorowicz provided an apologia for his earlier celebration of absolutism in his biography of the medieval Hohenstaufen emperor Frederick II. For a similar argument, see Ruehl, "'In This Time without Emperors.'"

28. *TKTB*, 25, 26.

29. *TKTB*, 29, 31.

30. Shakespeare, *Richard II*, 4.1.203ff., quoted in *TKTB*, 36–37.

31. *TKTB*, 39.

32. Lorna Hutson, "Not the King's Two Bodies: Reading the 'Body Politic' in Shakespeare's *Henry IV*, Parts 1 and 2," in *Rhetoric and Law in Early Modern Europe*, ed. Victoria Kahn and Lorna Hutson (New Haven; Yale University Press, 2001), 166–98.

33. In addition to the passages already cited, Kantorowicz calls the idea of the king's two bodies a fiction on 18, 21, and 23 in chapter 1 on Plowden.

34. *TKTB*, 25–26.

35. *TKTB*, 27.

36. See *TKTB*, 41, on Essex. Kantorowicz writes, "It would not have been surprising at all had Charles I himself thought of his tragic fate in terms of Shakespeare's *Richard II* and of the king's twin-born being" (41). See Sean Kelsey, "The Death of Charles I," *Historical Journal* 45 (2002): 707–54; on 748, Kelsey shows that Charles did indeed allude to *Richard II* during his trial.

37. Ernst Kantorowicz, "The Sovereignty of the Artist," originally published in 1961 and republished in Ernst H. Kantorowicz, *Selected Studies* (Locust Valley, NY: J. J. Augustin, 1965), 352–65, here 354. I am grateful to Rachel Eisendrath for calling this passage to my attention.

38. *TKTB*, 362; Dante, *The Divine Comedy*, trans., with a commentary by Charles Singleton (Princeton: Princeton University Press, 1973), 3.1.29.

39. Of course, one might argue that Kantorowicz himself is too susceptible to the rhetoric of the king's two bodies and doesn't see the way in which Shakespeare asks us to question this fiction. As Lorna Hutson has argued, "Kantorowicz emphasizes the pathos of Richard's assumption of his God-given status. Quoting Richard's assertion, 'The breath of worldly man cannot depose/The deputy elected by the Lord' (3.3.54), he comments 'Man's breath appears to Richard as something inconsistent with his kingship.' If we attend to the 'legal cast' of the play's plot, however, it becomes evident that the status of divine vicariousness asserted by these words is being offered to the audience's skeptical, equitable judgment of the circumstances leading up to it." Contrary to those critics who have argued that equity was equivalent to royal prerogative and that the view of the king as the vicar of God was widely accepted in Shakespeare's England, Hutson shows that such political theology was subject to widespread criticism, not least of all through the insistence that the king was not so much the representative of God as the guardian of the common weal. For these critics of political theology, equity was not simply associated with royal prerogative but also with the common law. In Hutson's view, the king's two bodies is a fiction but the more powerful equivalent of legal fiction-making in Shakespeare's England was the equitable judgment exercised by judges, juries, and citizen play-goers as they hypothesized the

intention of the law-giver. See Hutson, "Imagining Justice: Kantorowicz and Shakespeare," *Representations* 106 (2009): 118–42, esp. 136.

40. In "*Richard II*, Bracton, and the End of Political Theology," Anselm Haverkamp argues for a parallel critique of political theology in Kantorowicz and Blumenberg, linking "Kantorowicz' metaphorological topic—the juridical allegory of the king's two bodies" to Blumenberg's "final refutation" of Schmitt in his revised 1974 edition of *The Legitimacy of the Modern Age*" (315). Haverkamp also argues that *Richard II* does not so much stage the doctrine of the king's two bodies as reveal the moment when this doctrine is being supplanted by law, i.e., by the analysis of kingship articulated by the medieval jurist Henry Bracton (317). On Blumenberg and Schmitt, see also Graham Hammill, "Blumenberg and Schmitt on the Rhetoric of Political Theology," in Hammill and Lupton, *Political Theology and Early Modernity*, 84–101.

41. *T*, 87. Benjamin discusses the creaturely dimension of the *Trauerspiel* on 85: speaking of the sovereign in the *Trauerspiel*, he writes, "However highly he is enthroned over subject and state, his status is confined to the world of creation; he is the lord of creatures, but he remains a creature." On the element of the creaturely in Benjamin and *Richard II*, see Zenón Luis-Martinez, "Shakespeare's Historical Drama as Trauerspiel: *Richard II* and After," *ELH* 75 (2008): 673–705, esp. 674–75 (with reference to Kantorowicz) and 686–89. Luis-Martinez is particularly good on how Shakespeare's *Trauerspiel* "represents history as a mournful experience," where mourning is "the effect of the dramatic discovery of a human condition that is essentially creaturely and time-bound" (675). Eric L. Santner also reads *Richard II* in light of the "creaturely" aspects of human existence in *The Royal Remains: The People's Two Bodies and the Endgames of Sovereignty* (Chicago: University of Chicago Press, 2011). Richard Halpern also draws on Benjamin to explore Kantorowicz in "The King's Two Buckets."

42. On this allegorical image of Death, see Luis-Martinez, "Shakespeare's Historical Drama as Trauerspiel," 689.

43. *T*, 123.

44. *T*, 121, 74.

45. Lutz P. Koepnik, "The Spectacle, the *Trauerspiel*, and the Politics of Resolution: Benjamin Reading the Baroque Reading Weimar," *Critical Inquiry* 22 (1996): 289. Koepnik goes on to argue that "[i]f Schmitt defined the foundation of modern politics in the existential will to decide on the exception, Benjamin's monarchs forfeit resoluteness because, for them, the decisionistic formalization of politics turns out to be too narrow an approach to the complexity of rulership. Instead, they appeal to aesthetic sentiments in the poetic cloak of martyrs, thereby addressing their subjects with charismatic hopes for social renewal." Although this analysis suggests, incorrectly I think, that Richard decided not to decide on principle and simply turned to representing himself as a martyr in the "charismatic" hope of social renewal, it does capture the way the aesthetic trappings of martyrdom appear in the play as the logical conclusion of the failure of the decisionist model of sovereignty.

46. On the power of Richard's rhetoric, see Harry Berger, *Imaginary Audi-*

tion: Shakespeare on Stage and Page (Berkeley: University of California Press, 1990), 47–73.

47. Ibid., 157, 156.

48. William Shakespeare, *Richard II*, ed. J. Dover Wilson (Cambridge: Cambridge University Press,, 1939), quoted by Kenneth Muir, ed., *Richard II*, xxix. See also xxx.

49. *TKTB*, 494–95; Boureau, *Histoires d'un historien*, 167.

50. Sir William Blackstone, *Commentaries on the Laws of England* (Philadelphia: J. B. Lippincott, 1867), 390 (chap. 18, "Of Corporations").

51. For a different reading of this moment in *Richard II*, see Norbrook, "Emperor's New Body?," 340: "Kantorowicz's boldest strategy in his opening chapter is to argue that even the central moment of the Whig-liberal tradition, Parliament's declaration of war against King Charles in 1642, was in fact a product rather than a repudiation of absolutist mysticism. . . . The George circle's idealism triumphantly emerges here in the claim that on a higher metaphysical plane the English Revolution never actually happened." Norbrook sees Kantorowicz as a "counter-revolutionary" who is nostalgic for the moment of unity between the king's two bodies, and argues that Kantorowicz reads Shakespeare as a strong monarchist (342).

52. Johannes Fried, "Ernst H. Kantorowicz and Postwar Historiography: German and European Perspectives," in *Ernst Kantorowicz*, ed. Robert Benson and Johannes Fried (Stuttgart: Franz Steiner Verlag, 1997), 180–210. In this and the following paragraph, I draw on Ernst Cassirer, *The Philosophy of Symbolic Forms*, 3 vols. (New Haven: Yale University Press, 1955), esp. vol. 2, *Mythical Thought*; and Ernst Cassirer, *The Individual and the Cosmos in Renaissance Philosophy*, trans. Mario Domandi (1927; New York: Harper and Row, 1964).

53. Cassirer, *Philosophy of Symbolic Forms*, 2:26.

54. Ibid.

55. Cassirer, *Individual and the Cosmos*, 159, 161.

56. Ibid., 84, 87.

57. Ibid., 89, 91, 95.

58. Ernst Cassirer, *An Essay on Man* (New Haven: Yale University Press, 1944), 206 and 228, cited in Cassirer, *Philosophy of Symbolic Forms*, 1:65.

59. Cassirer did make a number of speeches in support of the Weimar republic between 1928 and 1930, and in 1932 he published a defense of the idea of natural law, which he linked to a cosmopolitan idea of humanity. See David R. Lipton, *Ernst Cassirer: The Dilemma of a Liberal Intellectual in Germany, 1914–33* (Toronto: University of Toronto Press, 1978), chap. 10.

60. Cassirer, *Myth of the State*, 141.

61. Ibid., 137.

62. *TKTB*, 463.

63. *TKTB*, 465. In his account of Dante's cosmopolitanism, Kantorowicz may have been influenced by Jacob Burckhardt's account of Dante in *The Civilization of the Renaissance in Italy* (1860), trans. S. G. C. Middlemore (Oxford: Phaidon Press, 1945). Vincent Pecora discusses Burckhardt on

Dante's secular cosmopolitanism in *Secularization and Cultural Criticism* (Chicago: University of Chicago Press, 2006), 195–97. Ruehl points to the racism of Kantorowicz's earlier, George-inspired analysis of Frederick II's campaign to fuse "German and Roman blood" in a vision of the *Volk* that excluded "gamblers, blasphemers, Jews, whores and minstrels" ("'In This Time without Emperors,'" 205, 203, on the Frederick biography). A full contextualization of Kantorowicz's reading of *De Monarchia* would probably have to take account of Hans Kelsen's early study of that work, as well as Kelsen's own contrasting of *De Monarchia* to the critique of absolutism in the work of Nicholas of Cusa in *What Is Justice? Justice, Law, Politics, in the Mirror of Science* (Berkeley: University of California Press, 1957).

64. *TKTB*, 493, 495.

65. Although the laurel in *Purgatorio* 27 is not explicitly described as the crown of poetry, it seems clear this is one of its connotations, given the usual connotations of the laurel and *Paradiso* 1.29, where the laurel is used to crown "o cesare, o poeta." On *Purgatorio* 27, see Albert Russell Ascoli, *Dante and the Making of a Modern Author* (Cambridge: Cambridge University Press, 2008), 329–56. Charles Singleton notes, "the crown and miter . . . were used in the crowning of an emperor, and . . . should not be construed as pointing to *two* powers, empire and church respectively." Singleton cites Kantorowicz on the use of the miter in the crowning of the temporal ruler (Dante, *The Divine Comedy*, 3 vols. [Princeton: Princeton University Press, 1970–75] 2:665).

66. Of course, it's also important to note that this moment of liberal autonomy is conspicuously staged as an interaction between Dante and his most authoritative precursor: Dante does not crown himself but instead requires the intervention of Virgil. This moment of heteronomy suggests the structural necessity of an external authority or third term in any scene of self-authorization. It suggests, in short, that self-authorization is itself a fiction, one that may be parasitic on theological or ecclesiastic notions of authorization. I return to this point later in the chapter.

67. Ernst Cassirer, *The Philosophy of the Enlightenment*, trans. Fritz C. A. Koelln and James P. Pettegrove (Boston: Beacon Press, 1964), viii.

68. Erich Auerbach, *Mimesis: The Representation of Reality in Western Literature*, trans. Willard R. Trask (1946; Princeton: Princeton University Press, 1953), 19–20.

69. Ibid., 193, 194, 193.

70. Ibid., 200, 201.

71. Ibid., 202.

72. Timothy Hampton argues that Auerbach's reading of Rabelais dramatizes the beginnings of a secular conception of literature in "'Comment a nom': Humanism and Literary Knowledge in Auerbach and Rabelais," *Representations* 119 (2012): 37–59. I have not been able to find any evidence that Kantorowicz knew Auerbach's *Mimesis* or his earlier book on Dante, but it is certainly possible, given his wide reading.

73. On this point, see Kantorowicz's remarks in "The Sovereignty of the Artist": "No one aware of the late medieval development of political theories

will be surprised to find an analogous development within the field of artistic
theories. The supreme human authority no longer was vested in the officer
alone, be he emperor, king, or pope. It was vested in man as well or, as Dante
would have said with Aristotle, in the *optimus homo* adorned 'with mitre and
with crown.' To be Man, in the emphatic sense of the word, had come to be an
officium, not only for the Neo-Platonists or for Campanella, but already for
Dante. And through the agency of Petrarch the *officium poetae* had become
a well-articulated notion. Every *officium*, however, in order to assert itself,
demanded or was in need of some kind of quasi-theological justification and
exaltation" (365).

   It's clear that much more remains to be said about Kantorowicz's reading
of Dante. A fuller discussion would probably need to take into account the
work of Friedrich Gundolf, another George acolyte and a well-known transla-
tor of Shakespeare's plays. Gundolf's essay "Dichter und Helden" (1911)
"singles out Alexander the Great, Caesar, and Napoleon as world-historical
figures in the realm of politics, and Dante, Shakespeare and Goethe as their
counterparts in the realm of language." See Carl Landauer, "EK and the
Sacralization of the Past," *European History* 27 (1994): 1–25, here 3. See also
Schiller, "Dante and Kantorowicz." Schiller reads Kantorowicz not as a nationalist but as a promoter of George's cultural "secret Germany." See also Mali,
Mythhistory, 202–8. It would also be interesting to explore the possibility of
a three-way conversation between George, Auerbach, and Kantorowicz. See
Auerbach, *Dante, Poet of the Secular World* (1929), the last chapter of which
begins by citing George's praise of Dante.

   74. See *TKTB*, 55, on the effect of chiasmus in political theology.

   75. Here Kantorowicz invites comparison with that other great maker of
myths about the early modern period, Jacob Burckhardt (whose own *Civilization of the Renaissance in Italy* begins with a discussion of Frederick II and
"the state as a work of art"), but that is another story.

   76. Claude Lefort, "The Permanence of the Theologico-Political?," in *Democracy and Political Theory*, trans. David Macey (Minneapolis: University of
Minnesota Press, 1988), 213–55.

   77. Ibid., 223, 224.

   78. Ibid., 225. Lefort's conclusion raises questions about the permanent
success of this distinction between the real and the symbolic and argues for the
destabilizing role of "the imaginary":

> Rather than seeing democracy as a new episode in the transfer
> of the religious into the political, should we not conclude that
> the old transfers from one register to another were intended
> to ensure the preservation of a *form* which has since been abol-
> ished, that the theological and the political became divorced,
> that a new experience of the institution of the social began
> to take shape, that the religious is reactivated at the weak
> points of the social, that its efficacy is no longer symbolic
> but imaginary and that, ultimately, it is an expression of the
> unavoidable—and no doubt ontological—difficulty democracy

has in reading its own story, as well as of the difficulty political or philosophical thought has in assuming, without making it a travesty, the tragedy of the modern condition? (255)

This argument is taken up by Slavoj Žižek, who discusses Kantorowicz and Lefort in *For They Know Not What They Do: Enjoyment as a Political Factor*, 2nd ed. (London: Verso, 2008), 253–73. Žižek argues that "there is always at work a remainder of an object which resists symbolization" and which explains why people subject themselves to "the sublime body of Power" (263). But he also argues that "one should also *reverse* the perspective by exhibiting how the King's body could also function as the very *guarantee* of the nonclosure of the Social the acceptance of which characterizes democracy" (267). This argument is developed by Eric L. Santner in *The Royal Remains*.

79. Lefort, "Permanence of the Theologico-Political?," 233.

CHAPTER THREE

1. Alison Brown describes Savonarola as the most influential figure in Florentine politics at the end of the fifteenth century in her introduction to *Selected Writings of Girolamo Savonarola*, ed. and trans. Anne Borelli and Maria Pastore Passaro (New Haven: Yale University Press, 2006), xv; the quotation from Savonarola is from xxii. In the following pages Ital. refers to the Italian edition of *The Prince* or *Discourses* in Machiavelli, *Il Principe e Discorsi*, ed. Sergio Bertelli (Milan: Feltrinelli, 1977).

2. See Girolamo Savonarola, *Trattato . . . circa el* [sic] *reggimento e governo della città di Firenze*, in *Prediche sopra Aggeo, con il Trattato circa il reggimento e governo della città di Firenze*, Edizione nationale delle opera di Girolamo Savonarola, ed. Luigi Firpo (Rome: Angelo Belardetti, 1965), 477 (*mandato da Dio*), 446 (*culto divino*), 482 (*paradiso terrestre*).

3. See Brown, introduction to *Selected Writings of Girolamo Savonarola*, xxx.

4. *D*, 1.45.289.

5. Machiavelli, *The First Decennale*, in *Machiavelli: The Chief Works and Others*, trans. Allan Gilbert, 3 vols. (Durham : Duke University Press, 1989), 3:1444–57, here 1448.

6. See Friedrich Meinecke, *Machiavellism: The Doctrine of Raison d'Etat and Its Place in Modern History*, trans. Douglas Scott (New York: Praeger, 1965), 31. The book was first published in 1924.

7. Ibid., 39, 19. On *kratos* and *ethos*, see Meinecke, introduction to *Machiavellism*, esp. 4–6, 11. One of Meinecke's chief examples of this kind of historicist thinking is the work of Hegel. On Hegel and Machiavelli, see Meinecke, 34 and 343–69.

8. Ibid., 425, 433, 431.

9. For the specifically Nazi connotations of political theology, see the introduction to this book, n. 40; and Karl Loewenstein, *Hitler's Germany: The Nazi Background to War*, 2nd ed. (New York: Macmillan, 1940).

10. See *CP*, 61. Schmitt analyzes Machiavelli as concerned with "technical

problems" in *Die Diktatur*, and he explicitly links this technical conception of politics to art:

> Out of this absolute technicity develops the indifference towards any further political purpose in the same manner as an engineer can have a technical interest in the production of a thing, without being in the least interested in the purpose that the product serves. Any political result—be it absolute domination by an individual or a democratic republic, the power of a prince or the political liberty of a people—is performed as a mere task. The political power organization and the technique [*Technik*] of their maintenance and expansion differ according to the various types of government, but always as something that can be brought about in a factually-technical [*sachtechnische*] manner, in the way an artist fashions a work of art according to a rationalist orientation.

This quotation comes from John P. McCormick, *Carl Schmitt's Critique of Liberalism* (Cambridge: Cambridge University Press, 1997), 131, quoting *Die Diktatur* (1921; Berlin: Duncker and Humblot, 1989), 8–9. McCormick shows that Schmitt moved away from the classical Roman idea of dictatorship as a temporary measure to supporting an absolute dictatorship a year later in *PT*. At the same time, "the exception [the extraordinary case that requires the sovereign's decision] changes from a purely functional-political problem for a regime to a kind of moment of divine intervention likened to a miracle" (McCormick, 133–35).

11. Franz Neumann, *Behemoth: The Structure and Practice of National Socialism, 1933–1944* (1942; rev. ed., 1944; New York: Oxford University Press, 1966), 465: "National Socialism has revived the methods current in the fourteenth century, when the first modern states, the Italian city states, were founded. It has returned to the early period of state absolut[ism] where 'theory' was a mere *arcanum dominationis*, a technique outside of right and wrong, a sum of devices for maintaining power. The leaders of the Italian city states in the fourteenth [*sic*] century: Machiavelli, the early seventeenth-century German lawyers (like Arnold Clapmar) were masters of this art." Neumann goes on to read the brief dictatorship of Cola di Rienzo in Rome in 1347 as an effort to establish a "fascist dictatorship."

12. Ernst Cassirer, *The Myth of the State* (New Haven: Yale University Press, 1946), 141.

13. Leo Strauss, review of Ernst Cassirer, *The Myth of the State*, *Social Research* 14 (1947): 125–28; republished in Strauss, *What Is Political Philosophy? and Other Studies* (Chicago: University of Chicago Press, 1988), 292–96.

14. See Leo Strauss, *The Political Philosophy of Hobbes*, trans. Elsa M. Sinclair (1936; Chicago: University of Chicago Press, 1963), 160–61. Strauss remarks, "It is thus not a matter of chance that *la volonté générale* and aesthetics were launched at the same time" (161 n. 2). This is only the most succinct formulation of what Strauss describes at 161 and elsewhere in his *oeuvre* as

"the emancipation of passion and the imagination" in modern philosophy and political theory.

15. See Daniel Tanguay, *Leo Strauss: An Intellectual Biography*, trans. Christopher Nadon (New Haven: Yale University Press, 2007), 203: for Strauss, "[t]he origin of modernity is not so much in Descartes as in Machiavelli. He effected the change in perspective characteristic of modern philosophy by replacing the primacy of theoretical reason with that of practical reason."

16. *TM*, 42, 109, 166.

17. *TM*, 118, 222.

18. Leo Strauss, *Liberalism Ancient and Modern* (1968; Ithaca: Cornell University Press, 1989), 20.

19. In summarizing Strauss's argument about Machiavelli, I have not addressed Strauss's claim that Machiavelli engaged in esoteric writing. While Strauss ultimately thinks that Machiavelli hid his critique of Christianity and his departures from the classical tradition, I think many of the compelling parts of Strauss's argument do not depend on the claim about esotericism. Like J. G. A. Pocock and many others, I think Machiavelli said explicitly what Strauss claims he hid. See Pocock, "Prophet and Inquisitor, Or, A Church Built upon Bayonets Cannot Stand: A Comment on Mansfield's 'Strauss's Machiavelli,'" *Political Theory* 3 (1075): 385–401.

20. But see "The Three Waves of Modernity" in *Political Philosophy: Six Essays by Leo Strauss* (Indianapolis: Bobbs Merrill, 1975), where Strauss argues it is not possible simply to return to earlier forms of thought; "the critique of modern rationalism or of the modern belief in reason by Nietzsche cannot be dismissed or forgotten. This is the deepest reason for the crisis of liberal democracy" (98).

21. Charles Singleton, "The Perspective of Art," *Kenyon Review* 15 (1953): 169. See Jacob Burckhardt, *The Civilization of the Renaissance in Italy*, trans. S. G. C. Middlemore (Oxford: Phaidon Press, 1945), 1–79, esp. 54–55.

22. Hannah Arendt, "What Is Authority?," *Between Past and Future: Six Exercises in Political Thought* (Cleveland: Meridian Books, 1968), 139.

23. For Arendt's hostility to art or poiesis as a model of politics, see the introduction above. See also Hans Sluga, "The Pluralism of the Political: From Carl Schmitt to Hannah Arendt," *Telos* 142 (2008): 91–109, on how for Arendt political philosophy endangers genuine politics: "Plato's critique of political praxis, his belief in the power of poiesis, and his profound desire to substitute the certainties of the ideas for the uncertainty of ordinary opinion had thus constituted the beginning of a process that has ended in modern technology, modern bureaucratic society, and the totalitarian state" (108).

24. See Robert Pippin, "The Modern World of Leo Strauss," *Idealism as Modernism* (Cambridge: Cambridge University Press, 1997), 216 n. 13: "Clearly, of course, from the modern point of view sights are raised, not lowered, particularly when the point of comparison is Scholasticism and papal or feudal politics. In the Kantian phrase . . . *sapere aude!*"

25. *P*, 17.48.

26. *P*, 6.16, 16–17.

27. This link between political autonomy and art reappears in the *Discourses* in Machiavelli's view that the success of Rome derived not from *fortuna*—construed either as chance or as fate—but from the purely human creativity of *virtù*. Here, too, Machiavelli frequently represents *virtù* in terms of art. Echoing his description of Moses, Machiavelli describes Numa as impressing a new form on the people of Rome, and he adds: "And without doubt anyone who at present wishes to build a state will find it easier among mountaineers, where there is no culture [*civiltà*], than among those who are used to living in cities, where culture is corrupt. And a sculptor will more easily get a beautiful statue out of a rough piece of marble than from one badly blocked out by someone else" (*D*, 1.11.225). See Mark Hulliung, *Citizen Machiavelli* (Princeton: Princeton University Press, 1983), who thinks Machiavelli misunderstands Livy's *fortuna* as chance, rather than destiny (266 n. 57).

In my reading of Machiavelli's Moses, I take issue with Graham Hammill's analysis in *The Mosaic Constitution: Political Theology and Imagination from Machiavelli to Milton* (Chicago: University of Chicago Press, 2012). Hammill argues that "[i]n *The Prince*, Machiavelli binds the state to divine authority" (31) and that "Moses exemplifies recourse to divine authority that enables the new prince to found the state" (32). Hammill is contradictory on the question of whether this amounts to an instrumentalization of religion. He sees divine authority as "manifest in the prince's capacity to regulate the beliefs of his subjects," which he describes as instrumentalization on 32; but on 39 he argues with Leo Strauss that Machiavelli is interested not just in the instrumentalization of religion but in why "a sense of religious duty persist[s] in the political landscape of the early modern and modern state." Moreover, in his introduction, Hammill explicitly rejects the view that early modern political theology involves the instrumentalization of religion (6). As I've argued, in contrast, I think Machiavelli's treatment of Moses's speaking with God is entirely ironic and that he is certainly recommending the instrumental use of religion for civic purposes.

28. *P*, 26.73, translation modified.

29. In *Leo Strauss*, Daniel Tanguay cautions that the defining characteristic of modernity for Strauss is not Christianity but the new anthropology that is first articulated by Machiavelli. He also refers to Strauss's letter to Karl Löwith of August 20, 1946, criticizing the identification of Christianity and modernity. Nevertheless, there is evidence elsewhere in Strauss's work that he thought Christianity informed the Enlightenment project of democratizing knowledge. Strauss also repeatedly drew attention to the similarity between the modern project of the "relief of man's estate" and Christian charity.

30. This is the view of Vickie Sullivan, who argues in *Machiavelli's Three Romes* (De Kalb: University of Illinois Press, 1996) that Machiavelli reinterprets elements of ancient Roman religion and Christianity to advance a new secular interpretation of human agency. I am sympathetic to this claim but think that Machiavelli was too much of a pragmatist to reject the political resources of religion.

31. See Gennaro Sasso, "Su un passo di Machiavelli, *Discorsi* 1 12, 10–14," in *Discorsi di Palazzo Filomarino* (Naples: Istituto Italiano per gli Studi Storici,

2008), 187–206; Alberto Tenenti, "La religione di Machiavelli," in *Credenze, ideologie, libertinismi: tra medioevo ed età moderna* (Bologna: Il Mulino, 1978), 175–219; and Ronald Beiner, *Civil Religion: A Dialogue in the History of Political Philosophy* (Cambridge: Cambridge University Press, 2011), 17–45.

32. A subset of this argument is the view that Machiavelli wants to radicalize the contemporary interpretation of Christianity by combining the military example of ancient Rome with Christian egalitarianism, thereby empowering the people. See John P. McCormick, *Machiavellian Democracy* (Cambridge: Cambridge University Press, 2011).

33. *D*, 191.

34. Lucretius, *De rerum natura* 1.928–29: "Avia Pieridum peragro loca nullius ante/trita solo." This passage also appears as the opening line of book 4. The Lucretius MS was first attributed to Machiavelli by Sergio Bertelli and Franco Gaeta in "Noterelle machiavelliane. Un codice di Lucrezio and di Terenzio," *Rivista storica italiana* 73 (1961): 543–55. For a good account of the ensuing debate, see Jérémie Barthas, "Au fondement intellectuel de l'irréligion machiavélienne, Lucrèce? Controverses, notes, et considérations," in *Sources antiques de l'irréligion moderne*, ed. Didier Foucault (Toulouse: Université Toulouse-Le Mirail, 2001), 67–90. For earlier discussions, see John M. Najemy, *Between Friends: Discourses of Power and Desire in the Machiavelli-Vettori Letters of 1512–1515* (Princeton: Princeton University Press, 1993), 337; citing Felix Gilbert, *Machiavelli and Guicciardini* (Princeton: Princeton University Press, 1958), 158 n. 9; Gennaro Sasso, *Machiavelli e gli antichi*, vol. 1 (Milan: Ricciardi, 1987), 202–16 (on the allusion to Lucretius in *D*, 2.5); Alison Brown, *The Return of Lucretius to Renaissance Florence* (Harvard: Harvard University Press, 2010); and Paul A. Rahe, *Against Throne and Altar* (Cambridge: Cambridge University Press, 2008), 32–45. I quote Lucretius from http://www.thelatinlibrary.com/lucretius/lucretius1.shtml; English quotations are taken from *On Nature*, trans. Russel M. Geer (Indianapolis: Bobbs Merrill, 1965). The line numbers in the English and Latin are the same.

35. Machiavelli also would have known that Dante put Lucretius in Hell, along with Frederick II and other heretics. See *Inferno* 10.13–15.

36. Epicurus and Lucretius did not deny the existence of the gods, only their interest in human beings. See, e.g., *De rerum natura* 5.156–234. But for most Renaissance readers, the denial of such providence amounted to atheism.

37. This is Virgil's "indirect praise" of Lucretius in *Georgics* 2.490–92, according to Brown, *Return of Lucretius to Renaissance Florence*, 17.

38. On "naturae . . . ratio," see Lucretius, *De rerum natura* 1.148; cf. 1.498, 2.301–2. Machiavelli's comment was "from motion there is variety, and from it we have a free mind [*liberam habere mentem*]." See Brown, *Return of Lucretius to Renaissance Florence*, 74. Louis Althusser links the contingency of the encounter of *virtù* and *fortuna* with the Epicurean-Lucretian swerve of atoms, though he doesn't discuss Machiavelli's specific indebtedness to Lucretius. See Althusser, *Écrits philosophiques et politiques*, ed. François Matheron, 2 vols. (Paris: Stock, 1994), 2:542, 560 (on Epicurus, Machiavelli, Spinoza, and Marx). I owe these references to Miguel Vatter, who discusses Althusser's reading of

Machiavelli in "Machiavelli after Marx: The Self-Overcoming of Marxism in the Late Althusser," *Theory & Event* 7 (2004): paras. 41–42 and 46.

39. See Lucretius, *De rerum natura* 5.1203, on "placata . . . mente." See also 6.68–79.

40. See Brown, *Return of Lucretius to Renaissance Florence*, 14.

41. Ibid., 46.

42. See Girolamo Savonarola, "Apologeticus de ratione poeticae artis," in *Scritti filosofici*, ed. Giancarlo Garfagnini and Eugenio Garin (Rome: A. Belardetti, 1965); see also Mario Martelli, "La politica culturale dell'ultimo Lorenzo," *Il Ponte* 9 (1980): 923–50, cited in Barthas, "Au fondement intellectuel de l'irréligion machiavélienne," 85.

43. Savonarola, "Apologeticus," 253, 254.

44. "Schoolteachers, where you find in your books of poetry [mentions of] Jove, Pluto, etc., tell them [your students]: My children, these are fables." Cited in Peter Godman, *From Poliziano to Machiavelli: Florentine Humanism in the High Renaissance* (Princeton: Princeton University Press, 1998), 138.

45. Savonarola condemns Pulci in his *Prediche sopra Aggeo*, and Ovid et al. in *Prediche sopra Amos e Zaccaria*. He condemns the poets as purveying fables in the latter. These references come from Godman, *From Poliziano to Machiavelli*, 137.

46. Ibid., 139 n. 36, citing Savonarola's *Prediche sopra Amos e Zaccaria*: "vedi Livio che non scrisse perché quella scrittura significassi cose future, ma solo le passate."

47. Cited by Strauss in *TM*, 92. Machiavelli mentions Gregory in *D*, 2.5.

48. Savonarola, *Trattato circa el reggimento e governo della città di Firenze*, quoted in Donald Weinstein, *Savonarola and Florence* (Princeton: Princeton University Press, 1970), 302.

49. Brown, *Return of Lucretius to Renaissance Florence*, 55. Carlo Dionisotti sees Adriani (whom he calls Marcello Virgilio) as a follower of Poliziano who essentially lay low during the period of the Florentine republic and did not produce any humanist scholarship of significance until the return of the Medici. See Carlo Dionisotti, "Machiavelli, Man of Letters," in *Machiavelli and the Discourse of Literature*, ed. Albert Russell Ascoli and Victoria Kahn (Ithaca: Cornell University Press, 1993), 31–32.

50. *D*, 1.12.227; Ital., 164.

51. Dionisotti, "Machiavelli, Man of Letters," 27. In *Return of Lucretius to Renaissance Florence*, Brown notes of Ficino, "After he became a priest and a dedicated Platonist in the 1470s, he referred to Lucretius only to attack him, but the care he then devoted in the *Platonic Theology* to refuting Lucretius's arguments against immortality shows how powerful Lucretius's impact on Ficino as a young man had been" (23).

52. Dionisotti, "Machiavelli, Man of Letters," 27. Closer to Machiavelli's allegiances was the work of Bartolomeo Scala, chancellor of Florence from 1464 to 1497 and author of a fictional dialogue between himself and Machiavelli's father, Bernardo. See below. As Brown shows, "Bernardo" argues for "the expedient use of religion to enforce obedience" and gives "Lucretius's definition of religion which comes—he tells us—from *religare*, to bind, hence

his desire to 'free our minds from tight bondage to religion.'" (Brown, *Return of Lucretius to Renaissance Florence*, 29).

53. Godman, *From Poliziano to Machiavelli*, 176, quoting Adriani. On Adriani's reassertion of the link between humanist rhetoric and republicanism, see 157–59. In "Machiavelli and the *Verità Effetuale*," in *Writing: The Political Test*, trans. David Ames Curtis (Durham: Duke University Press, 2000), Claude Lefort argues that Machiavelli chose to write a commentary on Livy in part to counter the politically conservative interpretation of Livy by the older generation of the Orti Oricellari circle, where Machiavelli and his friends discussed politics (115).

54. In *Florentine Histories* 5.1, Machiavelli wrote that the preference for literature and philosophy over arms was the sign of corruption in a state: "the strength of well-armed spirits cannot be corrupted by a more honorable leisure than that of letters" (trans. Laura F. Banfield and Harvey C. Mansfield Jr. [Princeton: Princeton University Press, 1988], 185). This seems more of a commentary on the Neoplatonic literary culture of Florence than on literature per se; Godman thinks it may be a reference to Marcello Virgilio Adriani, who abandoned his republican convictions once the Medici were restored to power (*From Poliziano to Machiavelli*, 290).

55. Dionisotti also suggested that Machiavelli's ambition for literary greatness in one of the traditional literary genres—notably epic or lyric—was diverted by his recognition that he could never rival Ariosto. Hence, according to Dionisotti, Machiavelli's turn to prose. But Dionisotti also helps us see the political implications of the turn to Lucretius and Livy as specifically Latin authors. For an argument that Machiavelli was trying to counter an existing conservative interpretation of Rome and Livy, see also Dionisotti, "Machiavelli, Man of Letters."

56. *D*, 1.11.225.

57. On Numa, see John M. Najemy, "Papirius and the Chickens, or Machiavelli on the Necessity of Interpreting Religion," *Journal of the History of Ideas* 60 (1999): 659–81. Najemy writes, "As Livy says (1.19) of Numa's pious fiction, he knew he could not instil the necessary fear of the gods into Roman hearts 'without inventing some marvellous story' (sine aliquo commento miraculi). A *commentum* is a fabrication, fiction, or falsehood, but one associated with poetry; and a *miraculum* is a strange or marvelous thing capable of exciting wonder" (670).

58. *D*, 1.11.225–26. Or as Machiavelli says about Savonarola in chapter 12 of *The Prince*: "The man who said our sins were the cause [of the French invasion of Italy] said the truth; but they weren't the sins he thought."

59. *D*, 1.11.226; Lucretius, *De rerum natura* 1.941–42.

60. *D*, 1.11.225–26.

61. On Machiavelli's appreciation of Savonarola's self-construction as a new Moses, one who sanctioned the use of violence in political affairs, see Alison Brown, "Savonarola, Machiavelli, and Moses: A Changing Model," in *Florence and Italy: Renaissance Studies in Honor of Nicolai Rubenstein*, ed. Peter Denley and Caroline Elam (London: Committee for Medieval Studies, Westfield College, 1988), 57–72; rpt. in *Machiavelli*, ed. John Dunn and

Ian Harris, 2 vols. (Cheltenham, UK: E. Elgar, 1997), 2:425–40. There is also extensive evidence in Machiavelli's correspondence that he detested Savonarola and his subordination of politics to what Machiavelli judged to be hypocritical and factional religious ends. See Marcia L. Colish, "Republicanism, Religion, and Machiavelli's Savonarolan Moment," *Journal of the History of Ideas* 60 (1999): 597–616, esp. 612–13.

62. *D*, 1.11.226; translation modified. See also Machiavelli's comments on the gullibility of the Florentine audience listening to a Franciscan preacher who claimed to be a "prophet," in a letter to Vettori (Dec. 19, 1513), cited by Colish, "Republicanism, Religion, and Machiavelli's Savonarolan Moment," 612.

63. *D*, 1.12.227; Ital., 164.

64. *D*, 1.11.232.

65. *D*, 1.14.233; Najemy, "Papirius and the Chickens," 678.

66. *D*, 1.13.230.

67. Livy, *The Early History of Rome*, books 1–5 of *The History of Rome from Its Foundation*, trans. Aubrey de Sélincourt, ed. Betty Radice (Harmondsworth, UK: Penguin, 1984), 194 (3.10).

68. *D*, 1.12.231; Livy, *Early History of Rome*, 206 (3.20): "Fortunately, however, in those days authority, both religious and secular, was still a guide to conduct, and there was as yet no sign of our modern scepticism which interprets solemn compacts, such as are embodied in an oath or law, to suit its own conscience." This is a wordy and tendentious translation of Livy's "neglegentia deum."

69. *D*, 1.15.234; translation modified.

70. Machiavelli, *Asino* 5.115; cited by Alison Brown, "Philosophy and Religion in Machiavelli," in *The Cambridge Companion to Machiavelli*, ed. John M. Najemy (Cambridge: Cambridge University Press, 2010), 166. Of the examples of the Roman plebs and Papirius's interpretation of the Samnite oath, Najemy writes, Machiavelli's "point may have been that the plebs suffered the consequence of leaving the interpretation of religion to others and that they too ought to have engaged in some creative interpretation of their own. As for the Samnites, it almost seems that their defeat came about *because* they believed so sincerely—indeed blindly—in the efficacy of their rituals and the truth of their religion. In all these stories those who actually believe in their religion, who live it with complete sincerity, are defeated by political or military enemies who know how to use religion and to 'interpret' its rituals 'according to necessity'" (678).

71. See also in *D*, 2.2.331: "This [Christian] way of living, then, has made the world weak and turned it over as prey to wicked men, who can in security control it, since the generality of men, in order to go to Heaven, think more about enduring their injuries than about avenging them."

72. Livy, *The War with Hannibal*, books 21–30 of *The History of Rome from Its Foundation*, trans. Aubrey de Sélincourt, ed. Betty Radice (Harmondsworth, Eng.: Penguin, 1985), 262 (24.25). In *D*, 2.2, Machiavelli also recommends Xenophon's *On Tyranny* for its analysis of how "what benefits [the tyrant] usually injures the city, and what benefits the city injures [the tyrant]."

73. *D*, 2.2.330; Livy, *War with Hannibal*, 256.

74. Machiavelli does, however, attribute this sentence about how the mob is either a humble slave or a cruel master to Livy in *D*, 1.58, where he argues that this characterization fits princes as well but does not describe the Roman people when the republic was not yet corrupt.

75. *D*, 2.2.330–31. See Virginia Cox, "Rhetoric and Ethics in Machiavelli," in Najemy, *Cambridge Companion to Machiavelli*, on this strategy in *The Prince*. Cox argues that Machiavelli borrows *Ad Herennium*'s distinction between two categories of the decent: the objective or right and the subjective or praiseworthy. This allows "the orator to present value conflicts in political deliberation in terms of a tension not between advantage and decency (*utile* and *honestum*), as was usual in philosophic discourse, but, more narrowly, between security and reputation (*tutum* and *laudabile*). This had obvious strategic benefits, in that it allowed what was conventionally conceived of as the toughest of ethical dilemmas in political deliberation to be massaged into a more easily soluble technical conflict between what were essentially two kinds of 'advantage'" (180–81). I'm suggesting that, in the opposition between Christianity's weak truth and Rome's strength, Machiavelli effects a similar translation of truth into a less advantageous or less effective truth.

76. In *Civil Religion*, Ronald Beiner argues that Machiavelli's goal is to "paganiz[e] Christianity as a neo-Roman civil religion" (35). See also 21–28.

77. See, for example, Machiavelli's letter to Giovan Battista Soderini, September 1506 (the "Ghiribizzi"). I return to this letter below. Brown argues that "in Machiavelli's physiology, . . . imagination (*fantasia*) replaces the soul or 'spirit' (*anima*) in relationship with the mind or intelligence (*animo*)" (*Return of Lucretius to Renaissance Florence*, 82). As Brown notes: "Despite the emphasis placed recently on the role of imagination in Machiavelli's later plays in creating the self, or 'self-fashioning,' in his letters [*fantasia*] describes a process of critical psychological and political analysis that distinguishes the 'effectual truth' of a situation from appearance, much as Lucretius distinguished the reality of a man, 'the thing itself,' when his mask was ripped away through adversity" (82).

78. As Felix Gilbert observed years ago, Machiavelli's conception of *virtù* "contains the suggestion that in every well-organized society a spiritual element pervades all its members and institutions tying them together in a dynamic unit which is more than a summation of its constituent parts" (*Machiavelli and Guicciardini* [Princeton: Princeton University Press, 1965], 180).

79. *D*, 1.55.307.

80. As Brown notes, "Scala's discussion of natural law is indebted to the Epicureans, as we can see from his reference to the law of nature as 'a sign to keep us from swerving from what is right and honorable.' . . . *Sign* was the word used in Traversari's translation of Epicurus's natural precepts or maxims in Diogenes Laertius' *Life [of Epicurus]*, where the law of nature is described as 'a sign of expedience that you should not harm another or be harmed'" (*Return of Lucretius to Renaissance Florence*, 29).

81. Ital., 124.

82. Ital., 3.1.381; see also 379.

83. See *P*, chap. 6, on Savonarola's lack of arms and so inability to coerce belief.

84. *D*, 1.12.227.

85. "Inde fabulae adiectum est uocem quoque dicentis uelle auditam; motam certe sede sua parui molimenti adminiculis, sequentis modo accepimus leuem ac facilem tralatu fuisse, integramque in Auentinum aeternam sedem suam quo uota Romani dictatoris uocauerant perlatam, ubi templum ei postea idem qui uouerat Camillus dedicauit" (http://www.thelatinlibrary.com/livy/liv.5.shtml#22). The English translation is from Livy, *Early History of Rome*, 366.

86. English translation modified. The Italian reads: "parve loro udire quella risposta che alla domanda loro per avventura si avevano presupposta" (165).

87. *D*, 1.12.228.

88. *D*, 3.1.422; cf. 2.5.

89. Theodor W. Adorno, "The Actuality of Philosophy," trans. Benjamin Snow, in *The Adorno Reader*, ed. Brian O'Connor (Oxford: Oxford University Press, 2000), 36–37. Thanks to Rachel Eisendrath for alerting me to this passage. Shierry Weber Nicholsen translates "exakte Phantasie" as exact imagination in *Exact Imagination, Late Work: On Adorno's Aesthetics* (Cambridge: MIT Press, 1997).

90. See *Machiavelli: The Chief Works and Others*, 2:747. On the "Ghiribizzi," see Brown, "Philosophy and Religion in Machiavelli." See also Brown, *Return of Lucretius to Renaissance Florence*, for a discussion of the critical role of *fantasia* in Machiavelli's *Asino* (84).

91. Strauss also notes this point in *TM*, 288.

92. *D*, 1.10.220, translation modified.

93. *TM*, 51.

94. *TM*, 167, 188.

95. *TM*, 185. Although Strauss doesn't make this point, Machiavelli could also have drawn here on Lucretius's critique of the gods as "cruel masters" (*De rerum natura* 5.90, 6.60.)

96. *TM*, 188. Cf. Lucretius, *De rerum natura* 5.1194–95: "Unhappy human race, to grant such feats/To gods, and then to add vindictiveness."

97. *TM*, 189.

98. See Stanley Rosen, *The Quarrel between Philosophy and Poetry* (New York: Oxford University Press, 1987), preface and chap. 1. In an argument too complicated to summarize here, Rosen (a student and critic of Strauss) argues that the quarrel between philosophy and poetry is a symptom of their deeper compatibility.

99. See Leora Batnitsky, "Leo Strauss's Disenchantment with Secular Society," *New German Critique* 94 (2005): 122: "At the basis of Strauss's criticism of modern rationalism and what he asserts are its historicist after-effects is his contention that a fully *philosophically* justified law is unavailable. The perhaps negative insight that philosophy is necessarily *limited* when it comes to founding universal laws is for Strauss the basis of a true philosophical rationalism. . . . The morality of 'civilization' (of science *and* morality, philosophy *and* law, philosophy *and* society) is one of prudence: its aim is to forestall

catastrophe. Against both Christian scholasticism and modern Kantian claims, Strauss maintains that it is not possible to ascertain a morality and law whose *foundations* can be rationally grounded."

100. Machiavelli writes that he loves his country more than his soul in a letter of April 16, 1527, to Francesco Vettori. See *Machiavelli: The Chief Works and Others*, 2:1010.

101. Gilbert, *Machiavelli and Guicciardini*, 199.

102. I am indebted here to a helpful conversation with Andreas Kalyvas.

103. William Rasch, *Sovereignty and Its Discontents* (London: Psychology Press, 2004), 41. See 30 on how the understanding of the concrete order is itself subject to conflicting interpretations.

104. Rasch, *Sovereignty and Its Discontents*, 61.

CHAPTER FOUR

1. See Benjamin Lazier, *God Interrupted: Heresy and the European Imagination between the Wars* (Princeton: Princeton University Press, 2009). Lazier has argued that the interest in Spinoza was a reaction to the "crisis theology" of Karl Barth, whose existentialist approach to theology was perceived by contemporaries as a kind of Gnosticism. Against such Gnostic dualism, Spinoza—with his famous motto "Deus sive natura"—stood for pantheism and immanence. Although a Catholic, Schmitt was closer to Barth than to Spinoza. He rejected Spinoza's immanence as contrary to his own notion of the sovereign decision that intervened miraculously, as it were, in the world of politics. Strauss, by contrast, saw that crisis theology's argument for a *deus absconditus* was compatible with Spinoza's defense of philosophy. In a letter to Gerhard Krüger on October 3, 1931, he wrote, "My [Spinoza] book [was] a single answer [from the perspective of unbelief] to the belief of the Barth-Gogarten tradition, at least in its intent" (cited in Lazier, 106). On Barth and Gogarten, see also John H. Smith, *Dialogues between Faith and Reason: The Death and Return of God in Modern German Thought* (Ithaca: Cornell University Press, 2011), 205–35.

2. Carl Schmitt, *The Leviathan in the State Theory of Thomas Hobbes*, trans. George Schwab and Erna Hilfstein (Westport, CT: Greenwood Press, 1996), 56.

3. Ibid., 57, 48.

4. There may be an analogy here with Derrida's arguments for the inseparability of democracy and literature. See "'This Strange Institution called Literature': An Interview with Jacques Derrida," in Derrida, *Acts of Literature*, ed. Derek Attridge (New York: Routledge, 1992), 37–38; and Neil Saccamano, "Inheriting Enlightenment, or Keeping Faith with Reason in Derrida," *Eighteenth-Century Studies* 40 (2007): 405–24. Saccamano writes, "An enlightened philosophy thus also finds itself caught up with literature since, for Derrida, the possibility of literature is politically inseparable from democracy and of the 'unlimited right to ask any question, to suspect all dogmatism,' and 'to say everything publicly, or to keep it a secret, if only in the form of fiction'" (408, quoting Derrida's *Passions*).

5. *SCR*, 101, 86.

6. Leo Strauss, *"Hobbes's Critique of Religion" and Related Writings*, trans. and ed. Gabriel Bartlett and Svetozar Minkov (Chicago: University of Chicago Press, 2011), 111, 113. Strauss's further untranslated work on Hobbes from the 1930s is available in Heinrich Meier and Wiebke Meier, eds., *Hobbes' politische Wissenschaft und zugehörige Schriften, Briefe*, vol. 3 of *Leo Strauss: Gesammelte Schriften*, ed. Heinrich Meier, 2nd rev. ed. (Stuttgart: J. B. Metzler, 2008).

7. Leo Strauss, *The Political Philosophy of Hobbes*, trans. Elsa M. Sinclair (1936; Chicago: University of Chicago Press, 1952), 71. Also on this page, Strauss makes it clear that he thinks of Hobbes as a political theologian, if by this we mean a critic of appeals to divine revelation to shore up the authority of the state: "Hobbes's three presentations of political philosophy may with scarcely less justice that Spinoza's expressly so entitled work be called theological-political treatises."

8. *SCR*, 18: "Spinoza rejects both Greek idealism and Christian spiritualism. The Biblical God forms light and creates darkness, makes peace and creates evil; Spinoza's God is simply beyond good and evil. God's might is his right, and therefore the power of every being is as such its right; Spinoza lifts Machiavellianism to theological heights. Good and evil differ only from a merely human point of view; theologically the distinction is meaningless."

9. *SCR*, 19.

10. *SCR*, 15.

11. *SCR*, 1.

12. *SCR*, 5–6. See Nancy Levene on Strauss: "Athens and Jerusalem: Myths and Mirrors in Strauss' Vision of the West," *Hebraic Political Studies* 3 (2008): 124.

13. On Strauss's relationship to the Jewish Question, see among others Daniel Tanguay, *Leo Strauss: An Intellectual Biography*, trans. Christopher Nadon (New Haven: Yale University Press, 2007), 10–48 ("Zionism, Orthodoxy, and Spinoza's Critique of Religion"); and Steven B. Smith, *Reading Leo Strauss: Politics, Philosophy, Judaism* (Chicago: University of Chicago Press, 2006).

14. See "An Introduction to Heideggerian Existentialism," in Leo Strauss, *The Rebirth of Classical Political Rationalism*, ed. Thomas Pangle (Chicago: University of Chicago Press, 1989), where Strauss writes, "the only great thinker in our time is Heidegger" (29). For an argument that *SCR* needs to be read in the context of Strauss's relation to Heidegger (and not simply through the 1962 preface), see John P. McCormick, "Post-Enlightenment Sources of Political Authority: Biblical Atheism, Political Theology and the Schmitt-Strauss Exchange," *History of European Ideas* 37 (2011): 175–80.

15. Karl Barth, *The Epistle to the Romans*, translated from the sixth edition by Edwyn C. Hoskyns (London: Oxford University Press, 1933), 267–68.

16. Jeffrey Andrew Barash, *Martin Heidegger and the Problem of Historical Meaning*, rev. ed. (New York: Fordham University Press, 2003), 138.

17. In "A Giving of Accounts: Jacob Klein and Leo Strauss," *The College* (1970), Strauss describes the influence of Barth and Rosenzweig. Referring to

"the resurgence of Karl Barth," he comments, "The preface to the first edition of his commentary on the Epistle to the Romans is of great importance also to nontheologians: it sets forth the principles of an interpretation that is concerned exclusively with the subject matter as distinguished from historical interpretation. Wholly independently of Barth, Jewish theology was resurrected from a deep slumber by Franz Rosenzweig, a highly gifted man whom I greatly admired to the extent to which I understood him." Cited in Lazier, *God Interrupted*, 93.

18. Strauss refers to their "neues Denken." The term comes from Franz Rosenzweig's essay "Das neue Denken" in *Kleinere Schriften* (Berlin: Schocken Verlag, 1937). On Strauss's view of Heidegger, see among others Horst Mewes, "Leo Strauss and Martin Heidegger: Greek Antiquity and the Meaning of Modernity," in *Hannah Arendt and Leo Strauss: German Emigrés and American Political Thought after World War II*, ed. Peter Graf Kielmansegg, Horst Mewes, and Elisabeth Glaser-Schmidt (Cambridge: Cambridge University Press, 1995), 105–20.

19. *SCR*, 12. Elsewhere Strauss is critical of the secularization thesis for neglecting "the essential nature of modernity—that is, its will to break with the old theological world." In particular, Strauss rejects the traditional view that "the natural law of modern thinkers is a secularized version of Stoic-Christian natural law." See Tanguay, *Leo Strauss*, 101, 103; see also 109ff.

20. *SCR*, 17.

21. *SCR*, 28, my emphasis; 29.

22. *SCR*, 30.

23. In *Reading Leo Strauss*, Steven Smith construes this opposition as relevant to both ancient and modern philosophy: "The conflict between faith and reason, Jerusalem and Athens, is in the final instance not a theoretical but a moral choice" (79).

In proposing this argument, Strauss may have been drawing on the eighteenth-century critic of Spinoza F. H. Jacobi, the subject of his doctoral dissertation. Jacobi is now famous for having touched off the pantheism controversy by accusing Lessing of Spinozism. Lessing's good friend Moses Mendelssohn defended him against the charge. But the real issue at the heart of this debate, as Frederick C. Beiser has argued, was the autonomy of reason, its vulnerability or invulnerability to historicist and cultural relativism. The pantheism controversy, that is, was a dress rehearsal for the crisis of historicism in the late nineteenth century. See Beiser, *The Fate of Reason: German Philosophy from Kant to Fichte* (Cambridge: Harvard University Press, 1993), 44–105.

24. NCP, 53, 72.

25. NCP, 86, 92.

26. *CP*, 60, 86; NCP, 92.

27. Miguel Vatter summarizes Strauss's logic as follows: "If evil belongs to the state of nature only in the sense that it can be eliminated by a transition to the state of culture, then the Hobbesian ideal of civilization entails the loss of the absolute opposition between good and evil." See "Strauss and Schmitt as Readers of Hobbes and Spinoza," *New Centennial Review* (2005): 175.

28. As Heinrich Meier has shown, Schmitt altered later editions of *The*

Concept of the Political in response to Strauss's critique, including replacing various references to culture with "the political" or deleting them altogether. See Heinrich Meier, *Carl Schmitt and Leo Strauss: The Hidden Dialogue*, trans. J. Harvey Lomax (Chicago: University of Chicago Press, 1995), 30–32. Meier also points out that Schmitt addresses Strauss's complaint regarding his admiration for amoral animal power by adding a sentence on Hobbes, Spinoza, and Pufendorf and the state of nature as a state of perpetual danger to the 1933 edition of *The Concept of the Political* (Meier, 58 n. 60).

29. NCP, 58. Schmitt fails to see, according to Strauss, that the political "owes its legitimacy to the seriousness of the question of what is right" (NCP, 118). As Meier points out in *Carl Schmitt and Leo Strauss*, Strauss criticizes Schmitt for describing "the thesis of dangerousness as a '*supposition*,' as an 'anthropological confession of *faith*'" (58). "'But if man's dangerousness is *only supposed or believed in, not genuinely known*, the opposite too can be regarded as possible, and the attempt to eliminate man's dangerousness . . . can be put into practice. If man's dangerousness is *only believed in*, it is in principle *threatened*, and therewith the political is threatened also.' . . . Precisely for that reason Strauss opposes knowledge to faith, and for the same reason he categorically emphasized that faith does not suffice" (51; Meier's emphasis).

30. *SCR*, 31.

31. This is the argument of Smith in *Reading Leo Strauss*, 83.

32. Specifically, Strauss develops his idea of premodern rationalism through his encounter with medieval rationalism, in the work of Maimonides, Alfarabi, and Averroes, whom Strauss reads as closet Platonists.

33. Leo Strauss, *Philosophy and Law*, trans. Eve Adler (Albany: State University of New York Press, 1995), 31.

34. Ibid., 32.

35. Ibid., 138 n. 2.

36. Leo Strauss, "How to Study Spinoza's *Theological-Political Treatise*," in *Persecution and the Art of Writing* (Chicago: University of Chicago Press, 1952), 142–201. The essay was originally published as an article in 1948.

37. Ibid., 142.

38. Ibid., 157.

39. Steven B. Smith, *Spinoza, Liberalism, and the Question of Jewish Identity* (New Haven: Yale University Press, 1997), 25 and xiii.

40. See Ernst Cassirer, *The Philosophy of the Enlightenment*, trans. Fritz C. A. Koelln and James P. Pettegrove (Boston: Beacon Press, 1955), 183: "Consideration of the eternal and immutable norms of reason must go hand in hand with consideration of the manner in which they unfold historically, in which they have been realized in the course of empirical historical development. Real 'enlightenment' of the mind can only emerge from the reconciliation and opposition of these two modes of contemplation."

41. I am indebted to David Bates for helping me sort through the ideas in this paragraph.

42. In the preface to *SCR*, Strauss writes that Spinoza attempts a "synthesis of pre-modern (classical-medieval) and modern philosophy" (16). While Strauss doubts whether such a synthesis is possible, he is surely right that

Spinoza is trying to negotiate some kind of middle position between premodern rationality and postmodern skepticism, a skepticism that Strauss thinks follows from the assumptions of Baconian science and modern philosophy. I am indebted to Ethan Guagliardo for some probing questions on this point.

43. See *TTP*, introduction by Jonathan Israel, xvi. I have also consulted the Latin text of the *TTP* in *Benedicti de Spinoza opera quotquot reperta sunt*, ed. J. Van Vloten and J. P. N. Land, 3rd ed., 2 vols. (The Hague, 1914), vol. 2.

44. See *TTP*, 17.225: "Nature certainly does not create peoples, individuals do, and individuals are only separated into nations by differences of language, law and morality. It can only be from these latter factors, namely law and morality, that each nation has its unique character, its unique condition, and its unique prejudices."

45. For the view that Spinoza's target here is the Dutch Collegiant Bible critics, see *TTP*, 7.112n. In *SCR*, Strauss argues that Spinoza's target here is Calvin.

46. See Israel, introduction to the *TTP*, on the distinction between textual truth and the truth of fact (xi–xii).

47. Henry E. Allison, *Benedict de Spinoza: An Introduction*, rev. ed. (New Haven: Yale University Press, 1987), 108–9. See also Spinoza, *Ethics*, trans. Andrew Boyle and G. H. R. Parkinson (London: Dent, 1997), appendix to part 1, for further remarks on the imagination.

48. Yovel goes on: "and he thinks it is the philosopher's task to provide tools for dealing with the various forms of this transition—as he himself does in his theory of allegory, metaphor, and nonscientific discourse generally." See Yirmiyahu Yovel, *Spinoza and Other Heretics*, vol. 1: *The Marrano of Reason* (Princeton: Princeton University Press, 1989), 145. See also Antonio Negri, *The Savage Anomaly: The Power of Spinoza's Metaphysics and Politics*, trans. Michael Hardt (Minneapolis: University of Minnesota Press, 1991). In Negri's brilliant account, Spinoza's analysis of prophecy thus takes place on two levels: "the analysis and identification of the imagination as a constitutive function of falsity and illusion; followed by . . . the analysis of the ontological (differentiated, true) basis of the action of the imagination" (92–93); or, in other words, "a first, static level on which the imagination proposes a partial but positive definition of its own contents and a second, dynamic level on which the movement and effects of the imagination are validated as a function of the ethical constitution of the world" (94–95). See Willi Goetschel, *Spinoza's Modernity* (Madison: University of Wisconsin Press, 2004), chap. 3, on the role of the imagination in Spinoza's *Ethics*: "The imagination's role in the theory of affects casts cognition as the interplay of forces that occurs within the affectual economy and has important implications for aesthetics. . . . Spinoza's revalorization of the imagination accords the aesthetic a new ontological significance" (52). See also Jonathan Israel's introduction to the *TTP*: "Although such universals [in Scripture, such as 'there is a God, one and omnipotent, who alone is to be adored'] are historically determined and are therefore poetic concepts, inexact, limited and vague, and while it is totally impossible to infer from the biblical text 'what God is' or how he 'provides for all things,' nevertheless such universals are not just wholly fictitious or arbitrary intended meanings. To

[Spinoza's] mind, they are inadequate but still significant perceptions, that is, vague but natural approximations to the 'truth of things'" (xvi).

49. See *TTP*, 16.206: "The laws of nature are not accommodated to religion, which is concerned solely with the human good, but to the order of universal nature, that is, to the eternal decree of God, which is unknown to us."

50. See *TTP*, 17.212, on the "stratagem" of pretending government has been "instituted by God rather than by the consent and agreement of men."

51. In a sense this is already true in the theocracy established by Moses, which divided the state into priests and civil administrators: "Thus, God's pronouncements in the mouth of the high priest were not decrees but just responses; they gained the force of commands and decrees only when accepted by Joshua and the supreme councils" (17.217). See also 19.238: "religion has the power of law only by decree of those who exercise the right of government and . . . God has no special kingdom among men except through those who exercise sovereignty."

52. See Alexandre Matheron, "The Theoretical Function of Democracy in Spinoza and Hobbes," in *The New Spinoza*, ed. Warren Montag and Ted Stolze (Minneapolis: University of Minnesota Press, 1997), 215. See also, in the same volume, Antonio Negri, "*Reliqua Desiderantur*: A Conjecture for the Definition of the Concept of Democracy in the Final Spinoza."

53. Negri, "*Reliqua Desiderantur*," 231.

54. One important difference is that, while Spinoza has learned from Machiavelli about the manipulation of opinion in the realm of politics, Spinoza is far more concerned than Machiavelli with the individual's struggle against superstition.

55. For a different account of Spinoza's relation to Machiavelli, see Graham L. Hammill, *The Mosaic Constitution* (Chicago: University of Chicago Press, 2012). Hammill focuses on Machiavelli's and Spinoza's treatment of Moses and argues that "Spinoza's description of Moses as sincere lawgiver and promulgator of justice rebuts the latent cynicism of Machiavelli's portrait" (85–86). I think Machiavelli is less cynical (especially in his defense of republicanism) and Spinoza less theological (in his defense of democracy) than Hammill does. Where I do agree with Hammill is when he writes, "Imagination, Spinoza suggests, posits an external authority through which it receives its own images as obligation" (89).

56. Lewis and Short defines *syngraphum* as "1. A written contract, Plaut. As. 4.1.1; and 2. A passport, pass, Plaut. 2.3.90."

57. In *Civil Religion: A Dialogue in the History of Political Philosophy* (Cambridge: Cambridge University Press, 2011), 133–34, Ronald Beiner argues that Spinoza presents a Machiavellian argument for civil religion in *TTP*, chap. 16, and a defense of liberalism in *TTP*, chap. 20. Ultimately, however, Beiner argues that Spinoza is not a liberal regarding religion and the state. "The liberal idea is the idea of *separating* the realm of religion and that of politics; the civil-religion idea is the idea of empowering the state to legislate religious norms according to what is dictated by the state's own purpose and responsibilities" (140). Beiner goes on to assert, "What is unique about

Spinoza's political philosophy is that it maintains *both* Hobbesian civil religion *and* the beginnings of a properly liberal politics in an uneasy (and highly unstable) balance. Notwithstanding the Hobbesian moments in his political thought, Spinoza was the one who launched the crusade for liberalism. This long struggle had the outcome Spinoza intended. How do we know this? Because Freud's *Future of an Illusion*, unlike Hobbes's *Behemoth* and Spinoza's *Ethics*, was not published posthumously" (146). I take up Freud's indebtedness to Spinoza in chapter 5.

    58. See Neil Saccamano, "Inheriting Enlightenment."

    59. Levene, "Athens and Jerusalem," 149, 153–54.

    60. See Etienne Balibar, *Spinoza and Politics*, trans. Peter Snowdon (London: Verso, 1998), 36–42, on how Spinoza's notion of nature involves a philosophy of history.

    61. Herder, "Auch eine Philosophie der Geschichte zur Bildung der Menschheit," in *Werke in zehn Bänden*, ed. Martin Bollacher (Frankfurt: Deutscher Klassiker Verlag, 1985–2000), 4:33; "Über National-Religionen," in *Adrastea*, in *Werke in zehn Bänden*, 10:612; Herder, *Against Pure Reason: Writings on Religion, Language, and History*, trans. Marcia Bunge (Minneapolis: University of Minnesota Press, 1993), 88. These quotations from Herder are taken from Jonathan Sheehan, *The Enlightenment Bible* (Princeton: Princeton University Press, 2005), 219.

    62. Sheehan, *Enlightenment Bible*, 220. Sheehan traces how the Luther Bible became the cultural Bible in the nineteenth century. The Luther "German Bible simultaneously created a German religion, a German culture, and a German nation." The Luther Bible thus became "a Bible relevant and authoritative even separated from its original theological roots" (227). However, Sheehan also goes on to argue that the cultural Bible in Germany paved the way not only for a more spiritual view of culture but also for a "desecularization" or "revival of religion" (228). See also Smith, *Spinoza*, 15 and ff. on "the Enlightenment's project of emancipation through *Bildung*, or self-formation."

    Sheehan's notion that culture takes on attributes of the Bible is reminiscent of the argument that the discipline of aesthetics is a secularized version of the monotheistic God. But I think it's equally possible to argue that Spinoza reduces the Bible to the status of a cultural artifact, without assuming that this notion of literary culture is the *consequence* of the process of secularization. Spinoza turns Scripture into literature in order to save philosophy; but the tools by which he does so are the rational activity of interpretation and use, of reading and rhetorical analysis, that were available to early modern readers of literature and Scripture alike.

    63. See Smith, *Reading Leo Strauss*, 83.

    64. Ernst Vollrath, "Hannah Arendt: A German-American Jewess Views the United States—and Looks Back to Germany," in Kielmansegg, Mewes, and Glaser-Schmitt, *Hannah Arendt and Leo Strauss*, 58. On this understanding of *Bildung*, see also 47, 49, and 52. On Strauss and Arendt, see also the excellent article by Ronald Beiner, "Hannah Arendt and Leo Strauss: The Uncommenced Dialogue," *Political Theory* 18 (1990): 238–54.

65. Hannah Arendt, "The Crisis in Culture," in *Between Past and Future: Six Exercises in Political Thought* (Cleveland: Meridian Books, 1968), 197–226.

66. For a recent discussion of Arendt's relation to Schmitt and her hostility to political theology, see Samuel Moyn, "Hannah Arendt on the Secular," *New German Critique* 105 (2008): 71–96. See also Hans Sluga, "The Pluralism of the Political: From Hannah Arendt to Carl Schmitt," *Telos* 142 (Spring 2008): 91–109.

67. Arendt, "Crisis in Culture," 201–4.

68. Ibid., 220, 222.

69. Ibid., 223. Arendt further elaborated on this reading of Kant's *Critique of Judgment* in *Lectures on Kant's Political Philosophy* (Chicago: University of Chicago Press, 1982). Whether Arendt escapes the existential decisionism of Schmitt and, in some readings, Strauss is the subject of some debate. See Vollrath, "Hannah Arendt," 38, on the problem of a criterion of political judgment in Arendt.

70. Arendt lumps Spinoza with Hobbes, who equated politics with security. See "What Is Freedom?," in *Between Past and Future*, 150.

71. Louis Althusser, "The Only Materialist Tradition, Part 1: Spinoza," in Montag and Stolze, *New Spinoza*, 5; Louis Althusser, *Essays in Self-Criticism*, trans. Grahame Lock (London: Schocken Books, 1976), 136; and Althusser, "From *Capital* to Marx's Philosophy," in Althusser and Etienne Balibar, *Reading Capital*, trans. Ben Brewster (London: Verso, 2009), 17. Montag quotes *Reading Capital* in the introduction to *The New Spinoza*, xv. On Althusser's indebtedness to Spinoza, see Christopher Norris, *Spinoza and the Origins of Modern Critical Theory* (Oxford: Wiley-Blackwell, 1991). For further discussion of Spinoza, see also Althusser, *The Future Lasts Forever*, trans. Richard Veasey (New York: New Press, 1993), 215–20.

72. In the gloss of Terry Eagleton this means that "[c]riticism 'makes speak' what the work must at all costs repress simply in order to be itself. Its job [that is, the job of criticism] is not to extract some secret truth from the work, but to demonstrate that its 'truth' lies open to view, in the historically necessary discrepancy between its various components." See Eagleton, introduction to the English translation of Pierre Macherey, *A Theory of Literary Production*, trans. Geoffrey Wall (1966; London: Verso, 2006), viii–ix. See also 72–73 on how "Spinoza's notion of liberation involves a new attitude to language."

73. Friedrich Schlegel, *Dialogue on Poetry* (1800); *Gespräch über die Poesie*, in *Kritische Friedrich Schlegel Ausgabe*, ed. Ernst Behler, Jean Jacques Anstett, and Hans Eichner (Paderborn: F. Schöningh, 1958), 2:317.

74. Giorgio Agamben, *The Kingdom and the Glory*, trans. Lorenzo Chiesa with Matteo Mandarini (Stanford: Stanford University Press, 2011), xii.

75. Ibid., 188, 193, 194 (my emphasis).

76. Paul W. Kahn, *Political Theology: Four New Concepts on the Concept of Sovereignty* (New York: Columbia University Press, 2011), 120, 121.

77. Ibid., 120, 121.

78. Louis Althusser, "Machiavelli's Solitude," *Machiavelli and Us*, trans. Gregory Elliott (London: Verso, 2000), 123.

79. Ibid., 103.

CHAPTER FIVE

1. All references to the German texts of Freud are to Sigmund Freud, *Gesammelte Werke*, ed. Anna Freud, E. Bibring, W. Hoffer, E. Kris, O. Isakower, 4th ed., 18 vols. (Frankfurt: S. Fischer, 1968). The German text of "Leonardo da Vinci" appears in volume 8 of this edition; "The Moses of Michelangelo" in volume 10; *Civilization and Its Discontents, The Future of an Illusion*, and Freud's *Autobiographical Study* appear in volume 14; *Moses and Monotheism* appears in volume 16.

2. Freud compares the psyche to ancient and Renaissance Rome in the opening chapter of *Civilization and Its Discontents*. Freud's references to Shakespeare are legion. He discusses *Hamlet* in *The Interpretation of Dreams* (1900), *An Autobiographical Study* (1925), and in the essay on Leonardo, discussed below, as well as in his letters to Wilhelm Fliess.

3. Jacob Burckhardt, *The Civilization of the Renaissance in Italy*, trans. S. G. C. Middlemore (Oxford: Phaidon Press, 1945), 303–4: "Every disturbance of their inward harmony," Burckhardt wrote of the Renaissance Italians, "they feel themselves able to make good out of the plastic resources of their own nature."

4. "[A]ntiquity exercised an influence . . . not through its religion . . . but through its philosophy. Ancient literature, now worshipped as something incomparable, is full of the victory of philosophy over religious tradition. An endless number of systems and fragments of systems were suddenly presented to the Italian mind, not as curiosities or even as heresies, but almost with the authority of dogmas, which had now to be reconciled rather than discriminated. In nearly all these various opinions and doctrines a certain kind of belief was implied; but taken together they formed a marked contrast to the Christian faith in a Divine government of the world. And there was one central question, which mediaeval theology had striven in vain to solve, and which now urgently demanded an answer from the wisdom of the ancients, namely, the relation of Providence to the freedom or necessity of the human will" (ibid., 306–7). In particular, Burckhardt singled out Epicureanism, which, as described by Cicero and Lucretius, was "quite sufficient to make men familiar with a godless universe" (307). And he noted further that "the immediate fruit" of the study of Cicero "was the capacity to reflect on great subjects, if not in direct opposition to the authority of the Church, at all events independently of it" (309). Freud mentions Burckhardt in his letters to Fliess; see, among others, the letter of January 8, 1900 (*Complete Letters of Wilhelm Fliess to Sigmund Freud, 1887–1904*, ed. Jeffrey Masson [Cambridge: Harvard University Press, 1994], 394–96). He knew Burckhardt's cultural history of ancient Greece, *The Greeks and Greek Civilization*, well; he refers to Burckhardt secondhand in *MM*, 16 and 18, and in *Leonardo da Vinci and a Memory*

of His Childhood, trans. Alan Tyson, ed. James Strachey (New York: Norton, 1989), 9 n. 2. In "Freud's Reading of Classical Literature and Classical Philology," in *Reading Freud's Reading*, ed. Sander L. Gilman (New York: New York University Press, 1994), Robin N. Mitchell-Boyask demonstrates the importance of Burckhardt's work for *The Interpretation of Dreams*.

5. The term cosmotheism comes from Jan Assmann, *Moses the Egyptian* (Cambridge: Harvard University Press, 1997), 3 and passim. See Burckhardt, *Civilization of the Renaissance in Italy*, 307.

6. Burckhardt, *Civilization of the Renaissance in Italy*, 305, associates the "religious indifference" of Renaissance Italians with Lessing's parable of the Three Rings in *Nathan der Weise*. Since Nathan himself has been seen as a figure for Spinoza, perhaps here too Burckhardt anticipated Freud. The English quotations from Freud's correspondence are taken from Yirmiyahu Yovel, *Spinoza and Other Heretics*, 2 vols., vol. 2: *The Adventures of Immanence* (Princeton: Princeton University Press, 1989), 139. The first is taken from a letter to Lothas Bickel of June 28, 1931; the second from a letter to S. Hessing, in *Spinoza-Festschrift*, ed. S. Hessing (Heidelberg, 1932), 221; reprinted in Siegfried Hessing, "Freud's Relation with Spinoza," *Speculum Spinozanum, 1677–1977* (London: Routledge and Kegan Paul, 1977), 228. Freud also gestured toward Spinoza in *The Future of an Illusion*. Heine had famously referred to Spinoza as "a brother in unbelief" (an *Unglaubensgenossen*). In the conclusion to *The Future of an Illusion*, Freud called Heine an *Unglaubensgenossen*, thereby clearly establishing a line of descent from Spinoza to Heine to himself. (I return to these lines below.) See Yovel, *Spinoza and Other Heretics*, 2:163. In *FI*, 34, Freud also uses Spinoza's argument about how revelation has to be deduced from Scripture rather than presupposed. For the term *Unglaubensgenossen*, which Heine applied to Spinoza, see also *Jokes and Their Relation to the Unconscious*, in *The Standard Edition of the Complete Psychological Works of Sigmund Freud*, ed. and trans. James Strachey, vol. 8 (London: Vintage, 2001), 77.

7. Freud to Lou Andreas-Salomé, January 6, 1935, quoted in Bluma Goldstein, *Reinscribing Moses: Heine, Kafka, Freud and Schoenberg in a European Wilderness* (Cambridge: Harvard University Press, 1992), 100.

8. *Leonardo da Vinci*, 22, 11, and 23. This is also the view of Yirmiyahu Yovel, in his chapter on "Spinoza and Freud," in *Spinoza and Other Heretics*, vol. 2. For other treatments of Spinoza and Freud, see also note 19 below.

9. See *Leonardo da Vinci*, 83–84. At the outset of his essay, Freud mentions Vasari's description of Leonardo returning to the Catholic faith on his deathbed, only to dismiss it as implausible.

10. Ibid., 85. Freud might have said the same of Spinoza. The fact that he does not may suggest that Freud was working out his own indebtedness to Spinoza by finding Spinoza's achievement earlier in the Renaissance.

11. In the Standard Edition of Freud's works, James Strachey translated *Besetzung* as "cathexis."

12. *Leonardo da Vinci*, 33, 34, 35.

13. Horapollo's *Hieroglyphica* was supposedly a Greek translation of an

Egyptian treatise on hieroglyphics. On Horapollo, see Assmann, *Moses the Egyptian*, 18–19 and 221 n. 29.

14. *Leonardo da Vinci*, 44.

15. The other important text contributing to Egyptomania was the newly discovered *Corpus Hermeticum*.

16. Assmann, *Moses the Egyptian*, 127, 142.

17. Assmann establishes that Freud knew the classical sources that described Moses as either having Egyptian knowledge (e.g., Tacitus, Philo) or being Egyptian (Apian, Strabo) (*Moses the Egyptian*, 145). Assmann also writes that "as a Jew, [Freud] could not possibly have overlooked Schiller's essay on Moses," which was in turn based on some of the early modern arguments for Moses's Egyptian knowledge (146). In *The Legation of Moses*, Schiller argues that Moses betrays the Egyptian mysteries and lets an entire nation partake of the truth, but in a form in which they can believe it (rather than understand it by reason). Freud's own Egyptomania has been well documented by William J. McGrath in *Freud's Discovery of Psychoanalysis* (Ithaca: Cornell University Press, 1986). McGrath, following Leonard Schengold, argues for the importance of the story of Joseph in Egypt for Freud's self-understanding. He also reproduces some of the Egyptian illustrations from the Philippson Bible that Freud read as a child, argues for the importance of Moses's flight from Egypt for Philippson and Freud, and discusses the recurring Egyptian motifs in Freud's own dreams.

18. *Leonardo da Vinci*, 99–100.

19. On Freud's relation to Spinoza, see the probing remarks by Paul Ricoeur in *The Conflict of Interpretations*, ed. Don Ihde (Evanston, IL; Northwestern University Press, 1974), 191–92: "The fiction of the absence of motivation, by which consciousness supported its illusion of self-control, is recognized as such. The fullness of motivation is located at the same place as the emptiness of the freedom of consciousness. It is this process of illusion which opens, as does Spinoza, a new problematic of liberty, no longer bound to the arbitrariness of free will but to determination which has been understood. It seems to me, therefore, that meditation on Freud's work, if not on analytic practice and experience themselves, can restore to us a new concept of liberty very close to that of Spinoza. *No longer free will, but liberation.*" On Freud and Spinoza, see also Stuart Hampshire, *Spinoza and Spinozism* (Oxford: Clarendon Press, 2005), 110–11, 194–97; and Michael Mack, *Spinoza and the Specters of Modernity: The Hidden Enlightenment of Diversity from Spinoza to Freud* (New York: Continuum, 2010), esp. 193–216. Mack is less interested in showing the influence of Spinoza on Freud than the congruence of their critiques of Kantian rationalism and anthropocentrism.

20. See Yosef Hayim Yerushalmi, *Freud's Moses: Judaism Terminable and Interminable* (New Haven: Yale University Press, 1991), 41–43 and 75–79. Freud's letter to Karl Abraham is quoted on 42.

21. Freud to Jung, January 17, 1909; Freud to Ferenczi, October 17, 1912, quoted in Goldstein, *Reinscribing Moses*, 80.

22. Ibid., 13–14; translation modified.

23. This is the argument of Jean-Joseph Goux in *Symbolic Economies: After Marx and Freud* (Ithaca: Cornell University Press, 1990), 140. In light of our previous analysis, we could also say that Freud is taking the place of Spinoza, whom Feuerbach famously described as "The Moses of modern free-thinkers and materialists." See Yovel, *Spinoza and Other Heretics*, 2:51.

24. Giorgio Vasari, *Lives of the Artists*, trans. George Bull (Harmonds-worth, UK: Penguin, 1976), 345.

25. Julia Reinhard Lupton, *Afterlives of the Saints: Hagiography, Typology, and Renaissance Literature* (Stanford: Stanford University Press, 1996), 157. It may be significant here that Egypt was regularly associated with idolatry in the Bible, and that Jews were associated with Egyptians in the Renaissance.

26. "The Moses of Michelangelo," *On Creativity and the Unconscious*, ed. Benjamin Nelson (New York: Harper and Row, 1958), 24.

27. Ibid., 33.

28. Ibid., 37.

29. Here I differ from the interpretation of Goldstein, who argues that Freud's interpretation of Michelangelo's *Moses* Christianizes Moses (*Reinscribing Moses*, 90–92). Against this interpretation, I would point to the similarity between Freud's calculus of passion and restraint and Winckelmann's account of ancient Greek art, which Freud surely knew. See Gotthold Ephraim Lessing, *Laocoön*, in *Laocoön, Nathan the Wise, Minna von Barnheim* (London: J. M. Dent, 1930), 6: "The general distinguishing excellence of the Greek master-pieces in painting and sculpture Herr Winckelmann places in a noble simplicity and quiet greatness, both in arrangement and in expression. 'Just as the depths of the sea,' he says, 'always remain quiet, however the surface may rage, in like manner the expression in the figures of the Greek artists shows under all passions a great and steadfast soul.'"

30. Burckhardt, of course, did not argue that religion withered away in the Renaissance, only that the achievements of the Renaissance were not primarily religious but rather secular.

31. *BPP*, 79, 93, 71.

32. Here too we might think of Spinoza, specifically Althusser's comment that "Spinoza's 'theory' rejected every illusion about ideology. And especially about the number one ideology of that time, religion, by identifying it as imaginary. But at the same time it refused to treat ideology as a simple error, or as naked ignorance, because it based the system of this imaginary phenomenon on the relation of men to the world 'expressed' by the state of their bodies." Similarly, Freud saw illusion not simply as error but as the true expression of a wish fulfillment. See Louis Althusser, *Essays in Self-Criticism*, trans. Grahame Lock (London: Schocken Books, 1976), 136.

33. *FI*, 39. In thinking about Freud's analysis of religious illusion in *The Future of Illusion*, we can draw an analogy to Marx's distinction between the left Hegelians' criticism of religion and his own project of critique. As we saw in the introduction, for the left Hegelians such as Bruno Bauer religion was a mere illusion that needed to be dismantled, while for Marx critique involved revealing the conditions of possibility of such ideological mystifications. Like Marx, Freud is both a critic of illusion and an analyst of its enabling condi-

tions. This double valence of illusion is manifest in the constant play with the word, both in the essay and in Freud's later reflection on it. But ultimately Freud cannot resist passing judgment on religious illusion. Like ideology, illusions are everywhere, but some are more susceptible to rational disproof than others. In Freud's view, those illusions that cannot be disproved—like religion—are dangerous to civilization, while those that are obviously artistic, and created by humans (albeit geniuses like Michelangelo), are beneficial to civilization. In time, however, Freud would come to understand that artistic illusion is not always so benign or so easily separated from religion in the specific sense that, in some cases, art can itself give rise to the illusions of political theology.

34. See Ricoeur, *Conflict of Interpretations*, 124: "This refusal to accept an almost classical distinction is in itself very illuminating. There is no separation between the utilitarian enterprise of dominating the forces of nature (civilization) and the disinterested, idealist task of realizing values (culture). This distinction, which might have meaning from a viewpoint which differs from that of psychoanalysis, has none as soon as we decide to treat culture from the viewpoint of a balance sheet of libidinal cathexes and anti-cathexes."

35. For the conflation of civilization as mastery of nature and culture as ethical and artistic ideals, see also Freud's "Why War?," his open letter to Albert Einstein of 1933: "The cultural development [*Kulturentwicklung*] of mankind (some, I know, prefer to call it civilization [*Zivilisation*]) has been in progress since immemorial antiquity. To this process we owe all that is best in our composition, but also much that makes for human suffering. . . . On the psychological side two of the most important phenomena of culture are, firstly, a strengthening of the intellect, which tends to master our instinctive life, and, secondly, an introversion of the aggressive impulse, with all its consequent benefits and perils." *The Standard Edition of the Complete Psychological Works of Sigmund Freud*, ed. and trans. James Strachey, vol. 22 (London: Vintage, 1971), 197–98; *Gesammelte Werke*, 16:25–26.

36. *FI*, 17.

37. *FI*, 22, 23.

38. *FI*, 34.

39. *FI*, 38, 39, 40.

40. *FI*, 41, 57.

41. *FI*, 61, cf. 40; 65.

42. *FI*, 69–70.

43. *FI*, 71.

44. *FI*, 69. At least, Freud writes, this is true of religion that promises consolation; if we're talking just about a higher, inscrutable spirit, people will lose interest in this.

45. See Peter E. Gordon, *Continental Divide: Heidegger, Cassirer, Davos* (Cambridge: Harvard University Press, 2010), for Cassirer's view of Judaism as involving the criticism of myth in favor of ethical universalism (321).

46. I borrow the adjective "economic" from Freud, who uses it in *Beyond the Pleasure Principle* to describe the "consideration of the yield of pleasure" and the calculus of pleasure and pain in an individual's psychology (32), and from Ricoeur, *Conflict of Interpretations*, who uses it to describe one axis

of Freud's analytic approach to illusion and psychoanalysis more generally. "What is new in Freud's theory is an *economic* theory of illusion. The question Freud poses is not that of God as such but that of the god of men and his economic function in the balance sheet of instinctual renunciations, substitutive satisfactions, and compensations by which men try to make life tolerable" (131). See also 144 on how "the economic point of view takes account only of [the] relationship of energy [in sublimation] and not of the novelty of value promoted by this renunciation and transfer. " As Freud writes in *CD*, "man's judgements of value follow directly from his wishes for happiness; . . . accordingly, they are an attempt to support his illusions with arguments" (111).

47. *FI*, 62, 63.

48. Ricoeur, *Conflict of Interpretations*, 145. In *Freud and Philosophy: An Essay on Interpretation* (New Haven: Yale University Press, 1970), Ricoeur offers an extensive argument against Freud's critique of religion, asserting that "psychoanalysis is necessarily iconoclastic, regardless of the faith or nonfaith of the psychoanalyst, and . . . this 'destruction' of religion can be the counterpart of a faith purged of all idolatry" (230). See also 524–51.

49. For the Freud of *Civilization and Its Discontents*, the earliest gods are "cultural ideals" (*Kulturideale*), and this in turn means that religion is a part of culture, rather than transcending it. *CD*, 23, 44; *Gesammelte Werke*, 14:450, for *Kulturideale*.

50. Philip Rieff, *Freud: The Mind of a Moralist* (Chicago: University of Chicago Press, 1979), 287.

51. *CD*, 36, 38, 45, 33.

52. See *CD*, 67. Freud's various accounts of the origin of society in *CD* sound remarkably like Hobbes's account of the origin of society from the state of nature. See, e.g., 33, 55. At the same time, there is a Rousseauesque line of argument in Freud, according to which man was happy before civilization, which shackled him in chains of repression. See Ricoeur, *Freud and Philosophy*, for an eloquent account of Freud's tragic sense of culture.

53. *CD*, 79.

54. *CD*, 30, 39.

55. *CD*, 50.

56. Hegel opposes the notion of fate as contingency, characteristic of modern tragedy, to the classical idea of the "rationality of destiny" in Greek tragedy. See *Hegel on Tragedy*, ed. Anne Paolucci and Henry Paolucci (Garden City, NY: Anchor Books, 1962), 71–72, 208–9, 325. For the role of fate and contingency in Renaissance tragedy, see Alan Sinfield, *Faultlines* (Berkeley: University of California Press, 1992), and Jonathan Dollimore, *Radical Tragedy*, 3rd ed. (London: Palgrave Macmillan, 2010).

57. Freud, *Gesammelte Werke*, 14:457. See Freud's linking of Paul's universalism with intolerance toward the excluded (*CD*, 72–73). He also opposes the intolerance of Pauline Christianity to the tolerance of Roman religion. This line of argument is clearly at odds with the effort to see Paul as a defender of a tolerant universalism on the part of many participants in the modern debate about political theology. See below for Freud's remarks on Paul in *Moses and Monotheism*. On the coerciveness of Pauline universalism, see Daniel Boyarin,

A Radical Jew: Paul and the Politics of Identity (Berkeley: University of California Press, 1994).

58. *CD*, 70; see also 109, where Freud tells us that the commandment "Love thy neighbor as thyself" is impossible to fulfill.

59. *CD*, 70; Freud, *Gesammelte Werke*, 14:482; cf. *CD*, 106, where Freud distinguishes between the conflict between egoistic and altruistic interests and the conflict between eros and death. The former Freud thinks can find a resolution; the latter cannot.

60. *CD*, 111.

61. *CD*, 112.

62. *AS*, 83; *Gesammelte Werke*, 16:33.

63. Prefatory note I to part 3 of *MM*, 55.

64. See also Freud's remarks in prefatory note 2 to part 3 of *MM*, 57–58. Samuel Weber discusses the publication history and quotes the letter from Stefan Zweig in *Targets of Opportunity: On the Militarization of Thinking* (New York: Fordham University Press, 2005), 64 and 139 n. 7. It is sometimes argued that, with his subtitle, Freud is gesturing toward Thomas Mann, whose Joseph novels he was reading at the time he composed *MM*. One wonders if Freud is also alluding to Berthold Auerbach's *Spinoza, ein historischer Roman* (1837). Auerbach translated Spinoza's work into German in 1842. Freud refers to one of Auerbach's works in a letter to Eduard Silberstein of August 15, 1877.

65. *MM*, 41, 43.

66. *MM*, 10–11, 62. See chapter 6 of *The Prince*.

67. *MM*, 43.

68. Michel de Certeau, "The Fiction of History: The Writing of *Moses and Monotheism*," *The Writing of History*, trans. Tom Conley (New York: Columbia University Press, 1988), 308–9. See also 331: "Theory, for Freud, is exercised both from and within fiction (dreams, legends); its work traces within the foreign language of these fantasies a 'knowledge' that is inseparable from them but which becomes increasingly capable of articulating them *historically*, that is, through a practice of inversions and displacements."

69. On the way the Freudian theory of displacements and conflict affects the theory itself, see also Samuel Weber, *The Legend of Freud* (Minneapolis: University of Minnesota Press, 1982).

70. Assmann, *Moses the Egyptian*, 163, 164.

71. *TTP*, 2.38.

72. Like Spinoza, Freud comments on the contradictions and corruption of the scriptural text, but he goes further than Spinoza when he argues that these contradictions reveal the specifically political origins of monotheism. "In Egypt," Freud writes, "monotheism grew up as a by-product of imperialism: God was a reflection of the Pharaoh who was the absolute ruler of a great world-empire" (*MM*, 65).

73. See *MM*, 17, where Freud refers to his argument as "a bronze statue with feet of clay." See also 19 where he describes "the insatiable appetite of the Egyptians for embodying their gods in clay, stone, and metal," a passage that suggests Freud is allying himself with Spinozist and Egyptian cosmotheism

rather than monotheism. Freud also referred to *MM* as a statue built upon feet of clay in a letter to Arnold Zweig of December 16, 1934; cited in Goldstein, *Reinscribing Moses*, 94.

74. Religion is more like neurosis than like art because religion and neurosis share the "characteristic of compulsion, which forces itself on the mind along with an overpowering of logical thought—a feature which did not come into account, for instance, in the genesis of [an] epic" (*MM*, 72).

75. *MM*, 48.

76. Freud continues, "In the further development the animal loses its sacredness and the sacrifice its relation to the celebration of the totem; the rite becomes a simple offering to the deity. . . . At the same time the social order produces godlike kings who transfer the patriarchal system to the state. It must be said that the revenge of the deposed and reinstated father has been very cruel; it culminated in the dominance of authority" (*TT*, 193).

77. Assmann, *Moses the Egyptian*, 168. While Assmann discusses the relevance of Spinoza in general terms to Freud, he has nothing to say about the *TTP*.

78. *MM*, 21: Egypt's "imperialism was reflected in religion as universalism and monotheism. Since the Pharaoh's responsibilities now embraced not only Egypt but Nubia and Syria as well, deity too was obliged to abandon its national limitation." See also *MM*, 66, on the monotheism of the chosen people.

79. *MM*, 87, 88, 136. In both cases, the trace of the murder is revealed by a literal reading of Christian figuralism, of Christian ritual and doctrine.

80. In "Freud's *Moses* and the Ethics of Nomotropic Desire," *October* 88 (1999): 3–41, Eric L. Santner also takes issue with Assmann's interpretation that Freud is breaking down the Mosaic distinction and advancing a Spinozist cosmotheism. Instead, Santner argues that Jewish guilt produces the compulsion of a "nomotropic desire," which explains both the ethical dimension of Judaism and the compulsive dimension of Freud's commitment to scientific truth. However, Santner does not see Freud's indebtedness to the Spinoza of the *TTP*.

81. *MM*, 136.

82. *MM*, 86, 88. Freud also says Christians hate Jews because they really did "kill God," if we understand this as the murder of the primal father (90). Freud then advances a different argument, suggesting that Christians were converted from "barbarous polytheism" and then displaced their hatred of the new religion onto Judaism, which was the source of Christian monotheism. The new converts' "hatred of Jews is at bottom a hatred of Christians, and we need not be surprised that in the German National-Socialist revolution this intimate relation between the two monotheist religions finds such a clear expression in the hostile treatment of both of them" (91). See also 134–36.

83. See *MM*, 129, where "historical truth" is equated with "illusion."

84. See *BPP*, 33, 38, 61. Here we need only to point to the fact that Freud's analysis is very strikingly interwoven with two prefatory notes in which he reflects on the political conditions in Vienna in 1938 that prohibited publication, and on his exile in London, later that year, that allowed him finally to publish his scandalous work. In this way, the text dramatizes the considerations of

political theology that are also its explicit subject. On Freud's relation to his father's observant Judaism, see Yerushalmi, *Freud's Moses*.

85. *MM*, 73. Here we would do well to remember Freud's own comments on form in the famous footnote to the 1925 edition of *The Interpretation of Dreams*, in which he reminded his readers that the meaning of a dream is equivalent not to its manifest or latent content but rather to the *form* of the dream, the displacement (*Entstellung*) effected by the dream-work. This is the form to which the psychoanalyst attends. See also Samuel Weber, *Legend of Freud*, 66, where the passage from *The Interpretation of Dreams* is discussed. Weber also argues that the theory of the unconscious "explains why the ego is the site both of cognition and of illusion, and why the one is difficult to separate from the other. If a distinction is possible—and this is, of course, the necessary premise of any theory, including that of Freud—it can only be by an effort of reflection that takes the topography of the scene into account" (19).

86. Yovel, *Spinoza and Other Heretics*, 2:162.

87. *FI*, 67.

88. *CD*, 29, 30.

89. *FI*, 47, 50.

90. The phrase "ars poetica" is Freud's; see Freud, "The Relation of the Poet to Daydreaming," in *On Creativity and the Unconscious*, 45.

91. Herbert Marcuse, *Eros and Civilization* (1955; Boston: Beacon Press, 1966), 185. Marcuse was also acutely aware of the ways in which art can support the status quo. See "The Affirmative Character of Culture," *Negations*, trans. Jeremy J. Shapiro (Harmondsworth, UK: Penguin Books, 1968). For an argument cautioning that Freud did not identify the reality principle with adaptation to the status quo, see Ricoeur, *Conflict of Interpretations*, 188.

92. Theodor W. Adorno, "Culture Industry Reconsidered," trans. Anson G. Rabinbach, *New German Critique* 6 (1975): 13.

93. On Freud's similarity to and difference from Feuerbach, see Goux, *Symbolic Economies*, 151–53. Freud mentions reading Feuerbach in a letter to Eduard Silberstein of November 8, 1874. See *The Letters of Sigmund Freud to Eduard Silberstein, 1871–1881*, ed. Walter Boehlich, trans. Arnold J. Pomerans (Cambridge: Harvard University Press, 1990), 70. On Feuerbach's influence on Freud, see McGrath, *Freud's Discovery of Psychoanalysis*, 104–9.

94. What Carlo Galli writes of Schmitt is then equally applicable to Freud. For both, it is not enough to identify civilization with play, for this ignores a dimension of seriousness or tragedy or the ineradicable remnant of myth. Instead, for both Schmitt and Freud, "the modern metaphor of civilization as play carries with it an unease." See Galli, "*Hamlet*: Representation and the Concrete," in *Political Theology and Early Modernity*, ed. Graham Hammill and Julia Reinhard Lupton (Chicago: University of Chicago Press, 2012), 78. In a comment on Feuerbach's critique of religion, Paul Ricoeur observes that, "when placed in contrast to the assertion of radical autonomy, dependence is perhaps the only possible truth of religion, an avowal of an element of passivity in my existence, an avowal that in some ways I receive existence" (*Lectures on Ideology and Utopia*, ed. George H. Taylor [New York: Columbia University Press, 1986], 32).

CODA

1. Yirmiyahu Yovel, in his chapter "Spinoza and Freud," *Spinoza and Other Heretics*, 2 vols., vol. 2: *The Adventures of Immanence* (Princeton: Princeton University Press, 1989), 136.

2. Ibid., 153, 154; quoting Freud, "New Introductory Lectures," lecture 31, *Standard Edition* 22:80.

3. Yovel, "Spinoza and Freud," 173. Yovel distinguishes between Spinoza's philosophy of immanence and a critical philosophy of immanence: Spinoza turns immanence into "a new absolute, adorning it with semireligious properties. Thus pantheism, either in Spinoza's or Hegel's version, is excluded by a critical view of immanence" (175).

4. Ibid., 172.

Index